White Race Discourse

White Race Discourse

Preserving Racial Privilege in a Post-Racial Society

John D. Foster

LEXINGTON BOOKS
Lanham • Boulder • New York • Toronto • Plymouth, UK

Published by Lexington Books
A wholly owned subsidiary of The Rowman & Littlefield Publishing Group, Inc.
4501 Forbes Boulevard, Suite 200, Lanham, Maryland 20706
www.rowman.com

10 Thornbury Road, Plymouth PL6 7PP, United Kingdom

British Library Cataloguing in Publication Information Available

Library of Congress Cataloging-in-Publication Data

Foster, John D., 1976-
  White race discourse : preserving racial privilege in a post-racial society / John D.
Foster.
     pages cm
  Includes bibliographical references and index.
  ISBN 978-0-7391-7598-9 (cloth : alk. paper) —ISBN 978-0-7391-7599-6 (electronic)
  1. United States—Race relations. 2. Whites--Race identity—United States. 3. Race
awareness—United States. 4. Racism—United States. I. Title.
  E184.A1F624 2013
  305.800973—dc23   2013011168

♾™ The paper used in this publication meets the minimum requirements of American
National Standard for Information Sciences—Permanence of Paper for Printed Library
Materials, ANSI/NISO Z39.48-1992.

Printed in the United States of America

Contents

Tables ix

Transcription Symbols xi

Preface xiii

Acknowledgements xv

1 Introduction: How Does Racism Continue to Exist in U.S. Society? 1

2 Bureaucrats of Whiteness 27

3 Rationalizing Segregation 57

4 Products of the Retrogression 89

5 Defending White Supremacy 121

6 Antiracism in Progress 155

7 Conclusion: Toward a New Race Discourse 173

Appendix 187

Selected Bibliography 191

Index 201

About the Author 207

Tables

Table 1.1   Relationships between Structures and Agents
             in Impression Management   6

Table 2.1   Questionnaire Results for Attitudes towards
             Racial Purity and Judgment   32

Table 3.1   Questionnaire Results for Attitudes towards
             Racial Integration and Intermarriage   62

Table 4.1   Questionnaire Results for Attitudes towards
             Race-Sensitive Policies   113

Table 5.1   Questionnaire Results for Attitudes towards
             Supremacist Groups and Protecting Liberty   129

Transcription Symbols

I	Interviewer
R	Respondent
word=	Latched utterances; No interval
=word	
[xxx]	Overlapping talk
[yyy]	
Wor-	Abrupt cutoff
(.)	Micropause
(1.0)	Timed silence in seconds
word.	Falling intonation
word,	Continuing intonation
word?	Rising intonation
↑word	Higher pitch
↓word	Lower pitch
wor:d	Stretched sound
wo̲rd	Emphasis
WORD	Louder talk
°word°	Quieter talk
>word<	Faster talk
<word>	Slower talk
wo(h)rd	Laughingly spoken
((word))	Transcriptionist's note and comment
(word)	Transcriptionist's uncertain understanding

Preface

In U.S. society today, many believe that we live in a time of tremendous progress and prosperity. More specifically, there is the notion that people are more racially tolerant than at any other time in our history. Previous studies of white racial attitudes, using surveys with large samples, have often concluded that whites' prejudice has declined since the 1950s. However, more recent studies have found that the racial attitudes may not have changed so much after all. These studies have discovered that white Americans answer survey questions on race matters in unprejudiced ways, but then contradict those answers when interviewed in more depth. How do we make sense of these contradictions? This study examines the numerous contradictions white college students exhibit as they discuss a variety of race matters, including their identities as white Americans, interracial dating, and affirmative action. Data for this project were derived from the in-depth interviews of 61 white college students. The findings suggest that they initially project ambivalence and tolerance towards these matters, but upon further examination, they cast images of themselves as intolerant of, victimized by, and suspicious of nonwhite (particularly black) Americans.

However, given the era of political correctness when communicating in public spaces, this sample of white Americans cannot express these antiblack feelings plainly and unambiguously. Thus, they must use a variety of verbal tools that aid them in making such statements. These tools give them the ability to appear not prejudiced while making prejudiced statements. Moreover, regardless of their intentions, this form of discourse rationalizes the racial status quo and undermines attempts to deal with systemic racism. This study exposes an important way in which racism reproduces itself in the post-civil rights era.

Acknowledgments

A project of this size would not have been possible without the assistance and encouragement from so many terrific people. First, I wholeheartedly thank the college students who chose to take some time out of their busy schedules to talk to me about issues many white Americans would rather avoid. We as white Americans need to understand that research such as this helps all of us, not just minority groups. This research also helps us to "practice what we preach."

I am deeply grateful for the wonderful professors who have mentored me over the years. I am especially appreciative of my dissertation co-chairs, Hernán Vera and Joe Feagin, for their insightful comments and suggestions as I underwent this endeavor. I also thank Barbara Zsembik, Connie Shehan, Kathryn Russell-Brown, Charles Gattone, Felix Berrardo, John Henretta, and Jay Gubrium for their expertise and assistance during my time in Florida.

I thank Yuko Fujino and Mike Loree for encouraging their students to participate in my interviews. Without their assistance, this project would not have been possible. I also thank those my wife and I befriended during our stay in Gainesville, including Ginger Battista, Kuniko Chijiwa, Dana Fennell, Clay Hipke, Melissa Mauldin, Amanda Moras, Guillermo Rebollo-Gil, and John Reitzel. Portions of this book appeared in an article in *Discourse & Society*. I thank the editor Teun Van Dijk and the reviewers who offered helpful comments and suggestions for improving the material. Additionally, I presented material from this project at numerous conferences, including those of the American Sociological Association, Society for the Study of Social Problems, and the Pacific Sociological Association. I thank the various people who offered comments during those sessions, including David Embrick, José Padin, Eileen O'Brien, Jennifer Mueller, and Glenn Bracey.

I also thank my new "pride" here at UAPB who have encouraged me and helped me in adjusting to life in Pine Bluff, Arkansas, including Jerry Ingram, Michael Lynch, Ebo Tei, Gurdeep Khullar, David Vaughn, Sharunda Thrower, and Angela Anderson. I also thank my sisters Jill and Jody and my mother Carol for their assistance and conversations about my project and my life. Finally, I thank my life partner, Srey. She has helped me remain strong and supported me in so many ways throughout this process. I am blessed to have her in my life.

Chapter 1
Introduction: How Does Racism Continue to Exist in U.S. Society?[1]

Empowered by the political success of Reagan and other conservatives in the 1980s, a plethora of authors and pundits, lavishly funded by conservative think-tanks like the Olin Foundation, emerged in the 1990s to declare "the end of racism" in American society.[2] Despite a strong pushback by well-researched scientists in academia,[3] the damage had already been done in that large numbers of white Americans came to believe that racism was (at least largely) a thing of the past. The counterattack against the Civil Rights Movement had been launched and was winning the battle, affecting policies and programs designated to enforce the creed that America was the land of opportunity for all its inhabitants.[4] Evidence that the United States remained a separate and unequal society existed, but much of it was either hidden from view or blamed on the victims for its existence.

But then along came Hurricane Katrina in 2005, or more consequently, the botched government response to the storm's aftermath. Americans of all races were presented media images of mostly black Americans trapped in New Orleans without basic necessities like food or clean water, a moment when conservatives struggled to maintain the "it's their fault" storyline.[5] Viewers saw pictures of dead bodies floating in floodwaters on city streets, while many elders died, waiting for assistance that never came.[6] For at least a brief moment, the reality of U.S. society could not be ignored: that it is both a racist and classist society.[7] Coupled with a war in Iraq that was going badly and a financial meltdown, Democrats enjoyed significant gains in Congressional races in the 2006 midterm elections and regained the White House in 2008 with the election of Barack Obama, America's first black President.

Despite overwhelming opposition to Obama during the campaign, conservatives turned his electoral victory into a positive for their cause: that we had elected a black man President, further proof that America is beyond race and racism.[8] The "we" here did not refer so much to conservatives per se but to white Americans; however, a majority of white Americans did not vote for

1

Barack Obama in that election.[9] The lack of support for Obama serves as another instance of white Americans opposing racial progress; another was whites' opposition to the March on Washington in 1963.[10] Nonetheless, shortly after conservatives used Obama's election to reinvigorate a narrative that had been shaken following the Bush years (i.e., that white conservatives were not hostile to people of color), they quickly moved to criticizing him at every turn, even using blatantly racist imagery when doing so.[11]

What are we to make of such contradictory events in this country's history? Is this a society hopelessly trapped in little more than a caste system in which whites prosper at the expense of blacks and other nonwhites? Extensive research tells us that Americans of color continue to lag behind their white counterparts in numerous indicators, including income, wealth, educational attainment, and health.[12] On the other hand, is there an inevitable progression to a truly just and equal society? While perhaps not inevitable, some gains have been made over the years, including an increase in the number of black elected public officials and years of formal schooling, an emergence of a black middle-class, and an almost universal condemnation by white Americans of overt antiblack action.[13] Obama's election was certainly a testament to the hard work and dedication of those before him who had fought tirelessly for racial equality.

The answer is neither and both at the same time; that is the peculiar nature of U.S. society, dating back to the days of Jefferson and Washington. "America" is a contradiction itself—a society with liberty and fairness as its foundation while simultaneously allowing, even promoting, the enslavement of human beings. Although slavery is no more, the contradictory nature of U.S. society continues. I stipulate that the subject matter of this book—contradictions within the racetalk[14] of white Americans—reflects the very nature of U.S. society.

An Introduction to White Race Discourse

While previous studies have exposed contradictions within the race discourse of Americans,[15] little is known about why white folks speak in such a way. Few sociological studies have analyzed this phenomenon in a systematic fashion. This form of racetalk is the focus of this book: how do we make sense of the myriad contradictions in the race discourse of white Americans? What purpose do these contradictions serve those who use them? In this book I examine this discursive phenomenon, employing a synthetic approach that attempts to avoid the pitfalls of previous studies.

Despite the gains achieved since the Civil Rights Movement, why has U.S. society failed to eliminate the racial gaps in areas such as education, income, and employment? Eduardo Bonilla-Silva argues that a "racial grammar"[16] exists so as to maintain racial domination even when more overt and blatant means fall out of favor with the public. He stipulates that racial grammar "is a distillate of racial ideology and, hence, of white supremacy."[17] This grammar teaches people the rules of engagement when discussing race matters, and these teachings take place within society's institutions while being verified, negotiated, and even modified or revolted against within daily interactions.[18]

Indeed, various social structures contribute to the perpetuation and maintenance of the racial order. They include mental or cognitive as well as social or "objective" ones, such as institutions.[19] These structures have an impact on how we interact with each other, and responses within such interactions. How can a racial group so large in white, non-Hispanic Americans support a particular social system while never expressing it, at least on the frontstage of social life? In order to address this issue, social scientists have begun to analyze the more covert forms of social action that maintain white supremacy; e.g., discursive forms that masquerade as antiracist and egalitarian, yet serve to perpetuate that supremacy.

Race discourse is important to examine because "discourse is a form of social action"[20] and "discourse is intimately involved in the construction and maintenance of inequality."[21] Discourse is a critical tool in the legitimation process of the social order. How do white Americans claim to support racial equality and fairness while simultaneously opposing programs and policies deemed necessary to achieve racial equality and fairness? How can they claim to have no problems with black Americans yet report so few quality[22] relationships with them? Such a conundrum forces whites to walk a discursive tightrope when discussing racial matters, and contradictions are commonplace. Race is a social fact, [23] and whites' race discourse is unique in various ways.

Following events like the aftermath of Hurricane Katrina, white Americans have a lot to answer for, given that these vast racial disparities in life chances continue in a society in which the proponents of racial equality had presumably prevailed and are celebrated today.[24] Whites must immediately find (through little effort or time) that their privileges far exceed those of black Americans. While it is understandable that whites might take considerable care to appear nonracist in formal interactions due to present day customs discussing racial issues, would whites just say anything to maintain an appearance of nonracism to avoid such a label (e.g., admitting that they receive unfair privileges)?

In fact, studies have documented how whites speak in certain ways to avoid an appearance of racism.[25] This is certainly true, but there is something more going on here: individual whites not only defend themselves within their repertoires but they also defend the racist social institutions that perpetuate white supremacy in U.S. society. Some linguists have pointed out that race as a conversation or interview topic is a delicate subject,[26] but little or no discussion of reasons for its delicacy takes place, as if the subject's delicacy is assumed. As it turns out, race as a subject in conversations is not treated as delicately by nonwhite respondents than by white ones, and there is an obvious reason to this: whites and the institutions they control have more to lose with the occasional gaffe as compared to nonwhites. Thus, when blacks[27] or other nonwhite respondents[28] uncover the myriad contradictions in the dominant race discourse (RD), they are more likely to acknowledge and speak to those inconsistencies; in fact, they might even expose the contradictions themselves. In contrast, when whites see contradictions between their stated values and their opposition to various actions to fulfill those values, they utilize certain discursive tools to both rationalize the existing social structure and do so while appearing "open-minded." It is this form of RD, used by whites, that I call white race discourse (WRD).

(Re)producing the Racial Order Through Discourse

Despite advancements made in the Civil Rights Movement of the 1950s and 1960s, how does racism continue to exist, and more importantly, how do individual whites rationalize such a social system? A useful way to understand this process of rationalization is through the utilization of the dialectic. In this process, a contrary point of view challenges an initial claim, which then produces a synthesis of the two. In this particular situation, individual whites acknowledge the existence of white-over-black racism (thesis), but then add a peculiar antithesis to the thought process: that blacks discriminate against whites, or that "reverse discrimination" occurs. This creates a synthesis that racism is natural and unavoidable, producing an ambivalence towards racism in U.S. society. The antithesis is usually based on speculation, antidotal evidence, or fabrications passed onto individual whites (or thought up themselves). Such an approach is helpful in understanding how white racism continues in U.S. society due to the (re)creation of the social world in the minds of white Americans, often constructed through "sincere fictions." However, this image of society does not come about willy-nilly, but rather for two primary reasons: rationalizing the racist social structure and saving face when delivering comments feared as being interpreted as "racist." Whites may also use this technique to integrate incompatible frames of race.[29]

As a result of these sincere fictions of the white self,[30] whites are ambivalent towards aggressive measures to end racial injustice. This ambivalence is a synthesis of two components: first, the thesis that black Americans have suffered due to systemic racism; and second, the sincere fictions that structures the antithesis. The example of whites' explanation of racial segregation as the natural order of things and people[31] exposes their ambivalence toward "man-made design."[32] Systemic racism is the product of white America and the white elites in charge, rather than merely a product of nature. In this section, I discuss how both individuals and social structures work together to defend white privilege, and then discuss how this form of racetalk is a form of social control.

Preserving Whiteness and White Privilege

Do individual whites make the distinction between themselves and the social system, and if so, when? Members of a privileged class may not differentiate themselves from the structure because, in a sense, they are the structure (or at least its creators). When a problem occurs, e.g. if there is a conflict between the interests of people and those of the mechanics of the system designed (at least initially), then agents may attempt to distance themselves from the structure. But the distance act may occur with fellow whites as well: if a problem occurs, such as the recent investigations of political corruption in Congress, then individual whites are labeled, particularly by members of the institution who fear a public backlash, as "a few bad apples." However, regarding the Katrina debacle, with so many individual whites in power, the focus shifts onto reified bureaucratic mechanisms that were too inefficient or too cumbersome for individuals to act adequately to the situation. Only then do we hear calls for structural inadequacies to be addressed.

Elites in this country, who remain largely white and male, are, with the help of the media among other social institutions (by all means structures and agents work together or cooperate, at least in this case), doing what they can to wipe Katrina out of the collective memory of Americans. Contradictions, at least in this context, serve as face-saving devices, whether for structures, agents, or for both when a distinction fails to have been made between the two. It should not be thought that white Americans are individualistic; it should instead be understood that individualism has more often served their needs in preserving their hegemonic power, both nationally and globally. Yet the moment the time comes, that individualism will be replaced with structural explanations once the need arises.

Do the agents feel separated from the social structure? Do they see the difference? Generally no, because is there really a need for white Americans to differentiate themselves from the structure. It is a structure they benefit from, despite gender, social class, or other differences between them. Since they have a stake in the survival of the structure, they do not generally want to see any changes, so how can one best defend that structure? A rationalization process is needed to legitimize the existence of that structure. One method to do this is to make it invisible: if a structure does not exist, it would be pointless to talk about it, much less allocate societal resources to change it.

The point is that white agents and social structures are interconnected: whites create the institutions, they oversee their operations, maintain, protect, and legitimize them, which in turn maintains their power. Even if white Americans give into pressure and say "okay, we are going to tweak some things here and there," with the machine of the media and gridlock in government, little of substance will ultimately be done to address these structural problems.

When discussing race, most whites avoid the issue as much as possible, and they do this in a way that resembles the efficiency, calculability, predictability, and nonhuman control of other bureaucratic (purposively rational) actions.[33] Indeed, patterns exist within their race discourse that perform the function of rationalizing the way things are concerning race relations in U.S. society. These patterns include *structured incoherence* to avoid admitting the existence of racism, mitigation statements to minimize societal racism, insistence that racial segregation is a natural phenomenon, and blaming racial minorities for social inequality due to their inferior cultures.[34] Another function of WRD is to present oneself as nonracist.

This study deals with interactions in which agents are involved (see Table 1.1). Depending on the context at hand, individuals are involved in the maintenance of their group position and, in turn, the institutions that make those positions possible. In this social phenomenon, the quest lies in the maintenance of white supremacy. Built within the habitus is the ability to shift gears in one's status with the superstructure of society. This ability unsurprisingly causes myriad contradictions to appear across the times an agent speaks to various racial issues in various social settings.

Table 1.1   Relationships between Structures and Agents in Impression Management

Type of relationship	Parties involved in the interaction
Consensus	Agents and agents Institutions and institutions Agents and institutions
Conflict	Agents versus agents Institutions versus institutions Agents versus institutions

On one hand, the blurring of the line between oneself and the superstructure serves the function of maintaining the status of that superstructure; on the other hand, pressure to address structural concerns leads whites to distance themselves with the superstructure in management of their own faces. This is the way hegemonic power is reproduced. This process also occurs in relation to other agents: the common practice is the reference to "a few bad apples" in regards to differences between fellow whites, yet when feeling one's face threatened, a distancing act takes place between one's own position and that of another.

Do institutions have faces, as do individuals? Do individuals engage in impression management of institutions, beside themselves, as well as for other people? Other functions of contradictions include integration of incompatible frames or repertoires, frame switching, and constructing a convincing argument.[35] However, these functions all become rationalizations of the status quo, whether an intended consequence or not. In addition, they all can serve as face-saving devices for the speaker. If they think that respondents engage in impression management for an individual, that is too limited a scope; impression management could also serve the social structure, as well as for individuals, whether for that immediate individual speaker but also for other whites as well, such as intimate whites defending a bigoted grandfather, saying "well, he's a good guy; he grew up in a different time," while stating that "people are more open-minded nowadays."

Thus, individual whites act as "optimistic robots"[36] when addressing racial issues or racialized social systems, and their actions are bureaucratic in form. Their (at least initial) optimism towards race relations in U.S. society assists in the legitimization of the status quo. Similar to loyal bureaucrats of an organization, they engage in impression management for the institutions that provide whites their privileges, while in turn those institutions speak glowingly of the "lily white," which often is defined and affirmed through the defined inferiority of the nonwhite Other. In addition, individual whites also speak (and defend) themselves, as well as for fellow whites whose face may be threatened. The way they speak in a particular social context depends on their relationship to the issue personally, the structure, and other white Americans.

In addition to fulfilling their bureaucratic tasks, whites often feel empty, confused, and dissatisfied during interviews; this is due to the emergence of the formal rationality that dominates their WRD and within other domains of their lives. In the neo-apartheid[37] system, white Americans simply do not have a reasonable explanation for racial inequality since biological racism is no longer a justification they can use. Thus, they simply do not know how to speak about race, so they try their best to avoid the issue of race at (nearly) all costs. White Americans learn a particular racespeak, based on the color-blind ideology, from various (white-dominated) social institutions such as the family, schools, and the polity.

Racetalk as a Means of Control

In addition to rationalizing the racial order, racetalk is a form of social control. More importantly, this form of discourse keeps progressive (or potentially progressive) whites from joining in the struggle against racial inequality, and (thus) is a key component in perpetuating the racist status quo in U.S. society. By all means, this should not be taken as a strictly structuralist view that sees agents as mere cogs in the machine, but that the structure of whites' racetalk has a significant impact on the way whites come across as they speak about race. Previous studies have shown the number of progressive whites to be a minority within the racial group[38]; nonetheless, their participation in the movement is essential to the legitimacy of the movement, as they were during the Civil Rights Movement of the 1950s and 1960s.

To address this issue, a necessary concept is the white habitus[39] in which whites develop a set of structuring mechanisms that creates a white bubble complete with sincere fictions of whiteness. Whites' racetalk has both external as well as internal constraints on the white subjects in which it exists (not to be reifying a form of discourse). However, this racetalk is more than just an external constraint, imposed upon white agents by various social structures. Whites' "iron cage" is not exactly locked with the key out of reach; in fact, whites benefit from its form in that it (1) keeps race from being discussed in much substance, and (2) allows whites to come off as innocently nonracist. Hence, this form of discourse is also a method of impression management in which whites, within a frontstage setting, can somehow disapprove of actions needed to curb racial inequality in society while looking fair and open-minded at the same time.

Although other racial groups may well utilize the various frames, mechanics, and story lines associated with whites' racetalk, there are a few key distinctions that make it clearly a white praxis and white only. For instance, blacks and other racial minorities may invoke the frame of abstract liberalism, or even stress some of the same explanations for the racial gap in life chances that whites do; however, one key difference is the recognition of race as a factor in life chances, suggesting that whites try not to acknowledge race as salient.

Ambivalence and Racial Apathy

Ambivalence is a concept that has been used in a variety of ways, and I believe a clarification of the term is an order. It can be defined in three ways, including a more recent conception I implement for this study, including: (1) ambivalence is not knowing due to conflicting frames of reference; (2) ambivalence is knowing but uncertain of how to present oneself; and (3) ambivalence is a deliberate projection of oneself in an attempt to appear innocent (e.g., nonracist). This type of ambivalence relevant to the subject at hand is called racial apathy,[40] as developed by Tyrone Forman.

The first conceptualization of ambivalence is the most limited in the discourse analysis of whites' racetalk. A good example comes from Hass and colleagues,[41] which defines ambivalence as "a situation in which one has strong, competing, incompatible inclinations or attitudes toward a particular object." This viewpoint towards ambivalence is superior over common sense definitions of the term, which is too simplistic (in that an individual is neutral or uncertain about a particular topic). This definition gives us insight into the ways whites grapple with competing interpretive frameworks, such as individualism and equality. However, it is limited in that it is too individualistic and does not explain the differences whites talk about race in various social domains.

The second definition of ambivalence is that people know about an issue, and even have an opinion on the topic, but are unsure in how to present themselves in front of someone else. This usage is better than the first because it does account for the various ways individuals behave in certain social contexts. Indeed, in this study there are moments when respondents appear unwilling to make a statement without some sort of clue in my own stance toward the issue. However, the problem with this definition (like the first) is that ambivalence is treated as a kind of condition, a state of being, that individuals possess (like a feeling).

The third definition of ambivalence is that ambivalence is a social construction that whites project in order to come across as "color-blind," even though they are not. Indeed, whites are often ignorant of the experiences nonwhite Americans have with systemic racism; however, in this study I present examples in which respondents are aware of such injustices and cast them away in defense of white privilege. Hence, this ambivalent "color-blind" display is not a characteristic but, rather, a constructed front or pretense[42] that whites use to project an image of nonracism. Tyrone Forman's concept of racial apathy corresponds well with my own conception of ambivalence these white college students exhibit in their interviews. He defines racial apathy as "indifference toward societal racial and ethnic inequality and lack of engagement with race-related issues."[43] Whether intended or not, "racial apathy and [w]hite ignorance are extensions of hegemonic color-blind discourses" and "the *strategic* avoidance of...knowledge about racial and ethnic disparities and the racialized realities that go along with them" (emphasis added). [44] In his study, Forman found evidence that racial apathy among whites is on the rise in U.S. society. Indeed, as I will present in subsequent chapters of this book, I found evidence to support Forman's findings that this is the case.

A Synthetic Approach to Understanding WRD

The way social scientists collect and analyze data is critical in the validity of the knowledge claims we make. Researchers must exercise praxis in our scholarly pursuits; that is, we cannot discuss our methodological approaches separate from our theoretical and/or ideological convictions. Whiteness studies, though still in its early stages of development, has generated enough scholarship to warrant investigation of its progress. The important point to bear in mind is that all whiteness scholars need to agree with one fundamental goal of their studies: that the findings by whiteness scholars are an essential ingredient to the elimination of racial inequality. The approach of this study attempts to bridge the divide between two camps within whiteness studies: the "constructivist" camp and the "systemic racism" camp. In this section, I provide the important contributions and limitations of each camp. Based on my analysis, I present my method of discourse analysis for this study.

The first of two predominant camps of whiteness studies I refer to as the "constructivist" camp primarily due to its emphasis on the fact that race is a social construction. Scholars from this camp argue that too often whiteness scholars produce scholarship that further reifies and essentializes whiteness.[45] Some from this camp[46] fear that discourse analyses like those of Teun Van Dijk or others from the "systemic racism" camp[47] have a tendency to engage in "essentialist theorizing," or "produce what was already postulated in advance."[48] Thus, those from the "systemic racism" camp espouse a kind of circular logic, meaning they assume that racism exists and therefore must exist, even if a respondent might deny its existence. The evidence must be grounded in the data itself rather than "through reference to speculative social and/or cognitive theories."[49]

Whiteness scholars from the "constructivist" camp also argue that those from the "systemic racism" camp fail to acknowledge the localization of race experience and the importance of context in affecting what we say, when we say it, and how.[50] Alastair Bonnett argues that too often whiteness scholars assume that whiteness is something all whites have, in equal amounts, and always oppress without ever facing oppression.[51] Indeed, intersections of race, class, and gender in race discourse have yet to be examined in great detail. In his groundbreaking study, John Hartigan conducted interviews of working-class white Detroiters who struggle economically and socially in a situation in which they are a minority in their city, while members of the school board, city officials, and other citizens in leadership positions are predominantly black.[52] The most important contribution of this camp is their willingness to examine and address the variability in experiences and discourse, when too often variability is either ignored or dismissed as a result of measurement error. In fact, this variability is often the result of different variables interacting with each other, such as race, class, and gender.

Despite the validity in its premise, a critical limitation in the "constructivist" camp is the denial of structural factors affecting individual lives. Although individual variations are important, I agree with Bonilla-Silva and Forman that the focus should be on whites as a group, one that receives unfair advantages at the expense of nonwhites in society.[53] In addition, critical discourse analysts such as Van Dijk[54] and Ruth Wodak[55] provide evidence of the ways whites rationalize white supremacy and defend whiteness through various linguistic techniques.

Meanwhile, the "systemic racism" camp focuses on the role of power and how racial identity places one in a social hierarchy, a social system that favors white over black. Despite Hartigan's contributions, his assertion that the experience of white Detroiters, who are just 20 percent of the city population, will increase in the experiences of more white Americans in the future, this has yet to be seen. Although the attention to the coming nonwhite majority on the horizon has increased in recent years (particularly from white conservatives nervous about the "threat" the newest immigrants represent to white hegemony[56]), this phenomenon is unlikely since whites often change the parameters of whiteness to include more under their tent in order to maintain numerical domination.[57] As past studies have found, many whites overestimate the number of blacks in society and in their immediate vicinity.[58]

An example of this propensity to overestimate the numbers of blacks in my research came from Irene,[59] who discussed the significance of racism in contemporary U.S. society:

Well, the thing is, it's all in the context of where you live, it's all based on geography, like in—where I live, in my school, it's like 80 percent Hispanics, a:nd

15 percent African American and 5 percent white so I'm the minority so as far
as, you know, I mean, there's no, there's not racial discrimination there

Irene claims that, based on her racial distribution of her high school, discrimination no longer exists. Like Hartigan and others from the constructivist camp, the
focus on localization of race downplays the social reality that race is a social
fact. Even when addressing the status of poor whites such as "rednecks" or
"hillbillies," they still profit from their whiteness that blacks and other
nonwhites lack.[60]

More recent developments in critical discourse analysis have made significant headway in understanding this discursive phenomenon. For example, the
discourse-historical approach concerns itself with understanding the contradictions within discursive structures.[61] Furthermore, in the critical tradition associated with the Frankfurt School,[62] this approach (1) understands "discourse" as a
method of solidifying and perpetuating the status quo, and (2) works toward
exposing and even challenging that status quo (if unjust inequalities exist). This
approach has three stages: first, prejudiced discourse is detected; second, discursive strategies of the interlocutors are explored; and third, "the linguistic means
and the specific context-dependent linguistic realizations of the discriminatory
stereotypes are then looked into."[63] This approach attempts to avoid the pitfalls
of previous critical discursive analyses, such as slipping into essentialism, while
avoiding postmodern relativism.

Reflecting the discourse-historical analytic approach, discourse analysts
must provide the necessary background information to effectively "ground" the
data and avoid knowledge claims based on preconceived assumptions. As
Reisigl and Wodak point out, this approach "attempts to integrate much available knowledge about the historical sources and the background of the social and
political fields in which discursive 'events' are embedded."[64] For example, in
her studies of anti-Semitism in Austria, Ruth Wodak contextualizes utterances
that, however implicitly, promote positive self-presentation and negative other-
presentation.[65] For this study, utterances were examined with the usage of a particular frame,[66] that of the "white racial frame," as presented by Joe Feagin.[67]

Discourse is a product of social action, and agents use frames to produce
discourse. Originating from the work of Goffman,[68] Deborah Tannen defines
frames as "patterns of expectation that are socio-culturally determined."[69] These
frames are ultimately so embedded in the mind that agents are often unaware of
them as they make decisions in their everyday lives. Among these frames are
images of "blackness" that are diametrically opposed to "whiteness." Furthermore, frames are both social and cognitive structures.[70] On one hand, individuals
have their own habitus that affect the way they interact with others; meanwhile,
there are also social structures that impose meanings on the actions of individual
agents. With most major social institutions dominated be white Americans,
meanings often portray whites more favorably than nonwhites. This combination
of structures forms what Feagin refers to as the "white racial frame," which he
claims is the key factor in the reproduction of systemic racism in U.S. society:

Central to the presence of systemic racism into the present day is the organized set of racialized habits that whites consciously or unconsciously express in their everyday attitudes and actions in U.S. society. These habits include the racialized framing of the social world that most use extensively, a frame that embeds an array of racist stereotypes, images, and emotions that are to a significant degree survivals of centuries-old anti-black and prowhite thinking.[71]

It is this frame that serves as the backdrop for whites as they speak about racial matters. This book examines the important functions contradictions serve in protecting the white racial frame via discourse: first, they provide white respondents with a method to blame nonwhites for various societal problems while (seemingly) maintaining an image of nonracism; and second, they protect the status quo despite pointing out particular instances of prejudicial and discriminatory actions.

To conclude this section, one of the most important contributions from the constructivist camp is the insightful analytic strategies devised by conversation analysts.[72] These researchers provide sophisticated techniques for analyzing racetalk. While some researchers from the "systemic racism" camp have adopted these strategies, many of these studies have not.[73] Thus, I wish to build off of the theoretical works of those from the systemic racism camp while adopting analytic practices from the constructivist camp—the latter coming primarily from the area of linguistics.

Research Design

For researchers in the past, the observation of variability in the responses of study participants was believed to be a result of measurement error, and needed to be "fixed" with a "better" research design: i.e., a survey questionnaire that suppressed any variations.[74] However, over time these contradictory responses could no longer be ignored. The primary danger of this particular set of contradictions was the fact that social scientists had been peddling these survey data to show how quickly white Americans had ended their support of various antiblack stereotypes, only to find that these contradictions, found predominantly by more qualitative research measurements, posed a threat to the validity of their claims of whites' decreased bigotry. How do we make sense of the contradictions and variability in the race discourse of white Americans? Unlike other studies that have tried to come to terms with these contradictions by hiding them from view or ignoring them, this study focuses squarely on these contradictions, arguing that they rationalize the racial order and aids the respondent in face maintenance.

This study utilizes the collection of data through in-depth interviews. Prior to the interviews, each respondent filled out a brief questionnaire asking them to score the level of importance of a social value (see the Appendix for the questionnaire). Like previous studies, I used this approach to expose any contradictions between their answers on the questionnaire and those given during the interview.[75] This approach exposes the ways whites speak about race in a frontstage setting. Interviewing is a way to expose the myriad contradictions in WRD and a method to get at the white racial frame by giving respondents an opportunity to express emotions and recall personal experiences. Furthermore, my approach also takes into account the issue of framing interview topics for respondents, and by giving respondents the opportunity to frame the issue themselves, gives them more control of the situation.

I chose to interview white college students enrolled in sociology courses for this project. I chose a purposive sample[76] for three primary reasons: first, this sample is a convenient one that was easier to obtain than a different sample. Meanwhile, rather than paying study participants, respondents were granted extra credit by their instructors for participation in the study. Second, social scientists use purposive sampling to collect information-rich data for in-depth analysis that often cannot be obtained through other sampling strategies. Collecting data on the way white Americans contradict themselves when talking about racial matters is impossible with surveys. Third, many Americans have a tendency to assume that younger whites are more egalitarian than older whites. This study shows how region, age, and other factors mean little when a set of structures exist that perpetuates white supremacy, such as the discursive structure characteristic of WRD. Younger whites indeed may speak less overtly than older whites when legitimizing the racist social structure, but the legitimation occurs nonetheless.

Qualitative researchers have argued that we as scientists should not only analyze what people say, but how they say it and in what context was an utterance delivered.[77] Following pioneering works in the field of whiteness studies, analyses since have often lacked the sophisticated methods of discourse analysis. For this study, I have adopted a coding strategy used by conversation analysts such as those in the edited volume Van Den Berg et al. (see Abbreviations section for the list of the coding strategy). This strategy is useful for discourse analysis because it gets deeper into the textuality of discourse, and brings to light the ways interviewer responses influence that of the respondents. For example, in the following exchange with Kaitlin, observe the series of "mhm"s and its potential effect on the her utterances:

R: Um, actually one of my roommates is black, and one of them is Spanish, and then my actual roommate because I live in [name of dorm] is um, is white, she's the one who actually lives in my room.
I: Mhm.
R: Yeah, I get kind of angry and I don't blame it on the fact that (.) she's black but she like always has all of her friends over and they're really loud
I: Mhm
R: And sometimes I want to say that "black people are really loud" like but I know that's not it
I: Mhm↓

R: But I just like (.) sometimes I want to blame it on that. but

In this excerpt, I first give a "mhm." with the "." indicating a falling intonation, which suggests my wish for her to continue following her descriptive information of her roommates. The second "mhm" does not have a falling intonation, which suggests I could have been responding to her recount of a "problem" caused by her black roommate. Despite the difference between the two, both tend to serve the same backchannelling function. Compared to the others, however, the third "mhm↓" suggests my displeasure towards her semantic move "And sometimes I want to say that 'black people are really loud' like but I know that's not it." Although in this particular response the "mhm↓" did not seem to phase her (she merely reiterated her point), she might have been influenced by my response.

Active Interviewing

At the center of this methodological approach is the in-depth interview, and there are some methodological issues concerning this method of data collection. A debate within sociology remains what the role of the researcher should be as s/he is collecting data. Should a researcher take the role of "disinterested scientist," and thereby passively observing and recording social phenomena? Then again, is such an approach possible? In reality, both the interviewer and respondent contribute to the creation of interview discourse, regardless of the interviewer's level of activity. As James Holstein and Jaber Gubrium point out, in the "active interview" both actors have a role to play.[78] I take the position that the interviewer should take a more active approach to the interview process, e.g. probing respondents as Ruth Frankenberg did in her seminal study of white women. Although Margaret Wetherell and others warn against this for fear of less honesty in research, and that researchers often practice "friendly interviewing" methods,[79] scientists need to understand that vast contradictions exist in WRD, and thus a little "prodding" of respondents might be needed.

To address the issue of framing interview topics for respondents, this study will take an approach influenced by the concept of the focused interview.[80] The design of the interview was to begin with relatively unstructured questions and move into more structured questions as the respondent discusses each topic. The focus of the interviews is on "the subjective experiences of persons exposed to the pre-analyzed situation in an effort to ascertain their definitions of the situation."[81] In addition to exposing the myriad contradictions within their race discourse, how do respondents react to these contradictions as they present them during the interviews?

Benefits and Limitations of the Method

One important benefit in conducting these interviews is the matter of convenience, both for myself and for the sample of college students. These students could meet me for an interview between their classes, while I did not have to travel to conduct them. Meanwhile, although I did not offer respondents monetary compensation for their participation in the study, they did receive extra credit from their instructors.

Another benefit of this approach is the advantages associated with the qualitative method. One benefit of a qualitative study is the hands-on process that allows researchers to make adjustments or changes to various components of the research design. An example of this advantage during this study was the probing techniques to use during the interviews. Some probes I discarded after brief usage (e.g., asking respondents how they would answer a child's question "Mommy/Daddy, what is racism?"), while other probes were added or used more thoroughly. Unlike rigid surveys that cannot be altered once it is proctored, in-depth interviews allow the researcher to improve the validity of the study.

A third benefit of this method is that, unlike autobiographical accounts written by respondents, I have an opportunity to ask follow-up questions during the interviews. Although many constructivists fear the framing of issues by researchers, sometimes providing a frame of reference for respondents aids them in their understanding of a question. Furthermore, sometimes the researcher does not fully understand the meaning of an utterance, and can seek out a clarification. This most certainly applies to concepts like "whiteness" or "racism" when interviewing white Americans; often responses involving these terms are ambiguous or incoherent. In the following passage, Odella's conceptualization of "white supremacy" was ambiguous and serves an example of failing to see racism occurring right under her nose. Initially she talks about an experience at her high school in which white students hung a "black doll" from a tree and lit it ablaze on school grounds:

> At my high school, there was a big news story about there was a uh southern boys group at my school, and they um hung a (.) black doll from a tree at my high school, and that caused a very big news story and a huge, huge problem, and (.) the two groups, the black kids at the school, and the southern boys group had to go through this huge counseling, and they were two really big groups, but it kind of affected the whole school, and um (.) there was a petition to make the confederate flag not allowed to be worn or put on cars at our school, so there was lot of debate over that, and it caused tension (laughs)

After this set of statements, many questions entered my mind, such as the effects of this experience on the respondent personally (note her usage of passive voice or third person accounts, such as "there was a petition" and "there was lot of debate over that"). Thus, I immediately began to ask follow-up questions:

I: Well like, it was like(.) as far as some of the details, I mean I'm not familiar

with the story but like you said that a black doll they- like this was on campus?
R: Yeah, it was at our school.
I: Okay. Like and they um just like (.) I mean it was like just a regular-sized doll?
R: No, like a human sized
I: Oh, okay. Hmm (.) What and it was like dressed in real clothing?
R: It was just like, it was like cloth and uh a trash bag in the shape of a person, hung from a tree, by the neck.
I: Right. God, that's interesting. And so there was just like I mean you mentioned like the principal and
R: Yeah.
I: They were all (.) mobilizing as far as to deal with it
R: Yeah, and yeah (laughs)
I: And what about parents, were there parents getting involved to with it and stuff
R: Yeah, it was like a whole, huge (laughs) huge like news story with news stations at the school, and um but it resolved itself pretty well in the end. Like everyone realized the (.) stupidity of it.
I: Yeah.

Although Odella continues to distance herself from the "action" in this account (e.g., "Like everyone realized the (.) stupidity of it"), I was able to get more texture to the experience. Were her initial statement written as an autobiographical account, it would have been unusable due to its ambiguity.

Despite the advantages of a method like this, there are at least four limitations associated with this methodological approach, and the first has to do with the limitations of a purposive sampling strategy. I present two particular issues related to the sampling strategy here: first, is the data gathered from this study generalizable to other white college students? Moreover, is the data generalizable to white Americans in general? A study such as this cannot be used to describe the discourse of *all* whites. Still, this data gives much-needed exposure to the way one group of white Americans discusses race matters within a frontstage setting. Second, bias is possible in the selection of the sample. For instance, who chose to sign up for an interview? Were they students who needed the extra credit for the class? Furthermore, of those who signed up, which students did not show up for an interview or were unavailable for the study altogether? It is impossible to answer these questions accurately; nonetheless, they should be taken into account. The main point is that, despite these concerns, the goal of this study is to take an in-depth look at how these white students discuss race matters, and more specifically, the contradictions that abound within their race discourse.

The second limitation comes from various conversation analysts' concern over the ways interviewers too often influence participants' responses by framing the issue of discussion.[82] For example, Tom Koole points out the way interviewers can co-construct or confirm a response.[83] A key difference between this study and others is that great effort was made to avoid any framing of the problems for the interviewees and instead gave them as much room to roam on the various issues as possible. Despite this attempt to avoid framing the problems for respondents, they often would have a difficult time talking about the issue at hand (e.g., racial privilege), so it was imperative that I probed respondents in a particular way to get them started while continuing to let them take the stories in a direction that they wished to go. There were some sections of the interview that were framed by the interviewer (such as the statement that respondents recall a time when s/he was "embarrassed to be a white person"), but most of the statements were designed to generate frames fully produced and presented by the respondents. The ability of study participants to fully contextualize their stories would provide a safeguard from misinterpreting their responses.

Another potential limitation is the issue of respondents speaking "truthfully" when during these interviews. While conducting the interviews, I found that there were instances of "slippage" or variability of discourse within this frontstage setting.[84] I conducted most interviews in my office, which is shared with multiple graduate students. Respondents on a couple of occasions lowered their tone of voice when someone entered the room, perhaps due to the race of the individual. Thus, rather than seeing the stage as either front or backstage, there are degrees of comfort within both stages, including the race of people involved.

The fourth limitation of this method is the liability of study participants' lack of response. When discussing "controversial" subject matters, respondents might restrain themselves in a way that limits the quantity and quality of their utterances. Sometimes respondents just did not seem interested and no amount of probing helped; fortunately, this was an anomaly: in fact, most respondents were at least somewhat talkative during their interviews.

The Sample

In order to recruit respondents, I spoke with teachers of sociology courses and they agreed to offer students extra credit for participation in my study. I then gave them slips of paper for willing participants to sign up for interviews. Instructors made the announcements during class, and passed out the slips of paper to volunteers. Based on a previous experience of sample recruitment, I found it easier for instructors to make the announcement themselves rather than making the announcement myself in their classes. I asked respondents for some personal information, including contact information so they could be contacted for an interview.

The sample for this study consisted of 61 white undergraduates enrolled in sociology courses attending a historically white university in the southeastern United States. I interviewed the respondents between January 2002 and February 2006. Respondents filled out a slip of paper asking for contact information, sex, and racial identity (asked in an open-ended format: "Race: _____"), and their current year in school. Volunteers, who received extra credit in their course for participating, were contacted for interviews either by phone or e-mail. An informed consent form notifying them of their rights as interviewees was administered before proceeding with the study.

Of those interviewed, all but one wrote either "white" or "Caucasian" for their racial identity. One male respondent (Davis) wrote "White/Franco-Italian." His life experience was unique in that he spent much of his life living abroad in France. Despite some critics that have suggested these studies reify and essentialize whiteness,[85] all respondents interviewed for this study thought of themselves as such; I never assumed they were white. Samples like these are beneficial because young whites are more likely to utilize the covert discursive forms, have more contact with people of color, and likely have greater potential for antiracism than older whites.[86]

The respondents were generally in the traditional college-student age group (twenty-something). Of the 61 respondents, approximately two-thirds were female. This gender imbalance is actually more representative of college students, particularly given that a majority of sociology students and majors are female.

Outline of the Book

In the remainder of the book I present a thorough analysis of contradictions in whites' race discourse, and how they assist whites in the rationalization of systemic racism and the legitimation of themselves, fellow whites, and social institutions that perpetuate racial inequality. The topic of focus in chapter 3 is the contradictions surrounding the issue of interracial interactions respondents recall during the interviews based on their personal experiences. I divide this chapter into three parts: first, how do respondents come to terms with living in a segregated society despite favoring integration? Second, how does this fundamental contradiction affect their descriptions of experiences involving nonwhite Americans? Third, how do they rationalize the racial segregation of the social structure?

In chapter 4 I examine the role of contradictions in their discourse when discussing racial inequality. In particular, I look at their awareness of white privilege and how their ambivalence leads to opposition towards programs and policies that attempt to deal with systemic racism. I highlight the ways that whites in this sample paint themselves as victims of "reverse racism" while questioning the claims of nonwhite Americans that they face injustices. First, I explore the ways in which respondents oppose policies designated to alleviate past racial injustices (including their comments on reparations). Second, I investigate the way the sample comes to see itself as victims of the "quest" for diversity. Finally, I shed some light on how they will likely reproduce the racist social order as potential employers in the future.

In chapter 5 I examine the contradictions within their discourse when talking about white supremacy and racism. More precisely, I look at how whites' racespeak creates a defense for white supremacists and ambivalence towards racism. Additionally, I examine the ways that respondents express ambivalence towards racist jokes and even engage in racist joking.

A common theme throughout this book is that the type of racetalk utilized by this sample of white Americans confines and restricts their boundaries on what exists and what their capabilities are; thus, WRD is a form of social control. In chapter 6, I provide instances in which respondents deviated from the script of WRD. While WRD is a structure that limits the respondents' abilities to effectively challenge systemic racism, there were moments in which WRD broke down or was not used (in fact, at times respondents seemed to fight against it). I present evidence that the respondents least likely to use WRD were those who reported more "quality" contacts with persons of color in their everyday lives, or who are themselves members of social groups who have experienced marginalization (e.g., Jewish or gay respondents).

In the final chapter I summarize the significance of these contradictions in WRD and offer a list of general "rules" of WRD. Furthermore, I present ways in which we can challenge this ambivalence towards the impact of systemic racism and discuss the possibility of moving beyond WRD and to a racetalk that is more constructive in increasing racial and ethnic equality. I also provide some recommendations for future research in this area of inquiry. In the next chapter, I examine contradictions within whites' racespeak when articulating their thoughts on whiteness and how they discuss their social identities as white Americans. I present in more detail the bureaucratization of WRD, and apply George Ritzer's theory of McDonaldization to the racetalk of the sample.

Notes

1. Portions of this chapter are adapted from John D. Foster, "Defending Whiteness Indirectly: A Synthetic Approach to Race Discourse Analysis," *Discourse & Society* 20 (November 2009): 685-703.

2. For example, Dinesh D'Sousa's *The End of Racism* (New York: Free Press, 1995) was funded by the Olin Foundation, a supporter of the American Enterprise Institute, of which D'Sousa was a fellow at the time.

3. Great examples include Joe R. Feagin and Melvin P. Sikes, *Living With Racism: The Black Middle-Class Experience* (Boston: Beacon, 1994) and Ruth Frankenberg, *White Women, Race Matters: The Social Construction of Whiteness* (Minneapolis, MN: University of Minnesota Press, 1993).

4. An example of this was the passage of Proposition 209 in California in 1996, which barred state institutions to consider race, ethnicity, or sex. Considered by many to be (at least in part) a result of Prop 209's passage, the enrollment of both African American and Latino students at UC schools has declined significantly. See Michael Dobbs, "Universities Record Drop in Black Admissions," *Washington Post*, www.washington post.com/wp-dyn/articles/A2830-2004Nov21.html (accessed August 4, 2011).

5. An especially candid moment was when Shepherd Smith, interviewed on location in New Orleans by Bill O'Reilly via satellite on O'Reilly's program, exasperatingly said

the slow response to provide assistance was unacceptable, and O'Reilly was clearly dis-gruntled by Smith's words. For a video clip and article discussing the difference between journalists in the "real world" and those back in the studios, see Steve Classen, "Report-ers Gone Wild: Reporters and Their Critics on Hurricane Katrina, Gender, Race, and Place," *E-Media Studies* 2, no. 1 (January 2009): journals.dartmouth.edu/cgi-bin/WebObjects/Journals.woa/2/xmlpage/4/article/336 (accessed August 4, 2011).

6. Michael Eric Dyson, *Come Hell or High Water: Hurricane Katrina and the Color of Disaster* (New York: Basic Civitas, 2006), 4.

7. Some like to engage in the "which matters more?" debates, such as "class versus race" or "race versus gender" (the latter, for instance, was commonplace in the news media during the 2008 Presidential campaign between then Senators Barack Obama and Hillary Clinton) but this approach to understanding oppression is flawed because these variables, while capable of operating independently, often operate in conjunction with one another.

8. For an analysis of various responses to Obama's election (including African Americans as well as white conservatives), see Wornie L. Reed and Bertin M. Louis, "'No More Excuses': Problematic Responses to Barack Obama's Election," *Journal of African American Studies* 13, no. 2 (June 2009): 97-109.

9. Obama lost the white vote in the election by a margin of 43-55 to John McCain. Despite the attempt by white conservatives to "claim" this historical moment for them-selves, in reality it was (at least in many instances) Obama's support from blacks and Latinos that put him over the top: e.g., white voters were essentially inconsequential in Florida, a key battleground state, while Latinos made the difference, going from double-digit support for George W. Bush in 2004 to double-digit support for Obama (a 26-point swing!). I wrote about the 2008 Presidential Election results in a blog available at racismreview.com/blog/2008/11/15/whitewashing-the-election-results.

10. According to a Gallup poll taken shortly prior to the March on Washington, 63 percent of whites opposed it. George H. Gallup, *The Gallup Poll, Public Opinion, 1935-1971* (New York: Random House, 1972). Found in Richard T. Schaefer, *Racial and Ethnic Groups*, 12th ed. (Upper Saddle River, NJ: Prentice Hall, 2010).

11. One example was a Republican official who pasted Obama's face onto a monkey and sent the image with the caption "Now you know why—no birth certificate!" In re-sponse to those calling for her resignation, she later said "I am not a racist. It was a joke. I have friends who are black." Wire Services, "Orange County GOP Official Refuses to Resign Over Racist Email," *Los Angeles Wave*, www.wavenewspapers.com/news/orange-county-racist-ape-chimp-email-gop-republican-obama-davenport-19993794.html (accessed August 5, 2011).

12. For example, on income disparities and the impact on access to health care, see Carmen DeNavas-Walt, Bernadette D. Proctor, and Jessica C. Smith, "Income, Poverty, and Health Insurance Coverage in the United States: 2007," *Current Population Reports* (Washington, D.C.: U.S. Government Printing Office), 60-235. Available online at www.census.gov/prod/2008pubs/p60-235.pdf.

13. Eduardo Bonilla-Silva, *White Supremacy and Racism in the Post-Civil Rights Era* (Boulder, CO: Lynne Rienner, 2001).

14. Bonilla-Silva defines "racetalk" as "the idiosyncratic linguistic manners and rhe-torical strategies used to articulate racial viewpoints," in *White Supremacy*, 68. Also see Kristen Myers, *Racetalk: Racism Hiding in Plain Sight* (Lanham, MD: Roman and Little-field, 2005).

15. There are numerous examples, including Frankenberg, *White Women*; Eduardo Bonilla-Silva, *Racism Without Racists: Color-Blind Racism and the Persistence of Racial*

Inequality in the United States, 3rd ed. (Lanham, MD: Roman and Littlefield, 2010); and Teun Van Dijk, *Communicating Racism: Ethnic Prejudice in Thought and Talk* (London: Sage, 1987).

16. Eduardo Bonilla-Silva, "The Invisible Weight of Whiteness: The Racial Grammar of Everyday Life in Contemporary America," in *Ethnic and Racial Studies*, 35, no. 2 (February 2012), 173-194.

17. Bonilla-Silva, "The Invisible Weight of Whiteness," 174.

18. Bonilla-Silva, "The Invisible Weight of Whiteness," 174-175.

19. Pierre Bourdieu, *Outline of a Theory of Practice* (Cambridge: Cambridge University Press, 1977).

20. Harry Van Den Berg, "Contradictions in Interview Discourse," in *Analyzing Race Talk: Multidisciplinary Approaches to the Interview*, ed. Harry Van Den Berg, Margaret Wetherell, and Hanneke Houtkoop-Steenstra (Cambridge, U.K.: Cambridge University Press, 2003), 120.

21. Margaret Wetherell, "Racism and the Analysis of Cultural Resources in Interviews," in *Analyzing Race Talk*, 13.

22. By "quality" I mean beneficial contact, meaning that the relationship (1) must be approved of authority figures (e.g., parents), (2) is one in which they have equal social status, and (3) is a situation of cooperation, not conflict. Gordon Allport, *The Nature of Prejudice* (Reading, MA: Addison-Wesley, 1954); Hugh D. Forbes, *Ethnic Conflict* (New Haven, CT: Yale University Press, 1997).

23. Eduardo Bonilla-Silva, "The Essential Social Fact of Race," *American Sociological Review*, 64, no. 6 (December 1999), 899-906.

24. This was certainly the case following the election of Obama, with numerous pundits and commentators even using it to declare the U.S. a "post-racial" society. See Adia Harvey Wingfield and Joe R. Feagin, *Yes We Can?: White Racial Framing and the 2008 Presidential Campaign* (New York: Routledge, 2009), 1.

25. Ruth Frankenberg, *White Women, Race Matters*; Teun Van Dijk, *Communicating Racism*.

26. For example, see Anita Pomerantz and Alan Zemel, "Perspectives and Frameworks in Interviewers' Queries," in *Analyzing Race Talk*, 215-231.

27. Bonilla-Silva, *Racism Without Racists*.

28. Melanie E.L. Bush, *Breaking the Code of Good Intentions: Everyday Forms of Whiteness* (Lanham, MD: Roman and Littlefield, 2004).

29. Eduardo Bonilla-Silva and Tyrone Forman, "I Am Not A Racist But...": Mapping White College Students' Racial Ideology in the USA," *Discourse & Society*, 11, no. 1 (January 2000), 73.

30. Joe R. Feagin, Hernán Vera, and Pinar Batur, *White Racism: The Basics*, 2nd ed. (New York: Routledge, 2001).

31. Eduardo Bonilla-Silva, *Racism Without Racists*.

32. Zygmunt Bauman, *Modernity and Ambivalence* (Ithaca, NY: Cornell University Press, 1991).

33. George Ritzer, *The McDonaldization of Society 6* (Thousand Oaks, CA: Pine Forge, 2011).

34. Bonilla-Silva, *Racism Without Racists*.

35. Van Den Berg, "Contradictions in Interview Discourse," 128-134.

36. This concept was influenced by the term "Cheerful Robot" as used by C. Wright Mills in his essay "Culture and Politics: The Fourth Epoch" (*Power, Politics, and People: The Collected Essays of C. Wright Mills*, ed. Irving L. Horowitz (New York: Oxford University Press, 1963), reprinted in Peter Kivisto, *Social Theory: Roots and Branches*,

2nd ed. (Los Angeles: Roxbury, 2003). I will address this link to Mills' term further in Chapter 2.

37. Bonilla-Silva has argued that a "new" racism has emerged that has replaced the "old" model of overt white racist action (which was openly defended by individual whites without fear of reprisal or social criticism) with a more covert system that continues to privilege whites over blacks (see Bonilla-Silva, *White Supremacy*, 137-139). Undoubtedly, white Americans continue to enjoy innumerable privileges without many of the overt discriminatory practices of the past. However, the adjective "new" to describe racism in contemporary U.S. society seems problematic, given that some changes in form have not occurred, including the concentration of wealth in whites' hands, separate and unequal neighborhoods, while incarceration and capital punishment now the "modern form" of white-on-black violence (for example, see Michelle Alexander, *The New Jim Crow: Mass Incarceration in the Age of Colorblindness* [New York: The New Press, 2010]). Anthropologist Jane Hill has also directed criticism towards this notion of the birth of a "new" racism (see Jane H. Hill, *The Everyday Language of White Racism*, West Sussex, U.K.: Wiley Blackwell, 2008). Thus, a different label may be preferable at this juncture. Since the "previous" racialized social system is often labeled "apartheid," perhaps a term we can use for the current one is "neo-apartheid," since it not only follows the original, but in fact is little more than a modified version of the former system. Referring to the current system as "new" seems to grant too much distance from the "old" system.

38. For example, Leslie Picca and Joe Feagin estimated that no more than one percent of their study of more than 9,000 diary entries from 626 college students reported a white antiracist response to an act of racial discrimination perpetrated by whites. See Leslie H. Picca and Joe R. Feagin, *Two-Faced Racism: Whites in the Backstage and the Frontstage* (New York: Routledge, 2007). Feagin has a short blog on this topic entitled "Taking Anti-Racist Action: Why Rare for Whites?" Available online at www.racism review.com/blog/01/09/taking-anti-racist-action-why-rare-for-whites.

39. "Habitus" is a concept developed by Pierre Bourdieu in *Outline of a Theory of Practice*. Bonilla-Silva defines "white habitus" as a "racialized, uninterrupted socialization process that conditions and creates whites' racial taste, perceptions, feelings, and emotions and their views on racial matters" in *Racism Without Racists*, 104. Also see Eduardo Bonilla-Silva, Carla Goar, and David G. Embrick, "When Whites Flock Together: The Social Psychology of White Habitus," *Critical Sociology*, 32, vol. 2-3 (March 2006): 229-253.

40. Tyrone Forman, "Color-Blind Racism and Racial Indifference: The Role of Racial Apathy in Facilitating Enduring Inequalities," in *Changing Terrain of Race & Ethnicity*, eds. Maria Krysan and Amanda E. Lewis (New York: Russell-Sage, 2004), 43-66.

41. R. Glen Hass, Irwin Katz, Nino Rizzo, Joan Bailey, and Lynn Moore, "When Racial Ambivalence Evokes Negative Affect, Using a Disguised Measure of Mood," *Personality and Social Psychology Bulletin*, 18, no. 6 (December 1992), 786-797.

42. The idea of the concept "color-blind pretense" came during a discussion with Joe R. Feagin, October 2006.

43. Tyrone Forman, "Color-Blind Racism and Racial Indifference," 44.

44. Tyrone Forman and Amanda E. Lewis, "Racial Apathy and Hurricane Katrina: The Social Anatomy of Prejudice in the Post-Civil Rights Era," *Du Bois Review* 3, no. 1 (March 2006), 175-202. Van Dijk also alluded to the phenomenon of whites claiming innocence via ignorance in his book *Communicating Racism*.

45. Examples include John Hartigan, Jr., *Racial Situations: Class Predicaments of Whiteness in Detroit* (Princeton, NJ: Princeton University Press, 1999), and Van Den Berg, "Contradictions in Interview Discourse."

46. Examples include Jonathan Potter and Margaret Wetherell, *Discourse and Social Psychology: Beyond Attitudes and Behavior* (London: Sage, 1987) and Michael Billig, Susan Condor, Derek Edwards, Mike Gane, Dav Middleton, and Alan Radley, *Ideological Dilemmas: A Social Psychology of Everyday Thinking* (London: Sage, 1988).

47. Examples include Teun Van Dijk, "Discourse and the Denial of Racism," *Discourse and Society*, 3 (1992: 1), 87-118; Frankenberg, *White Women, Race Matters*; and Alice McIntyre, *Making Meaning of Whiteness: Exploring Racial Identity with White Teachers* (Albany, NY: State University of New York Press, 1997).

48. Van Den Berg, "Contradictions in Interview Discourse," 123.

49. Van Den Berg, "Contradictions in Interview Discourse," 123.

50. For example, see Nina Eliasoph, "'Everyday Racism' in a Culture of Political Avoidance: Civil Society, Speech, and Taboo," *Social Forces* 46, no. 4 (November 1999): 479-502.

51. Alastair Bonnett, "Antiracism and the Critique of 'White' Identities," *New Communities* 22, no. 1 (January 1996): 97-110.

52. Hartigan, *Racial Situations*.

53. Bonilla-Silva and Forman, "I Am Not A Racist But..."

54. Examples from Van Dijk include *Communicating Racism*, "Discourse and the Denial of Racism," and *Elite Discourse and Racism* (London: Sage, 1993).

55. Examples from Wodak include "Daus Ausland and Anti-Semitic Discourse: The Discursive Construction of the Other," in *The Language and Politics of Exclusion: Others in Discourse*, ed. Stephen H. Riggins (Thousand Oaks, CA: Sage, 1997), 65-87; "Discourses of Silence: Anti-Semitic Discourse on Post-War Austria," in *Discourse and Silencing: Representation and the Language of Displacement*, ed. Lynn Thiesmeyer (Amsterdam: Benjamins, 2004), 124-156; and "Critical Linguistics and Critical Discourse Analysis," in *Handbook of Pragmatics*, eds. Jan-Ola Ostman and Jef Verschueren (in collaboration with Eline Verluys; Amsterdam: Benjamins, 2006).

56. There are many in this area, including Patrick J. Buchanan, *The Death of the West: How Dying Populations and Immigrant Invasions Imperil Our Country and Civilization* (New York: Thomas Dunne, 2002).

57. Eduardo Bonilla-Silva, "'New Racism,' Color-Blind Racism, and the Future of Whiteness in America," in *White Out: The Continuing Significance of Race*, eds. Ashley W. Doane and Eduardo Bonilla-Silva (New York: Routledge, 2003), 271-284; also see Bonilla-Silva, *Racism Without Racists*.

58. Stan A. Kaplowitz, Bradley J. Fisher, and Clifford J. Broman, "How Accurate are Perceptions of Social Statistics about Blacks and Whites?" *Public Opinion Quarterly* 67, no. 2 (Summer 2003): 237-244; Charles A. Gallagher, "Miscounting Race: Explaining Whites' Misperceptions of Racial Group Size," *Sociological Perspectives* 46, no. 3 (Fall 1997): 381-396.

59. All names used for the respondents herein are pseudonyms to maintain confidentiality.

60. David Roediger, *The Wages of Whiteness: Race and the Making of the American Middle Class* (New York: Verso, 1991); Joe R. Feagin, *Systemic Racism: A Theory of Oppression* (New York: Routledge, 2006).

61. This approach is outlined in Martin Reisigl and Ruth Wodak, *Discourse and Discrimination: Rhetorics of Racism and Antisemitism* (London: Routledge, 2001).

62. For example, see Jürgen Habermas, *Legitimation Crisis* (trans. Thomas McCarthy; Boston: Beacon Press, 1975).

63. Ruth Wodak and Martin Reisigl, "Discourse and Discrimination: European Perspectives," *Annual Review of Anthropology* 28, no. 1 (October 1999): 175-199.

64. Reisigl and Wodak, *Discourse and Discrimination*, 35.

65. Ruth Wodak, "Turning the Tables: Antisemitic Discourse in Post-War Austria," *Discourse and Society* 2, no. 1 (January 1991): 65-83; Ruth Wodak, "The Genesis of Racist Discourse in Austria since 1989," in *Texts and Practices*, eds. Carmen R. Caldas-Coulthard and Malcolm Coulthard (London: Routledge, 1996), 107-128; Wodak, "Das Ausland and Anti-Semitic Discourse," and Wodak, "Discourses of Silence."

66. Teun Van Dijk, *Ideology* (London: Sage, 1999); Also see Bonilla-Silva, *White Supremacy*, 141-153.

67. Feagin, *Systemic Racism*. Also see Joe R. Feagin, *The White Racial Frame: Centuries of Framing and Counter-Framing* (New York: Routledge, 2010).

68. Erving Goffman, *Frame Analysis* (Boston: Northeastern University Press, 1974).

69. Deborah Tannen, "What's in a Frame?" in *Framing in Discourse*, ed. Deborah Tannen (New York: Oxford University Press, 1993) 14-55. The quotation is from Van Den Berg, "Contradictions in Interview Discourse," 120.

70. Titus Ensink, "The Frame Analysis of Research Interviews: Social Categorization and Footing in Interview Discourse," in *Analyzing Race Talk*, 156-177.

71. Feagin, *Systemic Racism*, 230.

72. Prominent examples in this area of discourse analysis include Margaret Wetherell and Jonathan Potter, *Mapping the Language of Racism* (New York: Columbia University Press, 1992), and the edited volume *Analyzing Race Talk*.

73. Works that have utilized such analytic techniques include Bonilla-Silva and Forman, "I Am Not A Racist But..." and Bonilla-Silva, *Racism Without Racists*. Those that did not include Joe R. Feagin and Eileen O'Brien, *White Men on Race: Power, Privilege, and the Shaping of Cultural Consciousness* (Boston: Beacon Press, 2002), and Frankenberg, *White Women, Race Matters*.

74. James Fraser and Edward Kick, "The Interpretive Repertoires of Whites on Race-Targeted Policies: Claims Making of Reverse Discrimination." *Sociological Perspectives*, 43, no. 1 (Spring 2000): 13-28.

75. One study that used this approach was Bonilla-Silva and Forman, "I Am Not A Racist But..."

76. Michael Q. Patton, *Qualitative Evaluation and Research Methods*, 3rd Edition (Newbury Park, CA: Sage, 1990); Bruce L. Berg, *Qualitative Research Methods for the Social Science* (Boston: Allyn and Bacon, 2001).

77. Jaber F. Gubrium and James A. Holstein, *The New Language of Qualitative Method* (New York: Oxford University Press, 1997).

78. James A. Holstein and Jaber F. Gubrium, *The Active Interview* (Thousand Oaks, CA: Sage, 1995).

79. Wetherell, "Racism and the Analysis of Cultural Resources in Interviews," 28.

80. Robert K. Merton, Marjorie Lowenthal, and Patricia L. Kendall. *The Focused Interview: A Manual of Problems and Procedures*, 2nd Edition (London: Collier Macmillan, 1990).

81. Merton, Lowenthal, and Kendall, *The Focused Interview*, 3.

82. For example, see Tony Hak, "Interviewer Laughter as an Unspecified Request for Clarification," in *Analyzing Race Talk*, 200-214.

83. Tom Koole, "Affiliation and Detachment in Interview Answer Receipts," in *Analyzing Race Talk*, 178-199.

84. Picca and Feagin, *Two-Faced Racism.*

85. Margaret Andersen, "Whitewashing Race: A Critical Perspective on Whiteness," in *White Out*, 21-34.

86. Karyn D. McKinney and Joe R. Feagin, "Diverse Perspectives on Doing Anti-racism: The Younger Generation," in *White Out*, 233-251.

Chapter 2
Bureaucrats of Whiteness

I mean, look...I'm not a bigot. You know the kind of books I've written about the civil rights movement in this country. But when I get on the plane, I got to tell you, if I see people who are in Muslim garb and I think, you know, they are identifying themselves first and foremost as Muslims, I get worried. I get nervous.

—Juan Williams, October 18, 2010[1]

In the above quote, the speaker delivers a contradictory statement. Williams first claims that he is free of racial bias, adding for support that he has written books on the Civil Rights Movement (with the assumption that by stating "the kind of books," he meant material that spoke positively towards the Movement). Then in his next statement Williams delivers a line that becomes headline news in the U.S. media for several days: that he is afraid of Muslims (or at least those whom he knows are Muslim). In effect, he asserts he is not a bigot while simultaneously making a bigoted statement. Shortly thereafter, Williams continues to provide supporting evidence of his lack of bigotry towards Muslims by stressing that not all Muslims were responsible for the 9-11 attacks, that doing so would be tantamount to blaming all Christians for the terrorist actions of Timothy McVeigh, and that the U.S. was not at war with the religion of Islam.[2]

Williams delivered this statement on a cable television show called *The O'Reilly Factor*, a show quite popular with conservative viewers. During this conversation between Williams and the host, they discussed the trouble O'Reilly had gotten into with a comment he had made on a different program in which he had said, "Muslims attacked us on 9/11."[3] After Williams' coup de grâce along with his assertion that great care had to be taken on this apparently sensitive issue, O'Reilly retorted that he was "done" being careful.[4] Shortly after Williams' statement on *The Factor*, National Public Radio (NPR), a radio station that had employed Williams as an "analyst" for 11 years, notified Williams and the public that Williams was no longer part of their team.[5] The aftermath caused a hullabaloo, particularly with conservative media, who argued that Williams'

27

freedom of speech had been restricted and his employment with NPR had been unfairly terminated. Shortly following the firing Williams received a lucrative contract from Fox News—the same cable news network that airs *The Factor*—and Williams remains there as a "contributor."[6]

Why did Williams deem it necessary to add the disclaimer "I'm not a bigot" prior to his statement that seeing "Muslims" in an airport make him feel uneasy? While some pundits and show hosts like O'Reilly have more freedom to provide an unfiltered account of what they feel, apparently Williams is one who lacks such freedom—or at least did at the time of the statement. In fact, the seemingly invincible Bill O'Reilly must conform at least in some respects, even if less so than someone like Williams. Race is likely one factor in explaining the difference, as organizational theories of social inequality stipulate, because minorities cannot "make it" without learning how and what to do or say when involved in media production.[7] Whether desired by Williams or not, his status as an "analyst" and not a mere "pundit" may be another, in which too many statements like these could cost him some credibility playing the role of the former as opposed to the latter. Regardless, he said what he said how he said it; i.e., he tried to "soften the blow" by saying he was not a bigot. But did it work? Although he lost his job with NPR, he remains employed at Fox News. His reputation may have taken a hit with liberals, though many had been complaining to NPR about him prior to his statement on *The Factor*.[8] What credibility he lost with liberals he likely gained with conservatives, since the story fit their narrative of the liberal media bias towards conservative thought and people.

Statements like Williams' are the focus of this book. I must mention here that Williams is an African American, is generally thought (at least among conservatives) to be politically moderate—even liberal—on many issues,[9] and at times fails to "toe the line" with the conservative narrative of the day. By all means, the particular sort of racespeak I present in this book is not a repertoire limited solely to white Americans; in fact, other studies have shown nonwhite Americans using at least some aspects of this race discourse in certain contexts.[10] I have no intention of arguing that only white Americans speak this way when discussing racial matters. However, I do argue that WRD has a reality sui generis and requires examination and understanding in order to effectively challenge the racial status quo in U.S. society. Furthermore, this kind of racetalk is not something random, disorganized, and trivial; in fact, it is something rational, systematic, and significant in affecting the everyday lives of all Americans.

In this chapter I present in more detail the bureaucratization of WRD, and apply George Ritzer's theory of McDonaldization to the racetalk of the sample. I argue that, contrary to the individualistic notions of understanding how racism is reproduced in society, the kind of race discourse used by my white study participants reveals an almost robotic character. The remainder of the chapter focuses on the contradictions within respondents' racetalk specifically as to how they discuss their social identity and social position as white Americans. Respondents express much ambivalence initially during the interview, which leads them to speak of themselves and racial "others" in ways that are contradictory. This method is divided into two primary camps: first, the (at least initial) outright avoidance or ambivalence towards the conception of whiteness; and second, five common themes when defining whiteness, including (1) whiteness is natural; (2) whiteness is under attack; (3) whiteness is defined for what it is not (i.e., through the racial "other"); (4) whiteness is ethnically, culturally and nationally European, especially of Anglo-Saxon heritage; and (6) whiteness equates privilege (i.e., more resources). First, I begin with a closer examination of how the form of discourse these young whites use during their conversations about race is organized.

Bureaucratization of Whiteness

When first beginning this study, I was drawn to C. Wright Mills' concept of the Cheerful Robot[11] as a way to describe young white Americans today: i.e., young people through social action (such as discourse) rationalize systemic racism without reason (e.g., expressing disapproval of interracial families because of alleged "problems" biracial children have, though they cannot substantiate those claims with any evidence). In order to fully appreciate Mills' concept of Cheerful Robot, one must understand the influence from Weber's concepts of rationality and rationalization, leading us inevitably to the role of bureaucratic organization. The discursive actions of white Americans, I stipulate, resembles that of bureaucratic action in that the rules of the organization become so ingrained that people act uniformly and in a way similar to that of robots or laborers on an assembly line, (re)producing statements that protect white supremacy.

The bureaucratic organization that whites defend is the house of whiteness. Like any bureaucrat, the bureaucrat of whiteness performs specific, rigid tasks or duties for the organization (in this case, white-dominated republican society). This organization, in turn for its legitimation, produces certain privileges for the loyal bureaucrat. Hence, an exchange takes place between individual whites and the white supremacist social system they support. However, are whites indeed aware of these privileges? Do they even need to be? Either way, this ignorance creates the bubble young whites reside in today, and the ambivalence they project within their racetalk.

McDonaldization of Race Discourse

Applying George Ritzer's concept of McDonaldization—the notion that the ways of doing things in society are emulating the methods of the famous fast food chain[12]—to a type of discourse may seem questionable at first, since talk is something intangible, as opposed to animate objects like hamburgers. However, speaking of racetalk as McDonaldized is legitimate for two reasons: first, like hamburgers, discourse is both produced and consumed. Second, Ritzer has applied his orientation to the understanding of the discourse used by what he calls "non-people," or individuals employed in the proliferation of "nothing" who are, generally speaking, interchangeable and under the (often) close scrutiny of their employers.[13] One example of non-people are the employees at a McDonald's restaurant. Besides their identical uniforms and cooking methods, they also use (through training) identical greetings of customers at the cash register ("Welcome to McDonald's, may I take your order?") and other methods of communication with the customers (e.g., "Would you like fries with that?"). In the racetalk of white Americans, I contend that a similar "training" occurs that teaches whites to speak in similar predictable ways about racial matters, from parents to schoolteachers to Hollywood movie characters.

We live in a world that is being increasingly rationalized in virtually all aspects; i.e., our activities are increasingly organized in orderly ways influenced by modernity. Heavily influenced by Max Weber's concept of formal rationality, the process of McDonalization consists of four primary characteristics: efficiency, calculability, predictability, and control (specifically the replacement of human for nonhuman technology).[14] An additional characteristic that generally follows the others is the irrationalities of rationality, including the process of dehumanization, in which individuals become Cheerful Robots, as Mills had articulated.[15] Besides affecting the way people consume fast food, McDonalization has seeped into all kinds of activities, including how we earn college degrees, operate correctional facilities, or even how we worship.[16] But can we apply the concept of McDonaldization to help us better understand the racetalk of white Americans? That is the endeavor of this section.

The racetalk of white Americans resembles that of purposive rational action common to bureaucratic organizations. The first characteristic of McDonalization is efficiency, which means that one "chooses the optimum means to a given end."[17] While McDonald's paramount goal is to maximize profits while minimizing costs, WRD prioritizes the defense of the status quo—namely, white supremacy—above all else. This form of racetalk has within it a plethora of rhetorical devices that defend whiteness and white privilege. As we will see later, this occurs even when speakers are quick to "pick up the pieces" once the utterance has been delivered, even after an attempt to "soften the blow" prior to the statement (as Williams had tried to do). One way in which WRD is efficient is in the employment of particular frames such as the naturalization of racial segregation (e.g., "People tend to stick with their own") and the minimization of the effects of racism (e.g., "The past is the past").[18] For example, when discussing the issue of addressing the losses of certain racial groups who have been discriminated against, Jane had this to say:

> I think the government should address the losses of certain racial groups (.) who have struggled from discrimination but (.) sometimes I think that like um (.) races that suffer from racial discrimination (.) use that like (.) even when

they're not, you know, they like in the past, you know, in history we've been
discriminated against so that that makes, you know

She first utilized a disclaimer when she acknowledges the occurrence of racial
discrimination, but then presumes that people abuse the system for unfair advantages. Apparently she thinks that (1) racism existed only in the past, and that
(2) racism in the past does not matter. Also note how she appeals to the interviewer for recognition, for legitimation of her claim, and I instantaneously give
it to her. Whites interacting together (e.g., through interview discourse) co-construct images of the social world(s) they live in and those who live in it. Beliefs or attitudes only matter so much; the fact is that the respondent made a
claim that went unchallenged by the interviewer. Thus, the participant was able
to make a potentially "racist" claim due to its efficiency in delivery.

The second characteristic of McDonalization is calculability, or the ability
to quantify things, often replacing quality over time.[19] Calculability often makes
the efficiency more possible. While this characteristic assists McDonald's in
selling more hamburgers and increasing profit margins, WRD assists white
Americans in maintaining the racial order. WRD has calculability in that whites
quantify in particular ways that favor whites over blacks and other people of
color; this cuts both ways, depending on the function the calculation seeks to
achieve (a fundamental contradiction in WRD). When discussing white racism,
for instance, whites claim that there are "a few bad apples," but overall it would
be preposterous to assert that all whites engage in practices that justify and
maintain the racist status quo (i.e., there is a *systemic* nature to racism). Meanwhile, when discussing issues involving blacks, whites seldom hesitate to invoke
anecdotal evidence of laziness, carelessness, violence, or hypersensitivity that
they use to characterize all blacks.

Let us revisit the exchange between Kaitlin and myself that I first presented
in chapter 1. She had stated earlier in the interview that whites living in a retirement home she worked in "are really nice but (.) they're racist." This statement
shows her lack of reflection: would have her nonwhite co-workers seen "racist"
whites as "really nice?" Then when discussing her life in the dormitory, she responds this way:

R: Um, actually one of my roommates is black, and one of them is Spanish, and
then my actual roommate because I live in [name of dorm] is um, is white,
she's the one who actually lives in my room.
I: Mhm.
R: Yeah, I get kind of angry and I don't blame it on the fact that (.) she's black
but she like always has all of her friends over and they're really loud
I: Mhm
R: And sometimes I want to say that 'black people are really loud' like but I
know that's not it
I: Mhm↓
R: But I just like (.) sometimes I want to blame it on that. But

Thus, whites can be overtly racist and still be viewed as "really nice," while one experience with a black roommate causes Kaitlin to typify all blacks as "loud" and "weird." Note her usage of reported speech to distance herself from a potentially face-threatening statement ("And sometimes I want to say that 'black people are really loud' like but I know that's not it"), and how she differentiates herself from the activity of her roommate ("which I would never do with my frie(h)nds").

Third, WRD is certainly predictable in that whites, despite their various social backgrounds and experiences, utilize much of the same linguistic style and form that, whether intended or not, fails to challenge the racial structure via verbal communication. Previous studies (however implicitly) have shown the patterns common to WRD, such as documenting the usage of semantic moves or disclaimers by whites in order to present oneself as unprejudiced while making an antiblack or anti-Other claim, such as "I'm not a racist, but black people are dangerous."[20] A good example of this predictability is the study participants' response to the questionnaire statement "We should all judge people not by the color of their skin but by the content of their character" (see Table 2.1). Of the respondents, nearly all believed this to be either "essential" or "very important."

Table 2.1   Questionnaire Results for Attitudes towards Racial Purity and Judgment

Question	Mean
Society should maintain racial purity.	1.73
We should all judge people not by the color of their skin but by the content of their character.	4.76

As we will see though, WRD does have its fissures that create unpredictability; like other social structures, WRD is constantly being modified to better deal with the messiness of social worlds (we see this in their response to the statement "Society should maintain racial purity," in that while many respondents said it was unimportant, there was more variability). WRD comes to resemble the predictability of credit cards in that, once familiar with its method, it is easily recognizable.

Fourth, preserving systemic racism in U.S. society required overt purposive action from whites; now, this oppressive system is maintained through nonhuman technology, or at least that which resembles something as nonhuman. WRD resembles something of a machine that churns out the garb needed to preserve the "organization" that is the racial status quo. In addition, now whites need only to rely on the normative structure in order to preserve the superiority of whiteness. Similar to Weber's famous statement of the Puritan's calling to work,[21] the white supremacist of previous generations had the overt values to defend in everyday interactions, whereas today most purposive, rational, white supremacist action is carried out by an increasingly centralized normative structure, with faceless bureaucrats pulling the levers. Most whites would (at least publicly) be horrified to find that their actions (or lack thereof) perpetuate white supremacy and racism in U.S. society and across the globe, yet this is the case.

McDonaldization has affected the production and consumption of discourse as well as other cultural products. In short, this form of racetalk is a kind of "nothingness" that is (1) centrally conceived and disseminated within key social institutions such as media and education and (2) is lacking in substance.[22] Ritzer postulates that "mass manufacture and batch processing are intimately associated with all forms of nothingness."[23] I should mention that this is not totally a bad thing: for instance, less overtly racist discourse is uttered as a result of this process, and as I mentioned earlier, Bill O'Reilly is not foolish enough to be truly "done" being careful. Slogans circulated within social circles such as "I don't see race" or "I don't care if he's black, brown, yellow, or green"[24] become crystallized and require little forethought or reflection, while bigots may be more reluctant to openly express their true feelings on racial matters.[25] However, such a method allows its speakers (or at least those from the privileged positions) to either become ambivalent towards societal measures designed to fight racial oppression or at least fail to actively resist racist societal practices. In the next section, I address the apparent ambivalence of white Americans toward racial matters.

White Ambivalence

Of course, white Americans are human beings, not robots, even if their discourse has been mechanized in certain ways. However, this mechanization process is not completely out of their control; indeed, whites can (and as this study shows, occasionally) challenge their own discourse and modify it. Unfortunately, too many white Americans are either unable or unwilling to throw away the "cloak" of whiteness and the vehicles it wields for survival and prominence. But despite the power of whiteness, it would be foolish to claim that white Americans today occupy an "iron cage of whiteness." The reality is that whites benefit from whiteness, and these privileges continue to create different social conditions for members of the various races in contemporary U.S. society.

Through WRD, white Americans defend whiteness and its privileges by claiming ambivalence towards and distance from racial injustices.[26] After claiming ignorance of such injustices—both past and present—whites often oppose and resent black Americans and others who address the continued significance of racism in U.S. society. For example, if whites refuse to see whiteness and the benefits gained by those who possess it, why bother to policies or laws designed to aggressively thwart white supremacy, such as race-sensitive admissions policies for colleges and universities or hate crime legislation? Despite claims of being nonracist, white Americans oppose rigorous efforts to curb white-on-black discrimination and violence. In other words, despite the fact that whites claim to support democratic principles such as equality and freedom for all, they wish to do so only as long as the house of whiteness remains intact.

This kind of racetalk is significant because it at least partially provides an image of the interlocutors themselves. More specifically, it reflects their identities as white Americans. Given the back-and-forth character of WRD, whites in this sample seem to have split personalities in that one moment they are knowledgeable of what whiteness is while ignorant of its existence the next. In the next section, I discuss this contradictory image of white identities, first with a brief review of the literature in this area of inquiry, and then analyzing the results from my sample of respondents.

Split Personalities

Among all other racial groups in America, only whites assume to be devoid of race, or to be "postcultural."[27] Whites think that race is something other people have, while failing to acknowledge their own. Race is also a feature that marks a group in inverse proportion with power, so that the less power a group has—whether political, economic, or social—the more race one is likely to possess.[28] Thus, whiteness is invisible to whites because it does not appear to whites as "race" but the definition of what is the norm. Race, then, is something whites notice only in relation to what others possess.

Paradoxically, the continuing existence of white privilege relies on not seeing the social mechanisms that maintain it. Peggy McIntosh conceptualizes white privilege as "an invisible weightless knapsack" of tools that helps them navigate through society in the pursuit of educational opportunities, jobs, and the like.[29] The very privileges that facilitate the ease with which whites are able to negotiate everyday life make it difficult for whites to acknowledge their existence. White privilege, therefore, includes the ability to not see whiteness and its privileges. Although race is not truly "real" in a biological or ontological sense, it creates very real social consequences.[30]

In addition, because whites have an insider's status, they have "few incentives to cultivate a 'double consciousness.'"[31] That is, they neither see themselves clearly nor the way white privilege appears to those they categorize as "other," whereas people of color have an outsider's status and a clear view of whiteness and white privilege. Thus, most discursive repertoires of whites regarding whiteness and white privilege are, ultimately, more likely to be "privilege-evasive," while the discursive repertoires of people of color are more likely to be "privilege-cognizant." Color-blindness, or the color- and power-evasive discourse, is considered to be the dominant discourse of whites in contemporary U.S. society.[32] Those who comply with this discursive repertoire refuse to acknowledge racial differences. Analyzing this repertoire is crucial because this discourse ultimately leads whites "back into complicity with structural and institutional dimensions of inequality."[33] Hence, racial hierarchies remain unchallenged while even reinforcing what color-blindness had presumably set out to destroy: essentialist racism, or the belief in inherent natural (biological) differences between the various races.

Innocence and (Declared) Ignorance

The key to understanding this type of race discourse is to first pinpoint its essential trait: that noticing one's race is wrong, or a sign of prejudice. The problem with this is that whiteness is generally defined as normative.[34] Since the Other continues to be viewed as a deviation to the norm (white), the inferiority of the Other is automatically assumed. This inferiorizing of the Other then continues to influence white beliefs and attitudes towards people of color, and expressed through discourse. However, since the height of the Civil Rights Movement openly expressing such beliefs is unacceptable, and actually sullies whiteness since such overtly racist remarks are viewed as wrong and undesirable. A variety of methods are employed to avoid the label of "racist" while at the same time defending whiteness, including the declaration that race is something beyond their comprehension, embracing ignorance on the issue.

Selective Consciousness of Whiteness

Although many whites will claim color-blindness when addressing racial matters, in reality they will selectively acknowledge racial differences, particularly when the matter at hand involves the defense of white privilege.[35] Many respondents were ambivalent when addressing the statement "I can recall a situation or interaction that later made me think about my whiteness." For example, Casey began his interview this way:

R: I gotta think about it for a second.
I: Okay↑ (2.0) Which one are you thinkin' about?
R: The first one. (("Some people have certain advantages, based on their racial identity, that others don't have in this society."))
I: Okay.
R: (4.0) I do, I think some people have a certain edge in education of racial identity, that others don't have.
I: How so?

R: I think, like, people look at you differently when you're white, like, if you go for a jo- like as sad as it sounds, like, I know from like, like experience, like I think if you're white it helps, like 'cause I know some people are still like, have a lot of stereotypes that are still ingrained in their mind and they can't get rid of it, 'cause it's been passed down from generation and generation but like, I don't think that's fair, 'cause like, I can see past all that, so I mean (1.0) just like Huck Finn, for example, it's so ingrained in his mind he can't see past it.

After this first exchange, Casey appears to (1) recognize a concrete instance of the way blacks are at a disadvantage in the workforce due to lingering antiblack stereotypes, and (2) distance himself from those stereotypes. However, immediately following this exchange, I ask him about whiteness in his life:

I: Yeah. (3.0) How about the second one (("I can recall a situation or interaction that later made me think about my whiteness.")), like um, what would whiteness like, in your life personally, how has whiteness affected your life?
R: Umm, I don't really think about it to tell you the truth. I don't think it really matters. It's only [what] a person says who they are. I don't think, I don't really think about my color. (1.0) if that makes sense, I don't know.
I: Like how would you define whiteness?
R: Just the color of your ski(h)n.
I: The color of skin?
R: Yeah. That's all I see it as.

Casey contradicted his previous statement by asserting that whiteness is nothing more than skin color, and does not matter in life (or at least his own). How can someone shift from race-conscious statements to classic color-blind statements? Almost like a machine, Casey utters these statements, and then appears dissatisfied with their legitimacy. This excerpt resembles efficiency, with a color-blind statement ("It's only [what] a person says who they are") followed by an ignorance claim ("If that makes sense, I don't know"). Excerpts like these provide evidence that the house of whiteness is built upon a weak foundation, as he questions the reasoning behind the sequence of utterances he delivers.

In Casey's statements, he stated that whiteness was not an issue, despite noticing a particular instance in how people of color are detrimentally affected by antiblack prejudice (which is perpetuated by superior notions of whiteness). In George's response, he not only cites an example of the way people of color suffer from white racism but also provides an example of whiteness having an impact on his life experiences, yet still expresses ambivalence towards the concept. He first responds to "Some people have certain advantages, based on their racial identity, that others don't have in this society" this way:

R: Um, I think that's (.) probably true uh because I've had uh a couple of friends uh (.) one uh in middle school, I had a uh, a friend that was from uh (.) Panama and they were actually twins and uh, they were mainly black and so uh I noticed that uh like just one of my teachers didn't like them and I thought it was mainly because of their race um and so I don't know, because they were

really bright kids and so that's just one instance where I've seen that from an
early age, that was in middle school I believe, and
I: Like can you recall maybe any specific things that went on with the teacher?
R: Well, it was anywhere from reactions on papers, like writing papers, to little
comments in class. Like uh (.) I felt like it was really unnecessary so it was
I: Like what kinds of comments I mean, you guys had class discussions?
R: Yeah, exactly. And um what made it stick out was that they were the only
two black kids in the class and so (.) anything that they would say she would
kind of undermine it. So, I don't know, I can't think of any specific examples.

Despite his professed inability to recall specific instances, he recalled his experience in middle school with clarity, in which two classmates received differential
treatment by their teacher because "they were mainly black." He then completes
this exchange with an ignorance statement, despite just mentioning such an example. Also note his use of the diminutive "just" to limit the charge of racism to
one of their teachers. But then he addresses the statement on whiteness in this
manner:

I: What role, you know, if any has whiteness played in your life?
R: Um the only situation I can think is uh probably participating in events such
as like when I was younger I participated in little things such as golf, little golf
things where uh everybody would get together and teach you how to golf and
just let you like into that (.) like good ole boy club, so to speak so, I don't
know.
I: Yeah.
R: Other than that, that's about as much experience as I've had with that uh I
can't really recall anything that's made me feel white.

In this exchange he recognized that playing golf is, and largely remains, a recreational activity for affluent white males, and also how such recreational activities help their participants establish social networks.[36] However, he then delivers
an ambivalent statement that rivals that of Casey's. This example appears as if
he backed off, having given too much acknowledgment to the reality of whiteness as a social force.

Majority/Minority Games
A few respondents mentioned their status as a minority, perhaps as a way to
downplay their membership of the dominant racial group. Linda, for example,
mentions her status as a woman in the following except:

I: Right. How about the second one like what role if any has whiteness played
in your life?
R: Umm↑ (2.0) I can't really think of any that made me think about my whiteness but (.) I think I'm still like kind of a (.) I know this is about race, but like
I'm still kind of a minority because I'm a girl but like I don't know, I can't really think of anything that's made me think about the fact that I'm white (1.0) so

I: Right. (1.0) Okay.

Here, Linda avoids self-reflection as a white member of U.S. society. Apparently whiteness only affects those who do not possess it. Meanwhile, Mandy cites her minority status as a Jewish American:

> I: What role if any has whiteness played in your life?
> R: Umm (2.0) I don't think it played that big of a role. I guess it has (1.0) um but I come from a town that's mixed, I mean we have Latinos and all sorts of Spanish background, African American um (.) I was- from where I'm from I'm the only Jewish girl so everyone's like "oh, I know one other Jewish person," like I was like the token Jew I guess so (.) being white I've actually felt like a minority in some cases? Because of my religion but (.) otherwise I guess I'm from an accepting area where everyone works hard to get where they are.

Despite their ability to speak of their status as members of social minorities, why would they struggle to speak of their status as white Americans?

This brings us to the color-blind contradiction: since "seeing" race is bad, we should not talk about it. The best example of this was Irene who, through most of her interview, refused to go into any depth on the various statements. This evasiveness caused me to get rather frustrated with her lack of response. This culminated with the following exchange:

> R: ((Reads "I recently watched a movie that made me think long and hard about race in America.)) No. I remember when I felt embarrassed—n:↑o ((Reads "There was an event that took place where I work(ed) that made me think about race.")) No. ((Reads "I remember one instance in which I felt angry about race in America.")) No. ((Hands slip back))
> I: ((Getting rather annoyed at this point, I must confess)) You've ne—you've never been angry about race, like, in America, like, something happened (1.0) maybe you saw it on t.v. or maybe you (1.0) saw someone do something or whatever, like and you felt angry about it. (3.0)
> R: According to race? No.

Her response to the statement regarding embarrassment was most intriguing, with the rising intonation while saying no, suggesting disapproval with such a possibility.

Meanwhile, some respondents expressed anger towards discussing race at all. Elizabeth, for instance, appeared to be directing the disapproval towards me during the following comments:

> Um, I get angry when I think about like (.) like just the ways in which people continue to like bring it up and say that it's like, um (1.0) like, the way that- if you don't want race to be an issue, why do you continue to like bring it up? I don't know, that's what I think, but (.) I don't know ((trails off))

Responses like those from Irene and Elizabeth assist them in their defense of color-blind ideology and its discursive vehicle, whether they are aware of it or not. According to this ideology, if one does not talk about race, then it does not exist.

Constructivism as a Mechanism of Preserving Whiteness

In addition to outright hostility in discussing race, respondents also presented another contradiction: they could either reify racial categories as natural differences, or discount race as a factor in determining life chances through extreme social constructionism (if race is a social construct, then it does not matter). This discursive style is most disturbing, since it brings those respondents probably most progressive into a state of complacency regarding racism and white supremacy. Yannie, for example, recalled his experience when enrolled in his introductory sociology class:

> In intro, we read little inserts: Hispanics, African American, Asian American, Native American, and I'm like it's unfair to try and label individuals in such broad terms? Hispanic culture differs based on the nation you're from, um Asian Americans (.) Asia America typically could actually be applied to a Russian who moved to America, but no one ever thinks of that, so I remember getting angry about the way we label races in America, and that was a big deal for me, uh I don't know (.) I started reading in this thing about queer theory and how (.) gender and sexuality is socially produced? Or at least partially if not wholly? And it's the same with race, like we may different colored skin, but when you think of an Asian American, you don't think of a Russian or a Hindu, for the most part, um and then African American, um I have friends from Jamaica and they hate that te(h)rm, so I think like for the most part, the labels are a big deal, um when just dealing with race in general

Yannie points out that myriad differences exist within the various racial categories, and how race is indeed a social construction. However, this perspective "prevents sophisticated analysis of how different axes of power and subordination function and how race structured into the fabric of society."[37] Yannie and other white Americans need to understand the need to study these categories, and how they impact our everyday lives, such as the tendency to create social groups and affect our access to social networks and cultural capital.

Now You See (and Defend) It

One of the greatest strengths of this study's method is the ability to get a more accurate perception of where whites stand in terms of what they say, and perhaps of the attitudes behind them. Since the classic color-blind one-liners are so one-dimensional and ineffectual, most of the ambivalence and ignorance claims were initially made during the interaction, and were quickly discarded for other claims. However, as Casey's comments in the previous section shows, respondents often attach such color-blind (ignorance) claims to race-conscious claims. When making color-conscious claims, in what ways do these white college students perceive whiteness and their identities as white Americans? In this section, I present five of the most common themes respondents used when defining whiteness: the first four claims generally portrays positive self-presentation (often through negative Other presentation), and the last claim affiliates whiteness with privilege (i.e., access to more resources).

Whiteness Is Natural

When respondents did define whiteness, they did it in a number of peculiar ways. The first example were those who defined whiteness as simply "the way it is," thus naturalizing the social construction. Reification of racial categories disarms potential progressives from protesting the racist status quo. Some respondents, who had difficulty pinpointing whiteness, naturalized the concept by just saying "it's what I am" without further clarification. For example, Elizabeth had this to say about the role of whiteness in her life:

> Um, I don't really think about it that much but I guess it's just kind of (1.0) (set me up) for like where I am like I guess 'cause it's part of my background, like that's just part of who I am I guess.

Here I assume that she considers "background" to be synonymous with "ancestry." Kaitlin also commented on this issue in a similar fashion:

> I don't think it's done anything for me, I mean a lot of my friends are white but I just think that's 'cause (.) I don't know, 'cause I think people kind of (.) go with people (of) their own race, it's just kind of like habit.

Here, she rationalizes segregated social networks as a "natural" occurrence. When discussing embarrassment to be white, Harriet said "I mean, I'm not embarrassed because I am what I am, I can't change that."

Whiteness Is Under Attack

Many respondents defined whiteness as under attack. They did this in various ways: for example, Angie and I had this exchange during her interview:

> I: How about the second one, like the role of whiteness in your life?
> R: Uh (3.0) let me think about it ((laughs))
> I: Do you think that uh (.) whiteness has um as far as played a role that it's um, what's the word I'm looking for? Um, like do you think it's been something crucial like, is it something important like in society as far as (.) um, like whiteness in society as far as affecting opportunities or those kinds of things?
> R: Um, like where I grew up and stuff like my high school was half like black and Hispanic and I'd be in the minority sometimes ((laughs))
> I: Sure.

R: But um, I guess it does seem like (.) better jobs for like white people.

After having initial difficulty responding to the question, she appears to associate "majority" with "dominant" group. Angie focused on the locality of race and failed to see the effects of race throughout the social system. She also uses the apparent agreement method ("it does seem like...") as a technique to appear non-racist, which really is in itself a semantic move.[38] Still, she appears unconvinced that whites get better jobs because of their possession of whiteness.

After failing to respond to my question about the impact of whiteness on her life, Odella associates whiteness with social stigma:

R: (6.0) I think there's a certain stigma, like (1.0) especially if you do (.) if there's like a lower- class (.) black area than if you are white, they kind of look at you like 'oh, the man, the bad person' (.)
I: Has whiteness played much of a role in your life as far as in your life in various ways?
R: I grew up in a white town, so (laughs) so I'm sure I have advantages that maybe people don't

Here she also appears to associate majority with dominance. This demonstrates how whites become ambivalent towards aggressive actions for racial integration, since problems do not seem to occur unless in the presence of black Americans or other Americans of color. Thus, some respondents implicitly assert that whiteness is under attack by their perceptions of nonwhites as threatening.

Despite respondents who thought whiteness (and those who possess it) is under attack when in the minority (a rare situation in social interaction), others turned the argument the other way around, suggesting that whiteness is under attack due to whites' status as the majority. For instance, Dina had this to say:

R: I think there (.) since, it's just like where we live there's so many Caucasians (.) that it's like, more desirable to have more direct- diverse, so like other people that aren't Caucasians sometimes have preferential treatment?
I: Okay.

Note here her rising intonation at the end of her utterance, often used as an appeal to the recipient for approval (which I give her). The best example of this contradiction (in that depending on the situation at hand, whites are disadvantaged for being the minority or the majority) was Irene, who first downplays the impact of whiteness in her life (due to diversity in her locality growing up) and then adds that whites are at a disadvantage due to their majority status:

I: Okay. (2.0) Okay, and how about whiteness, like, what (.) role, if any, has whiteness played in your life?
R: I mean, seriously, I come from such a place that's so culturally diverse that, if, I- I'm the minority, [so
I: [mhm

R: It's not really, I mean, I am considered a minority from where I live so it's, I mean if anything it's kind of a disadvantage (1.0) because like, colleges, people, a lot of [my] friends are all Hispanic and they got into college because they needed (2.0) minorities, so

I: Okay. I mean, would you say—I mean, outside of like, where you're from, like, nationally would you say that people benefit from racial privilege?

R: Certain things. Politics, [yes.

I: [Politics (2.0) okay (1.0)

R: Oh um (.) I wouldn't say in jobs or education (4.0) I don't know.

After pressing her to address national disparities based on race, she completes her exchange with "I don't know," which leaves the door open to go either way in future interactions—including during the interview—in order for her to avoid shameface if I challenge anything she had said.

To close this section, there were those male respondents who thought that the white man in particular is the only group not to jump on the proverbial victim bandwagon and today feel like they are the true victims.[39] In his response to the anger statement, Vincent said:

Um (2.0) like on MSNBC and CNBC (.) I watch those a lot, I guess when they keep um, I don't wanna say low-balling but they keep firing at corporate America, it's always the corporate white person that is you know always (.) enslaving their companies or taking away the pensions, and it's like 'ugh,' you know=I mean this could be any person, just 'cause he happens to be white, you can't really put it on them for that, that's probably what I felt angry about.

Vincent feels like the media unfairly criticizes white men, insisting that the corporate wrongdoers "could be any person." Unfortunately, it is highly unlikely that the wrongdoers could be "any person," since few corporate leaders are nonwhite or female. Besides, after watching extensive cable news coverage of various corporate shenanigans, I never recall criticism directed towards the whiteness of a corporate crook.

Troy continued this train of thought in his response:

Whenever I hear someone always pushing in, saying 'oh, it's the white man's fault, white man's fault,' like I don't know, that really gets annoying after a while 'cause (.) you know, I never really did anything, like I said my family never owned slaves or anything, you know I was never really (.) racial tension or anything (.) you know, goin' crazy (.) runnin' around black neighborhoods, settin' stuff on fire (.) but, you know, I always hear about how me as a white person, I'm keeping black America down, but (.) you know, I almost think they're doin' it to themselves

As we will explore in more depth later, Troy utilized reported speech both as a way to strengthen one's argument (by looking "factual") and a method to denounce the "other."[40] In this excerpt, Troy used the common storyline of color blindness "my family never owned slaves"[41] to dismiss charges of racism, while presenting an image of black Americans as savage or uncivilized to explain racial inequality. Also note his usage of the first person ("...about how me as a white person, I'm keeping black America down..."), suggesting that he takes the criticism personally and fails to recognize his membership in a racial group that remains dominant and perpetuates the value of whiteness.

Whiteness Defined Through the Other

Some respondents defined, if implicitly, white as normal. They often did this by defining black or "Other" as abnormal or deviant. For instance, Dina recalled her experiences as a volunteer this way:

> R: I never had a job in high school, the closest thing I had to a job was volunteering?
> I: Mm.
> R: And um (1.0) but when I volunteered it seemed like most of people that were there were Caucasian so (.) they're all the same race as me and I didn't really have an issue at all.

Note her shift in number of "Caucasians" from "most" to "all" in this excerpt; this could be a strategy to bolster the evidence for strengthening her argument. She also sounds as if the racial homogeneity of the people around her kept problems from occurring, as if had persons of color been present, problems would have occurred. Shortly thereafter this framing of nonwhites as problematic surfaces again when she describes one of the high schools she attended:

> But then the high school I went to for the last two years there's a lot of like (.) um (.) diversity I guess, but um it never really seemed to be like a problem at all, I was never put in a situation at all

Sometimes respondents recalled authority figures instructing them to fear blacks in their workplace. Frank, for instance, recalled an interaction with his boss at a tennis club:

> R: Yeah, I had a job at a tennis club and uh (.) this is in [large city in a southeastern state] it's in a section that's mainly a black neighborhood, and so, I guess a lot of people are considered kind of like more (.) uh, uh, not as nice neighborhood but I remember my boss telling me to make sure that I locked up and stuff 'cause he had, he thought that the, the, he had problems with like the black kids in the neighborhood stealing stuff in the shop and uh (.) I never saw any problem with it but
> I: Mm
> R: I guess he could have had a specific problem but I think it was kind of a stereotype=
> I: =Oh=
> R: =thing, but

Frank tries to rationalize his boss' comments, serving an example of the impression management of fellow whites. After initially concluding the comments were based on stereotypical antiblack images of the criminal young black man, he adds an additional "but" to leave open the possibility of "common sense" that backs up the original comments.

Respondents often defined racial Others to be strange or inherently different from the norm (i.e., lily white). Quilla discussed the role of whiteness in her life this way:

> I: How about the role of whiteness in your life? Like uhm has it played a role if any?
> R: Uhm I think I didn't really notice it until I left my um house in [city in state] because our neighborhood uhm it's predominantly white and Spanish, but I never noticed that until we had a black family move in and then everyone like (.) [unintellible] not that it was weird, it's just like I realized that (.) we hadn't had that before, it was just (.)
> I: Right.
> R: I realized like how like (.) white I guess our area was, it was weird↑
> I: Sure.

Unfortunately, I would liked to have followed up here for what she meant by "weird↑" but she nonetheless reminisced how odd it was to have a black family move in nearby. This shows the luxury whites have in how little they think about race in U.S. society.

Meanwhile, Vincent had this to say about whiteness as a factor in his life:

> R: (1.0) Mhm (2.0) u:h (4.0) I don't think about that that often.(2.0) What do you mean about my whiteness, like just 'cause (.)
> I: Well, I mean, as far as (.) like your white identity, like you're identity as a white person (.) I mean I guess more generally like your race, like what has like your racial identity played in your life, like what kind of role, u:m (.)
> R: Mhm. (1.0) U::h (.)
> I: As far as, you know, any kind of impact, has it had any kind of impact on (.) you know, your life in any way, shape, or form, or something like that? like (.) everything from friends you've had, to (.) um you know schools you've attended or neighborhoods you're lived in or whatever.
> R: I guess, I mean the neighborhood I lived in was (.) I only had one (.) there's one black family living down the street from me and that's the only one I can think of in my neighborhood, because (.) in my town, it's really small, but there's one little part that's about a four-block you know radius, and it's literally called "Blacksville," that is the name on the address=
> I: =Oh, wow.
> R: Yeah. It's really called that.
> I: ((laughs)) Wow

Note the role of interviewer in the creation of discourse. After an initial ambivalence statement about whiteness, I provide assistance in thinking about the impact of whiteness in his life, even providing a particular context (schools and neighborhoods). He then remarks how incredibly segregated his little town is, with the black part of town literally called "Blacksville." Like other respondents, Vincent defined whiteness through blackness.

Not only did respondents view persons of color as strange, but as racialized beings, while apparently seeing themselves as not racial. George was one participant who defined "race" as nonwhite:

> I: Okay. And how about you know did you ever feel angry about race in America before?
> R: Um (.) occasionally people bring up that 'oh, whites are becoming a minority now' and that race is growing, I don't think I really feel angry about (.) that the race, the racial mixture in America? I don't think I really think I feel angry in that sense but uh (1.0) nah, I don't think I've felt angry about (.) race in particular.
> I: Mm, okay.

Here it sounds as if George sees whites as raceless beings, untainted from racial markers. Some respondents, when addressing the statement on anger about race, associated "race" with a particular racial group (and apparently nonwhite racial groups at that). Kaitlin responded in the following manner:

> I: Well what about the last one like was there a time when you felt a:ngry um about race like something you saw (.) on TV or you saw somebody do something or you know or umm
> R: Like angry at another race?
> I: N:o just like I mean maybe but I mean just about race I mean something that made you upset
> R: Umm it makes me- this isn't really about like the other races=it's kind of about our race but

The white college students of this study defined race in the form of binary oppositions, such as normal/strange or clean/dirty, suggesting not only an inherent difference between the two, but also deference (in that one is superior to the other).[42] One example is Mandy, who recalled an experience with a black roommate:

> R: One summer I had a black roommate
> I: Mhm.
> R: Um (1.0) I mean our problems weren't over race our problems were more like little stuff like she turned the air-conditioning off.
> I: Oh
> R: (laughs) and um she didn't do, she did weave in the room too, so I guess that's a cultural thing but (.) she was a little more messy so there were clumps of hair that I found there and (outbreath laugh) grease on the doors so you can't ope(h)n the doorknob? But I mean (.) it was nothing like (.) hatred you know

After mentioning an initial "problem" with her roommate deciding on the temperature of their room, she proceeded into a negative evaluation of her roommate's "cultural thing" as something "a little messy." Here a depiction of white culture as "clean" is made through her depiction of black culture as "messy." Her semantic move following this evaluation is especially intriguing: would there be a reason to feel "hatred" in this situation?

Mandy continues immediately following this utterance with another that implicitly defines white over black through a negative presentation of the Other:

> I learned more about her culture and like she wanted to know (.) what Judaism was, 'cause she didn't even know (.) what it was, which surprised me that could get into (.) a university like such a prestigious university and not know that like Judaism is a religion, it kind of surprised me. Other than that (2.0)

Although she claimed that the experience gave her an opportunity to learn about her roommate's culture (thus suggesting she had something to learn), she does not give her roommate the same leeway, even criticizing the university for admitting her into school. Again we see a kind of semantic shift when she first admits her own ignorance of black Americans, yet quickly moves to criticize blacks for lacking knowledge about whites. Should have Mandy been denied admission into this "prestigious" university for her ignorance of black Americans?

In addition, some respondents defined white identity through the depiction of blacks as troublemakers. As I discussed earlier, Dina seemed to imply that non-Caucasian volunteers would have created "issues," but provided no details. However, later during the interview she went into a more detailed portrayal of nonwhites in as she recalled classmates "of a different race" who boasted about high test scores:

> I don't really think that (.) I've ever felt angry, I mean (.) I guess the closest thing I could say would be like in high school where like the kids would literally, like maybe get back our test scores, or if you wanted to the teacher would say it out loud and like, the kids that were (.) a different race wou- would say 'oh, I got a score because I'm this race,' but I mean, they're somewhat kidding but still, I mean it's just (.) that's obviously not true=I don't know=it just seems like they place a lot of emphasis on having things happen to them because this is their race? and that's why? Well, Caucasians I mean like of the experiences I've had that Caucasians don't really do that, it just seems like their race is a- seems to be a much bigger deal to them than our race.

According to Dina, blacks cause trouble by making race a factor whereas whites never do, at least based on her experiences. Meanwhile, Harriet recalled her experience in the International Baccalaureate (IB) program:

> I: Like maybe you saw something in a movie or on t.v. or maybe you witnessed something um you know and you felt angry about it afterwards um

R: I guess when they start food fights where you get hit with fried chicken in the cafeteria o(h)r something like tha(h)t, you get angry about that.

I: You guys had food fights in your cafeteria?

R: Not really big food fights but, there'd be like (.) every now and then, like fried chicken would just you know fly across the cafeteria and hit you, it wouldn't start anything big or like step on ketchup packets or stuff like that. Times like that made me angry (1.0) because a majority of the time it was the African American kids doing that, you know.

I: Right.

R: And sometimes they would pick on the kids in IB or wou- not pick on 'em, but you know

I: Oh.

R: Stuff like that (laughs)

I: How so? Like, how would they

R: Like one of my friends is white and he's probably like 5 feet tall, he's really small, and one day this big like (.) African American guy just came and picked him up and started carrying him off (laughs)

I: Yeah (laughs)

R: So they do things that that (laughs) Sometimes stuff like that would happen.

It is interesting how she said this experience upset her because black students were the culprits (would she have been less upset if the suspects had been white?). Here statement "so they do things like that" is another play on pronouns: she could either have been speaking about the black kids from school or, especially since the verb is present tense, about all blacks in general.

As harmless as Dina and Harriet's examples might seem, this typification of blacks as troublemakers can be extended to include criminal behavior. As a result, whites can use the image of the criminal black person to rationalize differential treatment and racism, such as racial profiling by the police. For example, Amy said the following during her interview:

As far as cops pulling over a black guy and searching his car versus pulling over a white guy and not searching his car, (.) history just (.) if you were to search both cars, chances are (.) the black person just according to history the black person would have something and the white person wouldn't, I mean it might not be fair but if you don't have anything, don't be so mad if they're searching your car, and if you do, then you're guilty anyways, so you can be mad about it all you want, but if you're guilty you're guilty.

Like many other white Americans, Amy is convinced that blacks are more likely to possess illegal materials, whether drugs, guns, etc. This kind of repertoire contradicts the common repertoire of supporting law and order. Looking throughout U.S. history, whites have often chosen the value of white supremacy over law and order, such as the Omaha riot in 1919 in which white men lynched Will Brown who was suspected of raping a white woman.[43]

In addition to defining blacks as deviant, strange, and criminal (and thus whites as normal and law-abiding), some respondents argued during their interviews that blacks complain too much and have group leaders who seek selfish goals for themselves (namely, to get rich). During the time of the interviews, hip-hop star Kanye West made the comment during a Hurricane Katrina fundraising telethon that "George Bush doesn't care about black people." I asked several respondents if they had heard his comments (and the firestorm of criticisms against him, particularly from whites in the press). When addressing the anger statement, Linda had this to say:

> R: Yeah, well I think a lot of times (.) people who are like (1.0) people talk about how they've been like so discriminated against but really like (.) it's only a couple of people who have discriminated against them it's not like everyone I think there are just like a few main people who like start it and then (.) there are some followers and then there are some people who are just like "that's crap" like (.)
> I: Mhm.
> R: But that's the only time I can think of that. So (.) what was that (.) the thing (2.0) other like George Bush like some guy got on (.) what was it (1.0)
> I: Oh, Kanye West?
> R: Kanye West, yeah. (1.0)
> I: Yeah, what did you think about that?
> R: I didn't really know what to think about that 'cause I'd heard about it from several different people who actually saw it?
> I: Mhm.
> R: So I was like (.) I didn't really know [if] he was trying to be funny? Or like (1.0)
> I: Yeah, I think he was serious, definitely. I (.) yeah, um (2.0)

Apparently Kanye West violated the "golden rule" for black men in U.S. society: do not ever get too serious; otherwise, white folks will start getting nervous. Black entertainers can earn good money and even some respect for their services, yet cannot engage in any social action that leads to the criticism of a white leader. I discuss the responses to West's comment in more detail in chapter 5.

The final image of the racial other articulated by the respondents is the image of their leaders as self-serving and either unable or unwilling to "make things right" in their community. Interested in profits, they blame the white man for their racial group's difficulties in attaining parity with white Americans. Troy's response to the anger statement was most intriguing, showing how perceived poor leadership is linked to irresponsible behavior for the entire group:

> I don't know, some of the people that really annoy [me] are like Jesse Jackson and Al Sharpton um (.) I really fee(h)l that they're ju(h)st (.) they're doin' their thing for profit you know they're not really bringing people together u:h from what they're doin' I see more division, you know, and one of the things that really annoys me is always uh (.) you know, of course like (.) you know, blacks in American have problems, but (.) you know...just by the culture that you see

today on television, uh flip on black entertainment television where they're
showin' a bunch of people glorifying drugs, violence, you know (.) talking
down about women, ho, bitch, whatever, uh (.) you know, the problem is you
gave young kids growin' up now uh even the kids that aren't in the inner city,
you know, little suburbs and whatever you know they're African American and
they see these guys on television doin' that so (.) you know, a lot of times they
start dressing the same way and speak the same verbal stuff and um I don't
know, that's just kind of a problem right now 'cau(h)se (.) you know, majority
of blacks are all about you know just doin' everything [gangsta] doin' whatever
it takes to (.) you know, get money, whatever it takes (.) you know, get your
money and flash it out, you know, whatever.

In this excerpt, Troy brings up a host of antiblack images, including the stereotype of blacks to seek out quick profits. Furthermore, he suggests that this behavior of young black Americans reflects the poor leadership within the black
community. This discourse, when coupled with the previous images mentioned
such as exotic and law breaking, comes together to paint an image of the racial
other as threatening to U.S. society.

Whiteness is European (Especially Anglo-Saxon)

When filling out information for job applications, I noticed that for race identifi-
cations "white" included North African and Middle Eastern descent, and it got
me thinking: why were these groups included in this racial category?[44] I thought
that perhaps this is one way for white elites to claim that whites face discrimination, too (since the number of hate crimes directed towards Arab Americans
exploded following the events of September 11, 2001). This phenomenon does
prove the fluidity of race in U.S. society, in that groups once defined nonwhite
have become white over time. Nonetheless, whiteness has generally been defined as that stock and/or culture of Europe, and more specifically northern and
western European (e.g., Anglo-Saxon).[45] Some respondents did get more specific about the way whiteness is and has been conceptualized; for example, Elizabeth had this to say:

I: And how about the second one, like what kind of (.) ro:le has whiteness
played in your life?
R: Um, I don't really think about it that much but I guess it's just kind of (1.0)
(set me up?) for like where I am like I guess 'cause it's part of my background,
like that's just part of who I am I guess.
I: Like when you think about your background and that kind of thing like (.)
when you think about whiteness, like what comes to mind, like what kinds of
objects or what kinds of (.) beliefs, or values, or whatever.
R: I don't really know if anything is strictly white that I would think of, I mean
other than just something like (.) from England, you know, that kind of thing
you know, but I don't really have (.) specific examples ((trails off))

This conceptualization represents the way whiteness has been traditionally defined in American society; that is, that English-Americans have always been defined as white in U.S. society.

In recent years the white reactionary backlash has turned its attention towards immigration, and particularly the images of brown people crossing the southern border undocumented, overwhelmingly to work low-paying jobs. Another important privilege from possessing whiteness is the assumption of one's legality of entire existence: that one has the right to be here, and not face questions about one's legality. Hence, despite the reality of the immigration situation (in that people of various races reside in the country without "proper" documentation), folks with brown faces are assumed to be "illegal," as suggested by Vincent in the following excerpt:

> R: I was a landscaper at a golf course, so I worked around a bunch of uh illegal immigrants (.) they actually helped me get an A in Spanish in high school, they were great, they were very helpful, so (.)
> I: Did they uh I mean like how'd you know that they were illegals, like did they get in trouble?
> R: Well, no, I just uh they uh well, I've seen them being paid under the table like their hours that they work, like I always get a check, you know, with (.) you know, my taxes taken out and they got cash. They just got straight cash. And they all showed up in o:ne, one Van. And they were great guys, they were really nice. I had no problems with them at all, I mean, 'cause when I saw what was happening, I asked my boss I was like 'is that cool?' and he's like 'don't worry about it' wha↑tever. If it helps them, cool. And they were making more than I was, so (.) 'cause they were there all the time.

The probe following his initial statement ("how'd you know that they were illegals") and its response ("Well, no, I just uh they uh well") show how active interviewers can influence the production of discourse in interview settings. At least in this instance, I refused to legitimize his utterance "I worked around a bunch of uh illegal immigrants" and he struggled to reestablish rapport with me. Assuming his reported observations are truthful, he fails to challenge the structure of this exploitative system (in which "illegals" not only supply his boss with illegal labor, but also provide him free Spanish lessons to boot). But more than that, he rationalizes the structure to preserve the face of whiteness (and himself, not to mention his boss) by claiming, "if it helps them, cool."

Whiteness Is More Resources

A few respondents defined race through the privileges whites have and the resources they have at their disposal. Jane, for example, discusses the advantages in education many whites enjoy:

> R: U:m, well I went to private school in my life and like (.) I don't know whether it has to do with like (.) the cost of it, but there was a lot more white

kids than black kids and I grew up around like black kids but it wasn't predominantly black, it was definitely predominantly white

I: Mm

R: So (.) it makes you not as like open, you know you're more sheltered

I: Oh, okay

R: And like, that kind of stuff (.) I think, and you're not used to like dealing with racial like inequality stuff as much, because you don't really see that (.) unless you went to a public school

I: Right.

R: You're a lot more like [?] I guess.

Jane admits how whites have the ability to be close-minded and "stick with one's own" if they so choose. She also recognizes whites' ability to ignore wealth disparities and poverty, living in the white bubble. Samantha provides a better example: that white Americans have had more time (i.e. generations) to accumulate wealth compared to black Americans:

Um (.) well, my family has had the opportunity you know before a- African Americans were able to start establishing themselves in society, and (.) making good careers, my family has been able to establish a name before they had the rights to (1.0) politically in the United States

Whether aware of it or not, Samantha provides a good point of argument for reparations for the ancestors of slaves.

Other respondents focused on the more favorable treatment whites receive in various social domains. For instance, Xena provided the specific example of shopping:

Even like just everyday things, like going places, like (.) if I'm out, just like with my mom say shopping, and at the mall, you know, like (.) I'll get better service (.) at a store, you know, their gonna look at me and say 'oh, she's a better customer,' or (.) compared to like someone of an ethnic race, and like I mean it's (.) I think it's definitely like and that's (.) not just where I'm from, like even when I go (.) you know, travel, I feel like certain areas (.) like, I've been to New York City a lot, and that's definitely like (.) so many cultures there, and I think you know they should be more accepting of it there, but when you're out doing things, it's definitely like they're gonna (.) I think just being white like you're automatically perceived as like (.) more intelligent, or wealthier, you know. Like, you definitely get better services or people are nicer to you, or don't suspect you of doing like (.) they're not gonna think 'oh, she's gonna shoplift, so I don't need to keep an eye on her,' so (.) it's sad, I mean it shouldn't be like that

She mentioned how whites receive preferential treatment since they are perceived as "more intelligent" and "wealthier." Zachary also said "I've never really had to deal with any racism" during his interview.

Vincent mentions the proliferation of the criminal black male image in the news media:

> When I always watch the local news, it's always you know 'this crime hap-
> pened, and it was a black person, this crime happened, and it was a black per-
> son.' Why did you just say that? Why didn't you say he was a 5'10" male (.)
> that did this and just (.) you know, keep that out of the equation, 'cause that's
> really not information we need to know (.) I mean (.) or just 'a person' commit-
> ted this crime, so (.) that has made me [feel] angry

Unfortunately, this form of news coverage affects the way many white Americans see black Americans, and it continues throughout the country. He probably
learned about this media bias in his sociology course. Meanwhile, Renee cites
her sociology course as crucial in getting her to think about her whiteness and
the impact of race in people's lives:

> R: I know that I'm like (.) probably have more advantages than like=actually in
> My minorities in society class we actually talked about whiteness and that was
> the only time that I er that was like the first time my teacher like asked us to
> think about (.) if we've been- about our whiteness and I guess it's (.) I've prob-
> ably had a lot easier life than minorities because I've never really had to deal
> with being an outsider or (.) anything like that.
> I: Like what kinds of things come to mind when you think of whiteness?
> R: Not being a minority I guess like (.) I don't know, I grew up in a city where
> there was not a lot of (.) minorities? And then I moved to a different city for
> high school and I actually was it was like all mainly like Hispanic people so I
> was kind of a minority in high school? But I wasn't like made fun of or put
> down or anything I never felt like (.) subjected to racism or anything like that
> and I think that black people: deal with that a lot more.

Despite the assumption held by many whites that blacks discriminate against
whites (i.e., engage in "reverse racism"), Renee insists this is not the case, based
on her own experience in a predominantly nonwhite high school. She adds that
life is easier for white Americans because they never have to live as an outsider
in society.

Summary

In this chapter, I described the contradictory nature of the way whites see
themselves in U.S. society, and in turn how they see members of other races.
Their racespeak resembles bureaucratic action, possessing efficiency, calculability, predictability, and control. As if they were robots (in that their responses
were eerily similar), study participants often began their responses to the whiteness statement with considerable ambivalence, but this (color-blind) approach
proved futile due to its ineffectiveness, providing little more than a cloaking
device for white supremacist sentiments. I presented five major themes within
their conceptualizations of whiteness: whiteness is natural, whiteness is under
attack, whiteness is defined through the racial other, whiteness is European, and

whiteness is privilege. Respondents contradicted themselves when claiming color-blindness and simultaneously exhibiting race-consciousness. Meanwhile, they hold some of the most common and traditional stereotypes about African Americans, such as being strange, criminal, and complaining too much. The bureaucratization of their discourse does not seem to prepare them for hearty discussions on race, suggesting that their best bet to preserve whiteness is to avoid the topic altogether. In the next chapter, I present the contradictions within their discourse on interracial interactions.

Notes

1. Jack Mirkinson, "Juan Williams FIRED: NPR Sacks Analyst Over Fox News Muslim Comments," *The Huffington Post*, October 21, 2010. Available online at www.huffingtonpost.com/2010/10/21/juan-williams-fired-npr_n_770901.html (accessed July 23, 2011).

2. "Juan Williams FIRED."

3. See the video clip and summary of the incident at Devon Thomas, "Bill O'Reilly On 'The View': 'Muslims Killed Us On 9/11' [Video]; Co-Hosts Walk Off," *CBSNews*, October, 14, 2010. Available online at http://www.cbsnews.com/8301-31749_162-20019660-10391698.html (accessed July 30, 2011).

4. "Juan Williams FIRED."

5. David Folkenflik, "In 'Muzzled,' Juan Williams Tells His Side of the Story," *National Public Radio*, July 27, 2011. Available online at http://www.npr.org/2011/07/27/138761698/in-muzzled-williams-tells-his-side-of-the-story (accessed July 30, 2011).

6. Shortly after his firing from NPR Williams received a contract from Fox News reportedly worth two million dollars over three years. Matea Gold, "In Wake of NPR Controversy, Fox News Gives Juan Williams an Expanded Role," *Los Angeles Times*, October, 21, 2010. Available online at http://articles.latimes.com/2010/oct/21/news/la-pn-juan-williams-20101022 (accessed July 30, 2011).

7. Gaye Tuchman, "Women's Depiction by the Mass Media," *Signs* 4, no. 3 (Spring 1979): 528-542. Also see Margaret Anderson, *Thinking About Women*, 8th ed. (Boston: Pearson, 2009), 68-69.

8. "Juan Williams FIRED."

9. For example, Roger Ailes, Chief at Fox News Channel, remarked in regards to Williams that "Juan has been a staunch defender of liberal viewpoints since his tenure began at Fox News in 1997." Quote from Gold, "In Wake of NPR Controversy, Fox News Gives Juan Williams an Expanded Role."

10. For example, for the use of this form of racetalk by African Americans, see Bonilla-Silva, *White Supremacy*, chapter 6.

11. Mills, "Culture and Politics."

12. Ritzer, *The McDonaldization of Society 6*.

13. George Ritzer, *The Globalization of Nothing* (Thousand Oaks, CA: Pine Forge Press, 2004), 60-63.

14. Ritzer, *The McDonaldization of Society 6*.

15. One of the best known examples of the irrationalities of rationality includes Bauman's analysis of the Holocaust in Zygmunt Bauman, *Modernity and the Holocaust* (Cambridge, MA: Polity/Blackwell, 1990).

16. Dennis Hayes and Robin Wynyard (ed.), *The McDonaldization of Higher Education* (Westport, CT: Bergin and Garvey, 2002); Matthew B. Robinson, "McDonaldization of America's Police, Courts, and Corrections," in *McDonaldization: The Reader*, 2nd ed., ed. George Ritzer (Thousand Oaks, CA: Pine Forge Press, 2006), 88-101; John Drane, *The McDonalization of the Church: Consumer Culture and the Church's Future* (Macon, GA: Smyth and Helwys, 2008).

17. Ritzer, *The McDonaldization of Society 6*, 55.

18. Bonilla-Silva, *White Supremacy*, 149-153.

19. Ritzer, *The McDonaldization of Society 6*, pp. 79.

20. Bonilla-Silva and Forman, "'I'm Not a Racist, But...'"; Van Dijk, "Discourse and the Denial of Racism."

21. Max Weber, *The Protestant Ethic and the Spirit of Capitalism* (Los Angeles: Roxbury, 1996).

22. Ritzer, *The Globalization of Nothing*.

23. Ritzer, *The Globalization of Nothing*, 142.

24. Frankenberg, *White Women, Race Matters*, 149.

25. Merton presented his now classic typology on the relationship between attitudes and behavior in Robert K. Merton, "Discrimination and the American Creed," *Discrimination and National Welfare*, ed. Robert M. MacIver (New York: Harper and Row, 1949), 99-126.

26. Frankenberg, *White Women, Race Matters*.

27. Pamela Perry, "White Means Never Having to Say You're Ethnic: White Youth and the Construction of 'Cultureless' Identities," *Journal of Contemporary Ethnography* 30, no. 1 (February 2001): 56-91.

28. Martha R. Mahoney, "Segregation, Whiteness, and Transformation," *University of Pennsylvania Law Review* 143, no. 5 (May 1995): 1659-1684.

29. McIntosh, "White Privilege."

30. William I. Thomas, "The Relation of Research to the Social Process," in *W.I. Thomas on Social Organization and Social Personality*, ed. Morris Janowitz (Chicago: University of Chicago Press, 1966), 289-305.

31. Alison Bailey, "Locating Traitorous Identities: Toward a View of Privilege-Cognizant White Character," *Hypatia*, 13, no. 3 (August 1998), 28.

32. Frankenberg, *White Women, Race Matters*; Bonilla-Silva, *Racism Without Racists*.

33. Frankenberg, *White Women, Race Matters*, 145.

34. McKinney, *Being White: Stories of Race and Racism*. New York: Routledge, 2005.

35. Amanda Lewis, "Some Are More Equal Than Others: Lessons on Whiteness from School," in *White Out*, 159-172.

36. One article on the issue of the continuing racial divide was The Associated Press, "Even With Tiger Woods at No. 1, Golf Still Mostly White," *Boston Herald*, April 2009. Available online at www.bostonherald.com/sports/golf/view/2009_04_02_Even_with_Tiger_Woods_at_No__1__golf_still_mostly_white/srvc=golf&position=1(accessed July 29, 2011).

37. Bush, *Breaking the Code of Good Intentions*, 230-231.

38. Van Dijk, *Communicating Racism*.

39. Feagin, *Systemic Racism*; Feagin, Vera, and Batur, *White Racism*.

40. Richard Buttny, "Multiple Voices in Talking Race: Pakeha Reported Speech in the Discursive Construction of the Racial Other," in *Analyzing Race Talk*, 103-118.

41. Bonilla-Silva, *White Supremacy and Racism*, 158-159.

42. Jacques Derrida, *Of Grammatology* (Baltimore, MD: Johns Hopkins University Press, 1976); Jacques Derrida, *Writing and Difference* (Chicago: University of Chicago Press, 1978).

43. A good online source for information on the lynching of Will Brown is at www.nebraskastudies.org/0700/frameset_reset.html?http://www.nebraskastudies.org/070 0/stories/0701_0134.html.

44. Actually, Arabs and other peoples of "Middle Eastern" descent have been included in the white category of the U.S. Census for many years, showing the significance of racial formation by the U.S. government (for more on racial formation, see Michael Omi and Howard Winant, *Racial Formation in the United States: From the 1960s to the 1980s*, 2nd ed., New York: Routledge, 1994). This inclusion of peoples of North African and Middle Eastern descent continued with the 2010 count, while the term "Arab" does not even appear on the Census form (Tim Padgett, "Still Black or White: Why the U.S. Census Misreads Hispanic and Arab Americans," *Time*, March 29, 2010. Available online at http://www.time.com/time/nation/article/0,8599,1975883,00.html; Accessed August 4, 2011).

45. Joe R. Feagin and Clairece B. Feagin, *Racial and Ethnic Relations in the United States*, 9th ed. (Upper Saddle River, NJ: Prentice Hall, 2010).

Chapter 3
Rationalizing Segregation

In January 2012 a report on segregation in U.S. cities was released by the Manhattan Institute. In the report re-published verbatim by *Bloomberg View*, Edward Glaeser, economics professor at Harvard and Manhattan fellow, declared that "another great American division is finally healing."[1] Based upon two measures of segregation, dissimilarity and isolation, the researchers found that both indicators have been in a consistent decline since the 1950s. They made reference to the Fair Housing Act of 1968 as an important reason for this change, as well as more recent phenomena such as gentrification, immigration, and black suburbanization, with the latter having the greatest impact. Additionally, the report declares that the presence of all-white neighborhoods is "effectively extinct," while black ghettos, though still in existence, are in a state of decline. They argue that "the decline in segregation can be partially attributed to the reform of...government practices and partly to changes in racial attitudes that can be considered both cause and consequence of policy change."[2]

The report had its share of both supporters and critics. Some critics were quick to warn against declaring an end to American segregation, pointing out that the rate of integration for African Americans is on average slower than that for other racial-ethnic groups, including Hispanics and Asians. Douglass Massey, co-writer of the now famous sociological treatise on segregation *American Apartheid*, noted that "the average white lives in a neighborhood that is 78 percent white and seven percent black."[3] Nonetheless, many news outlets were quick to join in the party.[4]

While the discussion of residential segregation in U.S. society was certainly welcome, the problem with this discussion was in understanding precisely *why* the rates of dissimilarity and isolation were down. In a critical contribution to the discussion, Michelle Alexander, author of *The New Jim Crow*, wrote a reaction piece to the report.[5] She notes that while the trend lines of segregation are going down, the incarceration rate for blacks has skyrocketed since the 1970s. In effect, if the "War on Drugs" and "three strikes" sentencing guidelines never came into existence, the rate of desegregation would have flatlined, assuming all else being equal. How could such seemingly bright and learned researchers employed at prestigious U.S. universities have a blind spot such as this?

Another problem with the report was the assumption that racial attitudes are responsible for the "decline" in residential segregation. Is it safe to make this assumption? Are young white Americans truly less prejudiced, and thereby more willing to live in racially integrated neighborhoods? More generally, are they more open to intimate relationships with nonwhite people, particularly black Americans? In this chapter, I present the contradictions surrounding the issue of interracial interactions respondents recall during the interviews based on their personal experiences. I divide this chapter into three parts: first, how do respondents come to terms with living in a segregated society despite favoring integration? In this section, I discuss the important role of *beneficial contact* in the crystallization of the white racial frame. This lack of beneficial contact creates an ambivalence towards racial Others, which leads to a tendency to naturalize racial segregation, produces a façade of "virtual integration," and projects respondents' fear of, and contempt for, nonwhite (particularly black) Americans. Second, how does this fundamental contradiction affect their descriptions of experiences involving nonwhite Americans? Here I discuss their recalled experiences when growing up, discussing friendships—both real and imagined—and the racial tensions they have experienced. Third, how do they rationalize the racial segregation of the social structure? In this section, I present the way that respondents' misunderstandings and miscommunication with nonwhite Americans, along with putting the responsibility of segregating society on nonwhite Americans, leads to a validation of the white racial frame. Throughout the chapter, I present various ways in which respondents speak rooted within the bureaucratization of their discourse.

Why does Segregation Continue?

Despite the tendency of many white Americans to claim their belief in the value of racial integration, U.S. society remains deeply segregated by race. All major social institutions, including families, schools, neighborhoods, and churches are segregated. In fact, data suggest that *resegregation* is occurring as a result of various factors, including further deindustrialization and "white flight" from neighborhoods as blacks and other nonwhites move in.[6] Another important component to explaining this social phenomenon is the white racial frame in its impact on the way whites see black Americans. This frame impacts the way whites think and speak about race and, as we will see throughout this chapter, affect their interactions with black Americans. In this section, I discuss the significance of white contact with nonwhite Americans, and how the participants of the study interpret these experiences.

Low Beneficial Contact

The significance of interracial contact on white prejudicial attitudes has been the focus of many studies over several decades now. When contact with people of color is low, whites fail to see, question, or challenge white supremacist beliefs.[7] This includes failure to challenge the white racial frame, which affects actions as well as beliefs.[8] Even when some contact is taking place, some prerequisites must be met to improve antiblack attitudes that produce "beneficial" interracial contact.[9] For example, authority figures must approve of the interaction,[10] and the members of the interaction are of equal status. One analysis found that the prerequisites are not necessarily mandatory but important facilitating conditions.[11] The position here is that the conditions are still most likely to reduce white antiblack attitudes.

Contact with nonwhites can be a crucial factor in determining the perception of race, and hence the racial attitudes, of whites. When contact is low between white and black Americans, white attitudes are based on figments of the imagination created by hearsay, particularly with zero contact. According to Joe Feagin, "white isolation and lack of contact feeds negative stereotyping, and there is little chance to unlearn inherited antiblack attitudes."[12] In addition, most contact whites have with people of color is non-beneficial, such as a formal and superficial exchange in a service encounter. When contact increases, white antiblack attitudes can either increase or decrease depending on both the frequency of interactions and whether or not the prerequisites for beneficial contact had been fulfilled.[13]

But which types of contact would be considered beneficial? Gordon Allport argued that casual contact is likely to increase negative attitudes, since the contact is likely to be "frozen in superordinate-subordinate relationships."[14] In addition, peripheral contact, as developed by Michael Banton,[15] such as riding on a city bus or when grocery shopping, is another situation where "limited interracial interaction is expected and maintained by individuals."[16] Meanwhile, acquaintance contact may lessen prejudice because of a stronger likelihood that equal status would exist between the actors. Acquaintance contact, defined by Jackman and Crane as people that "keep in touch with or get together with occasionally,"[17] could be increasing due to an integration of much of the work force.[18]

Allport appeared to be arguing that friendships per se could lessen antiblack prejudice; meanwhile, Sigleman and Welch argued in their study of interracial contact that friends could be of equal status.[19] According to Christopher Smith, however, the assumption that members of friendships are of equal status is problematic. The fact is that most "friends" are actually acquaintances in which the interaction is formal, and even if the friendship exists there is that ecological distance whites have with people of color except in rare cases such as those involved in intimate relationships or who live in quasi-integrated neighborhoods.[20] Also, the prerequisites for "beneficial" contact are likely to cease to exist, such as parental approval of the relationship. Too often previous studies have used poor operationalizations for "friend" or "acquaintance," whereas Jackman and Crane focused more on behavior rather than mere perception of friendships.[21]

Residential contact interacts with age "to produce variable changes depending on region and education level."[22] However, region as a variable has diminished in more recent studies in that Southern attitudes have caught up with non-Southern attitudes.[23] Despite the sample for this study consisted of mostly white young adults from the southeast, region will not be considered a variable in affecting racial attitudes. Residential contact with people of color is low for the majority of white Americans. Despite John Hartigan's assertion that the experience of white Detroiters, making up just 20 percent of the city population, will increase in the future,[24] this has yet to occur for the average white American experience.

As a result of low beneficial contact, white Americans often express ambivalence when addressing various racial matters. Their separation from those who experience race in negative or non-neutral ways creates a "white bubble" for whites to honestly believe that racism is not a problem in U.S. society. This "bubble" has also been referred to as the "white habitus" (as discussed in chapter 1) in which whites do not generally see any problems with the racist status quo, and the problems presented by nonwhites are exaggerated and are said to complain too much. Furthermore, since race rarely is a problem for them, whites hardly bother to concern themselves with the conceptualizations of race, racism, whiteness, and white privilege. The "individualism" of U.S. culture serves whites well in perpetuating the status quo, since it benefits white Americans most.

This ambivalence allows whites to naturalize white or Anglo American culture, thereby allowing white supremacy to exist unabated and thrive.[25] Separated from the reality of multiracial and multicultural America, whites have the luxury of forming a kind of "dysconsciousness."[26] Because of white privilege, whites are able to shrug off concerns of white racism and forget about the gross inequities existing within their philosophies and the contradictions occurring throughout their repertoires on racial issues. This is a crucial process in the rationalization of the white racial frame, which reaffirms the entire process. Reinforcing white racism could be an unintended consequence of the ambivalence, while the manifest function is the management of one's face during a conversation. Still, the rationalization of the racialized social system takes place.

In order to carry out this task to protect both one's self-image and the white supremacist structure, whites employ various discursive moves that aid in reproduction and protection of the white racial frame. For example, see Cynthia's ambiguous statement on disapproval of interracial relationships below:

Not so much disapproval? Maybe I think expecting someone for you to marry someone of the same race, um (.) there might be some slight disapproval, but it wouldn't be completely unaccepting?

In this excerpt, Cynthia did two things that are common in discourse of this kind: the use of diminutives and impersonal nouns. Notice the question marks following her initial statement ("Not so much disapproval?") and final utterance within this excerpt ("but it wouldn't be completely unaccepting?"). This type of discursive action allows the speaker to downplay the significance of the disapproval, while opening a window to backtrack from the statement if challenged by the recipient of the utterance (simply for discussing racist behavior). Meanwhile, the impersonal pronouns "someone" and "you," coupled with the structure "there might be," hide the particular actors she is talking about. She could be, for example, talking about her own parents expecting her to marry a fellow white person, but due to her ambiguity, we do not know for certain. It is precisely these kinds of utterances that demand probes by the interviewer for specification.

Another move that highlights their ambivalence is structured incoherence.[27] Since white Americans tend not to discuss these matters in any detail in their everyday lives, they often have difficulties navigating their way through their thoughts to speak clearly about these matters. For example, study participants commonly contradicted themselves when filling out the questionnaire, considering both statements "A good society should be integrated" and "People should be able to attend racially segregated schools or live in racially segregated neighborhoods if they wish" as either important or unimportant values. It should be noted that the sample's support for racial segregation was almost as strong as support for parental support for interracial marriage (Table 3.1). When discussing interracial dates, Angie made the following statement:

> Yeah, I had friends from high school, they would date like black and Hispanic (.) people and, they were nice guys, I like them, it's a little weird, but we all make mistakes (laughs) it doesn't matter what race you are.

Here we see a great example of the incoherence often associated with whites' race discourse. After mentioning that her (white) friends dated interracially in high school and that she liked them, she then stated "it's a little weird" and said that "we all make mistakes." After presumably making a statement in opposition to interracial dating, she then added a semantic move "it doesn't matter what race you are," likely to protect herself from any charges of racism based on her prior comment.

Naturalizing Segregation

As a result of low beneficial contact, white Americans know little about the racial diversity of their society. This lack of knowledge leads to an ambivalence towards the segregation of their lives. When discussing racial experiences, respondents often realize the contradiction inherent within their discourse: how can they value integration while living such segregated lives? Thus, they need to explain how segregation exists despite their professed value in racial integration, while maintaining face by appearing nonracist.

Table 3.1   Questionnaire Results for Attitudes towards Racial Integration and Intermarriage

Question	Mean
Parents should encourage their children to marry someone of a different race if they choose.	2.50
A good society should be integrated.	3.76
People should be able to attend racially segregated schools or live in racially segregated neighborhoods if they wish.	2.43

One method is to naturalize the phenomenon. Some respondents tried to explain their segregated lives away as mere coincidence. Angie, for instance, recalled introducing a friend of color to her parents this way:

> R: One of my friends was (.) Hispanic, and he was interested in me, and he came over to my house (.) unexpectedly ((laughs)), so I had to choose an ordinance, not just for him, but for other reasons ((laughs)), but um
> I: Like was he like (.) Cuban, or
> R: Mhm (1.0) my mom's good friends with his mom ((unintelligible))
> I: Like how long ago was this?
> R: Um, like three years ago. (1.0)
> I: Okay.
> R: (3.0) I mean, yeah, I mean he's a good guy, he's just like any other friend.
> I: You guys had like dinner together?
> R: No, he just came over to say hi and stop in ((laughs))
> I: Oh.
> R: Hm, I mean I'm not really like (.) close friends with like any people of color but it's not (.) because of the reason [they are] that color (.) it's just that (.) um, it's just who I end up hangin' out with.

In this excerpt, Angie first describes a "friendship" with an "Hispanic" male (note how she did not—or could not—answer if he was Cuban or not). Her utterance about "an ordinance" was ambiguous, and unfortunately she was not probed for further explanation. After the interviewer's "oh" response, it appeared as though she needed to defend her lack of interracial interactions with the last utterance, insisting that her lack of nonwhite friends is a result of mere coincidence, not preference.

Oftentimes when recalling interracial interactions, respondents feel a need to mention how "normal" or "average" the relationships are. This discursive type attempts to avoid accepting that relationships of this kind remain rare in our society and respondents' maintenance of their color-blind images of U.S. society. A good example of this trend came from Jane when discussing interracial dates:

> Like my friend [name] started like (.) started to date this kid [name] and they didn't like stop dating because of any racial thing but I mean I hung out with them too and it wasn't like I was hanging out with anyone different than you normally would I mean it was fine and there was never any like (.) weirdness or you know

First, she feels a need to mention that race was not a factor in why her friend stopped dating a nonwhite individual. Second, she insists that there was no difference or "weirdness" due to the interracial intermingling. This shows how Jane seems to equate being different racially with being "weird." Wanda also delivered a quite peculiar response to "I can recall a recent interaction with a black student on campus" when she said "I was walking back from class with a °black° and uh it was like (.) nothing, like (.) obviously he was black, but it was like a normal conversation that I would've had with a white person, too." Here Wanda tells me he was "black" under her breath while feeling the need to say that the conversation was not anything "abnormal." Examples like these are prevalent throughout the data, and they expose a fundamental weakness of color-blindness: that recognizing race (often defined as "color") is "bad in and of itself."[28]

Another method of naturalizing segregation is by assuming inherent differences between black and white cultures, a kind of "biologization" process.[29] Respondents make these differences seem so large that they cannot be reconciled, and these differences steer individuals into particular groups. For example, George recalled someone who had expressed disapproval towards interracial sex or marriage:

> R: I've heard stories of, like my mother told me stories of where uh (.) her family would talk about like (.) uh a black man dating a white girl
> I: Mm
> R: And they would disapprove of it um
> I: Like did they um were there like any kind of reasons why maybe that there was disapproval for the relationship? [specific things or
> R: [Uh   I don't know. I think it's, it
> could be (.) I don't think they op- went out and said 'it's because he's black,' I think they were saying it's because uh (1.0) they're just in two different, two different cultures uh I don't know, I think it probably had a lot to with that.

In this instance, the person recalled by the respondent thought blacks and whites could not get along due to having come from different cultures. It is experiences like these that can reproduce beliefs that black culture is distinct from white culture, that the differences are irreconcilable, and therefore mixing should not take place.

White Fear

As presented in the previous chapter, whites identify themselves through the images of racial Others. This identification process produces positive self-presentation and negative Other-presentation. Specifically, since the view predominates that blacks are strange and criminal, whites must therefore be normal and law-abiding. What implications does this have on white attitudes towards black Americans? It is these negative images that (re)produces white fear of black people, a fear that creates such social phenomena as white flight from neighborhoods considered to have become "too black." This fear keeps white Americans from interacting with black Americans, particularly in more intimate relationships.

Respondents in this study exhibit their fears of nonwhites through the ways they talk about racial matters and situations (e.g., interracial interactions). These fears are borne out of the white racial frame, based on centuries-old images of blacks as hypersexual, primitive, less intelligent, and violence-prone. They will take great pains to deliver responses that insist in the availability and support (or at least not outright opposition) for interracial relationships in order to present an image of nonracism.

At times, however, respondents revel themselves beneath the mask of color-blindness. In the following passage, Amy tells a story of how she felt threatened due to a party that took place in her apartment building:

R: There was a big loud party going on, all black people, and they were all like they had a really loud DJ, we had like the cops come by and uh they said they weren't gonna do anything about the party that was going on, and this cop had like (.) gold teeth and everything, I was thinking like (.) I even called up and like 'can you send somebody else down here?' because (.) obviously like they're gonna side with them, and so the party went on, and it happened a second time I think, and both times we had to call the cops about it, and in this case they didn't do much.
I: Like what was the problem about it?
R: It was way too loud, like our (.) the floors in our apartments were vibrating, windows were vibrating, it was obnoxious, it was going on for a really long time, they were taking up (.) all the parking spots everywhere, not to mention parking on the grass, um (.) I felt for my safety, like (.) I didn't wanna go outside, they were all walking on the street, and being loud and stuff, and I'm sure there was drinking going on and whatnot, so (.)
I: So what ended up happening like I mean did cops come and (.) like I mean as

far as telling them to turn down the volume? Or breaking up the party altogether?

R: All the cops really did was ask them to turn down the music, and which they did until the cops left, and then it went back up again, and (.) other than that, nothing really happened, we just waited it out until it was over.

According to her own report, there was a party in which predominantly "black people" were having a party in which she "felt for her safety" and "didn't wanna go outside" because "they were all walking on the street, and being loud and stuff, and I'm sure there was drinking going on and whatnot." What precisely was the cause of her fear in this situation? I cannot help but recall walking with my wife in our apartment complex, with people outside a unit drinking, yelling (hence being "obnoxious"), and cooking in a grill out in the parking lot, and thinking how if they had been black, someone would have called the police for feeling "threatened." Furthermore, although the did not mention the race of the police officer, the point that he had "gold teeth and everything" and added "obviously like they're gonna side with them" shows her conception of the situation into an "us versus them" frame, and that the police had failed to protect "innocent" whites from "threatening" blacks.

Within the white racial frame, there exists a continuum of racial Others to be feared by whites, and the group feared most is black Americans. This applies to the issue of interracial dating, as in the instance of Wanda, who essentially considers her ex-boyfriend from South America as white when responding to the statement "I have been interested in a person of color romantically before (whether past or present)" she says "not personally," tells me they had dated for two years, and added "but like as far as having a relationship? I haven't wanted to pursue a relationship of color." She then adds the following incoherent statement:

But there are tim- like I think (.) like the mo- best looking at my school last year was like half black and half white (.) but I don't know like (.) it's not like "they're black, I can't °go with you°" and like my parents are more like strict on=like they're not like strict at all, but um (.) they obvi- they care more than I do, I care. [if] there's a black person that I like, then (.) I like them (laugh)

Despite her incoherence, it sounds as if she could not date interracially—or, at least a black person—because of the disapproval from her parents. She contradicts her earlier statement of not wanting to pursue an interracial relationship when she says "[if] there's a black person that I like, then (.) I like them." Or at least she would not pursue the relationship due to the pressure against such a relationship.

This association between "people of color" and "black" continues with Amy's experience in high school, in which she had a relationship with a Puerto Rican, asking me "is that a person of color?" Compared to the incoherence of Wanda's excerpt, Amy provides more texture to her differentiation between "colored" and "not colored" ("white") in considerable detail. After mentioning that she attended two different high schools, she described the first as "predominantly white and upper-class," while the second was

> probably the opposite, um it was more of a high school that pretty much everybody went to, it was you know, no one studied and um there was crime at that school and you know people (.) a lot of people had babies and stuff like that, whereas the first high school that I went to wasn't so much like that, and that's where I met this guy, and uh he wasn't I didn't think the typical Puerto Rican, he didn't (.) you know like um (.) he was just a really really nice, friendly guy and um his family was definitely very attached to their heritage like when I went over there, all they ever ate was Puerto Rican food, they were a lot different from what I was used to, but um they're very nice.

In this excerpt, Amy basically says (in so many words) that the second high school she attended was predominantly black, and that "black" is associated with slacking in studies, teenage pregnancies, and criminal activity. In this excerpt, she does show how members of other racial groups can be "black" when she describes her Puerto Rican boyfriend as a "really really nice, friendly guy" (and hence not the typical Puerto Rican). This shows the important distinction between race and color that race studies scholars need to recognize in the way whites see racial Others, and hence what position those Others will have within the racialized social system.[30] For groups like Puerto Ricans and African Americans, the descriptive statement "he wasn't the typical ____" does not bode well for their life chances in U.S. society, and the less intermingling with white Americans, the worse off they will be.

Segregated Lives

In this section I examine in more detail the extent of the segregation in the respondents' lives, and how they attempt to reconcile with that reality during the interviews. Although some respondents are honest about the little contact they have with nonwhite Americans, most try to evade the reality through various methods. One method is simply to ignore the social fact of segregation; I argue that the façade of integration (or virtual integration) aids them in this process. Furthermore, respondents also mention "friends" during the interviews, though upon further review, these are actually fictive friendships and more likely to be (or have been) acquaintances. Finally, in this section I examine the extent of tensions experienced by the respondents during their interactions in which interracial relationships was an issue.

Admitted Segregation

At times respondents admitted the segregation of their lives. Ursela, for example, mentioned the extensive segregation in the dorms on campus and in her neighborhood:

> It's definitely there, housing segregation ((in the dorms)). And (.) yeah, um there's definitely not a lot of black families that live in my neighborhood at all (.) or Hispanic families, whatever, um (.) and I can't really see my family living in a (.) really like ethnic community, so yeah, I could say that.

In addition to recognizing the segregation in the living spaces of her life, she adds that she could not imagine her family living in an integrated community, acknowledging that the antiblack prejudice of whites is a factor in the segregation of U.S. society, not merely a result of coincidence.

Some respondents were quite candid in their lack of interactions with a black person on campus. Still, respondents usually tried to cite instances of contact but could not. For example, George remarked that "there are [a] few people in my first year class that I've talked to but I can't recall any recent interactions with them." Meanwhile, Linda replied "<u>Umm</u> (1.0) not real- I mean I know I interact with other black students but I can't (.) think of any that were particularly memorable." I found it interesting when she added, "Like I'll talk to people and stuff, but (.)," and did not even complete the semantic move, as if she waited for me to bail her out by speaking up so that she would not have to finish the statement. Rather than having to admit that her interactions with black Americans are overwhelmingly brief, formal, and superficial, I bailed her out by continuing the interview.

In another candid reply to the same statement, Penelope replied this way:

> I: Uhm, can you think of a recent example? (2.0) I mean it could be like anybody, really, a recent (.)
> R: (3.0) No↑ I mean I don't wanna just pull something out of my ass and lie, so
> I: Oh, okay↑
> R: Not, not really (laughs and snorts)
> I: That's fine.

After taking some time to reply, Penelope's honesty was rather refreshing; still, it illustrates the reality of segregation on this large college campus. Despite the number of nonwhite students in their classes, most contact was not beneficial. After rationalizing her lack of interactions with blacks on campus, Harriet said "I know a lot of the (.) cleaning ladies...are black in my dorm, but they're really nice." The only contact she reported on campus was with blacks in subservient positions, contact that can further increase antiblack attitudes of whites.[31]

The inability to recall interracial relationships was particularly apparent when recalling interracial dates. Renee, for instance, tried to make-up for the inexperience by remarking that "I've had like (.) had crushes (.) on like people of color." Respondents often had difficulty admitting to the lack of interracial dating, since it exposes the reality of segregated U.S. society, while potentially (at least in their minds) labeling them prejudiced for not dating interracially. In an extensive attempt to maintain face, Ursela spoke about interracial relationships this way:

> I personally have never done that? I can't tell would I ever do it? But it just hasn't come along, like I haven't met that person that I felt we had a strong connection, and they happen to be of a different <u>race</u>, but I'm definitely not against it in any way.

Ursela first uses two appeals to the recipient as she begins her statement, as if she were walking on eggshells. She also tries to make her lack of interracial dating coincidental, insisting that if only the right person would come along, she would be willing to get involved.

At times respondents had epiphanies about the extent of segregation in the social spaces they had occupied. Kaitlin, for example, recalled a job she had at a restaurant in a retirement community and the racial make-up of the employees:

> R: And (.) I don't really remember anything specific like we had a- our head chef was a black cook and then the second guy down was Hispanic and then everyone else was basically white (.) we had a few dishwashers that were black.
> I: Mm.
> R: And we had an (.) Asian dishwasher and I don't think (.) <u>wow</u>, I don't think any of the servers were (.) black. One of- I think a few of- a few of the servers were (.) Hispanic, but I don't think there were any black ones. But that kind of all has to do with again the neighborhood thing like a lot of people around the place I live are white
> I: Mhm↓
> R: And those are the people who worked there.

Here, Kaitlin at first does not think anything peculiar until she actually thinks about it (apparently for the first time). She has the epiphany when she says, "<u>wow</u>, I don't think any of the servers were (.) black," and realizes how segregated her workplace was. Unfortunately, she tries to rationalize the segregated workplace by stressing the segregation within her neighborhood, which does nothing to explain the fact that the blacks who worked there were in positions with less pay and status.

Sincere Fictions of Integration

How can white Americans insist that U.S. society is integrated when the reality, as shown through the images of Hurricane Katrina's aftermath, paints us the opposite picture? Sometimes whites simply have blinders over their eyes, e.g. downplaying the disapproval of interracial marriage of their parents, while others use doubletalk to avoid looking "racist" while addressing the reality of their segregated lives.

One method to uphold this fundamental contradiction is to take the myriad images from the mass media as reality that portray society as racially integrated, tolerant, and egalitarian. A useful concept for understanding the mindset of white Americans is *virtual integration*, in which white Americans come to believe they interact with black Americans when they watch them on television or in movies (when in reality they have very few).[32] Programs like *E.R.* or *The Cosby Show* that portray black physicians or movies that portray a black "friend" (usually within a sea of whiteness) give whites soothing relief that America has successful blacks, and (hence) avoid the reality of white racism that continues to affect the lives of African Americans, promoting a color-blind image of U.S. society.[33] In reality, the common response from participants in the study would mention examples of how society is integrated based on examples from the media yet, when discussing more personal experiences, often contradicted those initial statements declaring racial integration.

A good example of this inconsistency came from Irene. A way to summarize her discourse is she believed that, due to living in a racially diverse social setting, racism was no longer a problem in our society. When pressing her to think of an example in which she felt angry about something involving race, she responded this way:

> I mean, I don't really watch t.v., but, as far as the news, in my hometown it's (1.0) pretty, racially equal as far as, I see just as many, African American anchors as I do white anchors like I just, it's pretty (1.0) equal.

Because of the numbers of black anchors she recalled on local news stations, she implies that U.S. society on the whole is racially integrated, and hence equal.

At times respondents would claim to have friends of other races but, upon further review, have few if any, reaffirming Jackman and Crane's finding that most whites overexaggerate their number of nonwhite friends.[34] A great example of this comes from Elizabeth, in which she says these interactions occur "all the time," only to be exposed as an imposter:

> R: Um, yeah. ((laughs)) Li(h)ke a(h)ll th(h)e ti(h)me. Totally fine, like (.) I don't know see it like (.) °blackness is like a difference° ((trails off))
> I: Well like, um, can you think of like a specific instance like, an interaction I mean, just recently?
> R: I don't know, I just [was] talking to my friend's roommate, before we went out last night.
> I: Mm, oh. Where'd you guys go?
> R: Um, we went t:o (.) um, to a homecoming party.
> I: And you guys went out as a group?

R: Oh↑ no, no no no, she was doing her own thing with um sort of her other friends, but I was just talking to her while we were getting ready.
I: Oh↑
R: So (.) I don't know.

After laughing off the statement as if the mere thought of not interacting with a black person on campus was ridiculous, she mentioned a specific instance in which she did not even go out with the same group.

High-Anxiety Interactions

Almost as ubiquitous as their lack of beneficial contact is the reports of tension in the experiences they did report. But the tension reported was not always with interactions with people of color, but rather with fellow whites when addressing, implicitly or explicitly, interracial interactions such as interracial marriage. For example, oftentimes whites do not explicitly tell fellow whites to avoid interracial dating or marriage. Instead, they express their disapproval through nonverbal forms of communication or more indirect verbal methods. Odella recalled one experience of one of her sister's friends:

R: [She] got engaged to a (.) black boy that she had been dating for four years, and her parents had never (.) disapproved of them dating, but (.) I guess they didn't think it was going to love onto marriage?
I: Oh, okay.
R: And then they kind of starting asking questions
I: Right.
R: They didn't outwardly say 'no,' but they (.)
I: Right. Like what kinds of questions did they start asking?
R: Like if you have a child, do you think the child will have problems, you know, with identity and things like that.
I: Yeah. How did she respond to that?
R: Um, I'm not entirely sure, but I know they're getting married (laughs)

Based on Odella's statement, her sister's friend seems to have not been affected by her parents' disapproval of the marriage. Still, such disapproval coming from parents could certainly create strains for the relationship.

Some respondents mentioned examples in which whites initiated the tension (though these were exceptions). Renee recalled an incident in which there was a fight outside of the complex she lived in during her freshman year:

R: My neighbors across the street were from like a really small town in ((part of state)) and they're just kind of (.) I don't know, maybe racist I think, a(h)nd they got in a fight with these kids right outside (.) and it was like a really big deal and the cops came and I don't really know why they got in a fight
I: I mean you think it was like because of racial tensions?

R: U::mm I think so, like I think I remember them talking about it later and like yeah, 'cause there was like no purpose for the fight, they just (.) crazy kids.
I: When they were talking like what things were they saying like about them?
R: It was kind of a long time ago (.) I don't remember I think they just honestly wanted to get in a fight with peo- somebody and like they were talking about how the n-word and say that he was the n-word (.) how they were coming to their apartment and like causing trouble and they didn't want them there or something (.) it's terrible.

Renee rationalizes the neighbors' behavior due to where they came from, implicitly suggesting they were "rednecks" or "hillbillies,"[35] and her laugh in Line 2 is rather ambiguous: she may have been a bit tense while recalling the incident, or (more likely) it was due to her dismissal of such "redneck" behavior. Of course, racist actions are never laughable for those who are victims to them. She also dismisses the perpetrators for being pathological, and hence defining racism in purely individualistic terms while neglecting the structural nature of the problem.

Kaitlin also downplayed the tension caused by whites with another common excuse: that the whites involved were old people who lived in the past. After downplaying the segregation of her workplace, she downplays the impact of racist comments from the residents at the retirement community:

R: And the old people are really nice but (.) they're racist. Like you can hear them talking like when you serve them they'll just be having a conversation about (.) I don't know, something.
I: O(h):h.
R: Uh hu(h)h
I: Like did the (.) the folks that worked there did they ever have like problems with like (2.0) um people that lived there like make comments or something and they got upset or something like that?
R: No↑t that I saw. I mean (2.0) th:e head chef went out a lot of times and talked to people and everyone was always really friendly to him, so I don't think it's (.) I don't know, I don't know why they=I mean, it wasn't all of them obviously that were racist=there was just a select few that you would hear talking about him but (.) not, like not anything I saw=I mean something definitely could happen, I only worked there a year so I definitely (laugh) could have missed stuff, but
I: Right.
R: But not really that I saw.

She begins this excerpt with a classic contradiction "[they] are really nice but (.) they're racist," and then works to minimize both the prevalence and damage of their racist comments. She claims that there were only a few bad apples in the mix, and she never saw anything happen. If racism only exists when white Americans see it, then it likely will never exist.

In one instance of antiracism in which a respondent fought for a nonwhite woman to rush at her sorority, Samantha recalled the tension with her fellow sorority members:

> R: I live in a sorority (.) and we had a lot of tension because (.) we're not letting other races in?
> I: Mhm.
> R: And it was supposedly not on purpose? But we did tell it was? And I became an executive] and we fought for a girl (.) to be in our house, so (.) I've always lived in the sorority house so I haven't lived in a dormitory or an apartment building, but it was kind of along the same lines where (.) there is just like (.) people (laugh)
> I: That's interesting how it's like (.) like it was kind of like backdoor? Like I mean it wasn't just ["oh, we're letting them in, but"
> R: [Yeah.   It was like the you know the people (.) upstairs and they call them that, always pick who are in the sororities, and their excuse or their (.) reaction to it is that (.) you know, there are (.) the (.) multicultural sororities and stuff and then not many people other than (.) white females come through rush

In this exceptionally rare account, Samantha realizes (apparently along with other members) that leaders within the organization were intentionally keeping nonwhite women from rushing. In addition, when confronting them about it, they rationalized the racist action by claiming nonwhite women rushed for "multicultural" sororities anyway. Like Renee's excerpt, this respondent recalled a situation in which whites initiated the tension. However, as we will see in the next section, whites often view racial Others with contempt and suspicion, and as the initiators of conflict and the people responsible for segregation.

Rationalizing Segregation

In this section, I map the way respondents rationalize their separation from people of color—in particular black Americans—however implicitly it is done. First, the respondents mention examples when recalling interracial situations in which there was miscommunication and misunderstanding. Second, respondents often projected the responsibility of integration onto black Americans, and complaining of alleged characteristics of nonwhite Americans that make integration difficult or impossible to achieve. Third, I present some important extracts from the interviews in which respondents validate the components of the white racial frame, and how their misunderstandings often turn into contempt for nonwhite Americans. Finally, I present a passage from Betty, the only study participant with an intimate relationship with a black American, and how her experience has provided her an understanding of segregation that the majority of the sample lacks.

Misunderstandings and Miscommunication

Due to the limited amount of beneficial contact with black Americans and, more generally, the representations of black folks' experiences, ordinary whites often create distorted images of African Americans and pass them on to future generations of white Americans. Thus, when whites do come into contact with black Americans with an opportunity to experience beneficial contact, there is often confusion and miscommunication due to the misrepresentations of the African American experience.

Sometimes respondents reported experiences with black roommates that had caused unpleasant moments. Let us revisit the passage from chapter 2 when Mandy spoke of one roommate she had a previous summer:

> R: Um (1.0) I mean our problems weren't over race our problems were more like little stuff like she turned the air-conditioning off.
> I: Oh
> R: (laughs) and um she didn't do, she did weave in the room too, so I guess that's a cultural thing but (.) she was a little more messy so there were clumps of haiˆr that I found there and (outbreath laugh) grease on the doors so you can't ope(h)n the doorknob? But I mean (.) it was nothing like (.) hatred you know

In this passage, Mandy was responding to the statement asking for recent interactions with blacks on campus. I should note that this statement followed the one asking for experiences of tension in her dormitory or apartment building, which might explain why she and other respondents continued to think of instances of tension with black Americans; still, the reason why they continue to frame their interactions with blacks in this way is intriguing. After stating that her problems with her roommate was not racial (note the usage of the pronoun we to make the misunderstandings appear equally shared), while mentioning an example of something unrelated to race (turning the air conditioner off), she does mention the example of hair weaving that is related to race, and even admits it ("so I guess that's a cultural thing"). Despite her addition of the invariable "but" here to insert a semantic move, she adds another point of contention against her black roommate for being "a little more messy" (note the diminutive "little" here to soften the charge). Then she completes the semantic move to protect her self-image by saying "it was nothing like (.) hatred you know." Even if we can take her comment that they did not hate each other (or at least Mandy did not hate her roommate) at face value, she nonetheless expresses some contempt for her roommate's actions.

Since whites rarely interact in any meaningful way with blacks, their images of African Americans often come from hearsay from fellow whites. Elizabeth also mentions an example of white girls' misunderstanding (and disdain) of hair weaving in the dorms. Mentioning this in response to the tension statement, she recalls a white friend's experience with a black roommate:

Um, well not for me but for another friend of mine, she doesn't live in my dorm um, she and her roommate like, she's umm (.) like white and her roommate's black and (.) like just in like (.) different like grooming things like her roommate has a weave or something like that and so like the hair glue and all that stuff is around and (.) she thinks that's weird but that's okay, like she's okay with it, but it's different, so that's the only thing I can think of really.

After failing to mention instances of tension in her own dormitory, she mentions this example, yet adds that her white friend is "okay with it." So why then would there be any tension to report? Unless she was merely trying to satisfy the interviewer by saying something, it sounds as if she was shielding her white friend's image by saying "but it's different," while calling the practice of hair weaving "weird," to legitimize the agitated feelings of her roommate.

On a different subject, Kaitlin spoke of her black roommate and the "weird" activities she and her friends (assumed here to be black, though Kaitlin does not explicitly mention this) did while in the room:

I: Like what kinds of things do they like to do, like this is on the weekends?
R: No, like all the time (laughs) they're over there, and they just do stuff that (.) I don't do, like they move the table and like da:nce in the middle of our room
I: Right.
R: Which I would never do with my frie(h)nds
I: Like listen to music?
R: Yeah, like rap which doesn't bother me like listening to rap music but I just find it kind of weird 'cause I wouldn't have my friends over and like break dance all over my living room like they do (laughs)
I: Oh. What do you like to do like do you have friends come over to you dorm?
R: Mm mhm↑. And we like play cards and watch movies and sometimes they watch t.v. with us together and stuff like that (.) it's not that (.) I don't like them or anything, it's just that it gets loud sometimes.
I: Do you guys ever like go out together like to parties or clubs or
R: Not really. We invited them (.) me and my roommate invited them one time to see a movie and they (.) already had plans or something, but yeah not really, we hang out in the room together but not really outside of that.

During this exchange, I did better than usual at challenging the respondent's remarks. First, I challenged her assertion that her black roommate and friends were "weird" due to their listening to music together. She replied that they listened to rap, which last I knew many young whites also listen to. Also note how she went from "da:nce in the middle of our room" to "breakdance all over my living room," in which "breakdance" here is a use of absurdity[36] to solidify a point she is trying to make; meanwhile, she uses the possessive pronoun "my" as though "they" have invaded her private space, despite the fact that her roommate lives there, too. She then provides "evidence" in how different she and her (white) friends are (considering the fact they often watch movies together in the room), and includes a semantic move to insist that she still likes them. Finally, Kaitlin mentions how little time they spend together outside of the dorm room.

In a similar vein, Linda complained of two black girls who live on her floor:

I: Like have you (.) witnessed or heard about any kind of tensions or anything?
R: No, I mean well there's (.) these two girls who are really lou:d and they listen to really loud music but I think
I: Mhm.
R: I don't think people (.) get annoyed with them because of like the fact that they're like black, I think it's just an- they're annoyed because they play loud music, you know so but I mean for the most part everything's fine.

Note here her noun "people" to distance herself from the annoyance. There are two important points worth mentioning that suggest the difficulties associated with declining antiblack attitudes of whites via beneficial contact (e.g., roommates on college campuses). First is the issue of imagined racial differences to provide an excuse for racial segregation. Although some important differences remain unacknowledged or misunderstood by whites, there are plenty of similarities that black and white Americans can identify with. Second, it is interesting how whites only interact with blacks when forced to (here, the result of being roommates). This poses a real challenge to Allport's contact hypothesis, in which whites can have relationships with blacks they do not see as "black" per se, and continue to harbor deep-seated racist images embedded within the white racial frame.

White misunderstandings often lead to miscommunication with black Americans. This miscommunication often leads to distrust and suspicion of the racial Other, even feeling like blacks only look out for themselves while even attempting to put whites at a disadvantage. In other words, whites think black folks are out to get them. In the following passage, Dina speaks of her experience with her black resident assistant:

I guess (3.0) I don't know, I feel like woa:h, when I lived over the summer in (.) in, on camp↑us, um my R.A. ((Resident Assistant)) was a different race than me? And all the R.A.s they were all the same race, and I have a lot of problems with her like, um, not (.) because of her ↑race, but just like we (1.0) like I had to call [a] judicial a lot about her? and I know like other problems, too, but um, I don't know, when they talked to me it seemed sort of like (.) they weren't, they weren't as understanding about the situation as if they would be if I was of the same race as them.

In this situation Dina reported feeling like her resident assistant was not as understanding as she could have been. Notice, however, her shift from singular to plural pronouns in the excerpt, as if she used the instance of one experience with a black person to generalize for the entire group. Fortunately, when failing to respond to the statement "I can recall a recent interaction with a black student on campus," I asked her to recall an interaction with her resident assistant, and also to elaborate on "the situation" she had mentioned earlier during the interview:

> R: Well, umm I guess it just seemed like my R.A. happened to be a different race than me but, the majority of the R.A.s were of a different than me but there's like the couple that were the same race as me? And the ones that were the same race as me like I talked to them all in a group because they were in office and the ones that were the same race as me seemed to be more on my side in the matter and the ones that were a different race seemed to be a little more reluctant to [like
> I: [What was the issue?
> R: Like I was, there was like a (.) fire safety inspection and my R.A. didn't (.) like they're supposed to come around first, and check all of your stuff to make sure you're not in violation and if you are they're supposed to give you a slip and then they come back the next day
> I: Like the stuff in your dorm?
> R: Yeah. Then they come the next day to give you (.) like, the violation like, the first time was just a warning and then the second time you're supposed to fix it, but then she came she told me all of my stuff was fine, but then I ended up not being fine when she checked thoroughly for the real thing, so I like never got documentation that my side was not fine=I never got the written warning, so it ended up=turned into a big deal because, um, everyone else got a written warning? And it was an accident obviously but, she like wouldn't, she was just like 'well, that's just the way it is,' and I was gonna have to go to a seminar and stuff, so it (.) is was just like I had to do, out of a whole bunch of people that were above her and I ended up getting it taken away but, the, like when I addressed everyone about it, and the R.A.s in the office it just seemed like the ones that were my race were more on my side and the other ones were like less understanding.
> I: So in the end, it was pretty much settled?
> R: In the end, yeah, it pretty much worked out like I didn't have much contact with her at all except for that one experience but, um, like (.) in the end I ended up just going through somebody that was above her that worked for judicial at [school] and they took it away so I didn't have to ask her about it or anything anymore.

After elaborating on what had happened, she basically saw her black resident assistant as unreasonable and out to get her. Her usage of reported speech of the R.A. "Well, that's just the way it is" is used to reinforce that image of unreasonable, and even more generally, socially deficient.[37] The most important point is how the respondents frame these moments as tense, while trying to downplay race as a factor.

Onus Placed on Blacks

When white Americans think of race, they usually think of nonwhite Americans, and thus when thinking or speaking of race "problems," they think of black or nonwhite "problems." Regarding the issue of integration, whites in the sample had a tendency to at least implicitly place the onus of responsibility on black Americans for integrating U.S. society. If whites and blacks do not intermingle with each other, it is due to blacks' desire to self-segregate, create racial conflict, and possess unfavorable attributes that make them undesirable associates. It is rarely (if ever) mentioned as a result of centuries of white racism.

When analyzing the interview discourse, it is intriguing in how the sample replied to the statement "I recall an experience involving some racial tension in my dormitory or apartment building" in that they often appeared to equate racial diversity with tense situations, and in particular people of color created the tense situations. Oftentimes respondents stamped blacks as the initiators of conflict. For example, Yannie recalled a situation in which his black friend visited him at his dormitory:

> Over the summer, [he] came into the dorm and I live in [name] so it's (.) pre-dominantly white it seems, um (.) and actually (.) interestingly enough, he caused the tension? But my black friend walked in and uhm sat down and talk to some of these people, and they were talking about the group that's for saluta-torians and valedictorians only? And he mentioned him being in the group, and the girl turns to him and was like 'you're salutatorian?' and he's like 'what? Surprises you that there's a black salutatorian?' So, he just kind of blamed [her] for that, and attacked her and she didn't mean anything along those lines by it, and he was partially kidding? Because it's just how he acts, but it like caused some tension? Um (.) 'cause he, he doesn't relent, that's how he acts, so it ac-tually resulted in um (2.0) uh, and the thing was really surprising is the girl was uh actually Asian, so she wasn't exactly (.) a majority either, so that I guess that was the interesting part of it, but there was tension, he (.) did get in trouble, they reported to the R.A.s, so (.) I guess like even jokingly it led to problems?

In this situation, Yannie failed to see how the Asian girl's question could have insulted his friend, while assuming that only white Americans are capable of racism (for instance, many Asian Americans are considered to be "borderline" whites). Yannie immediately defended the Asian girl, saying "she didn't mean anything along those lines by it," yet why would she ask the question in the first place? Is there any reason to believe that someone would lie about being a salu-tatorian? An interesting finding here is how whites can defend "borderline" whites as well as fellow whites. More importantly, Yannie uses this situation to describe his black friend's personality in that he is relentless and a troublemaker, so much so that the people there at the time notified the resident assistants about his presence.

Another instance of blaming black Americans for the inability to integrate U.S. society was the notion that blacks choose segregation, often the result of "black pride." For example, Wanda spoke of black girls living on her floor in her dormitory:

> They act different, like you can hear outside their doors like loud rap music, like you know (.) who's (laugh) which room is (.) but there's no tension on the floor, I mean, they don't- actually, there's no tension, but they're not like (.) as friendly as- I guess they feel that like there's only two or three on like a floor of like 30 (.) people? So I guess they are like major like minorities, so they don't like (.) even (.) like feel the need or want to get along with everybody? Not like just like they don't wanna be like friends, it's not like they don't want to have (.) it's not that they want to have like problems with people, they just don't choose to be friends with everyone?

Again, there is the association made between black people and loud rap music. Despite Wanda's initial statement that no tension exists on her floor, she contradicts herself when she says that the black girls are "not like (.) as friendly as-" (note how she does not complete the statement). She places the responsibility of the girls having friends with whites squarely on their shoulders.

Meanwhile, "black pride" was also cited as a cause of racial conflict, albeit indirectly. In an interesting statement, Betty speaks of her "best friend," whom she met this semester, and reasons why tense moments do not exist:

> And she's really awesome, and uh if you get her to talk about like just black pride in general, she can go off for hours on it, and uh it's not a bad thing, but um she does like realize that (.) she doesn't feel like necessarily discriminated against on campus, even though the campus is majority white from what we can see, and uh she doesn't feel discriminated against, she feels like she gets along with everybody, and but uh I think she's well-adjusted, and I enjoy her company (laugh)

First, Betty fails to complete the semantic move "it's not a bad thing, but" in reference to her friend's "black pride." We can conclude from her statement that she conceptualizes "black pride" as "feeling discriminated against" and not getting along with everybody. Hence, if black Americans would only stop complaining about experiencing discrimination would they then cease being discriminated against, be "well-adjusted" and then whites could "enjoy their company."

Some respondents equated "being black" with being hostile or unfriendly. For instance, Wanda described black kids at her high school:

> R: There was always tension between um they would just like turn over lunch tables and sit on top of them and like (.) just be loud (.) I, I was friends with them, so (.) there was separation, I guess they felt that like (.) they were (.) like black, and they didn't really hang out with whites, they kind of like made fun of us, so (.)
> I: Was the tension a pretty common occurrence, or was it um can you think of like a specific time or instance?
> R: Yeah, there hasn't been like fights in school or there haven't like (.) black person against a white person, but there has been at my school, but it wasn't like people would like walk by and be like 'you know, I don't like them,' it was

just certain people like, for the most part, they wanted to like °be black°, that's what they wanted to do, and it's not like the white people didn't like black people, they just felt like they had to like live up to their standard of being like a black person who would like dress a certain way or like act a certain way, especially (.)

Wanda typifies "being black" as not liking white people, though she insists that whites do not have a problem with them. She believes that blacks choose to segregate themselves from whites in society.

Some respondents also blamed blacks for whites' disapproval of interracial relationships. In one particular instance Jane reported parental disapproval of interracial dating. In the following excerpt, she defends fellow whites (her parents) for their disapproval, while blaming, albeit implicitly, black Americans for the racial separation:

> R: So (.) but um (.) my parents never wanted me to like, they still don't but, they like don't agree and like, if I wanted to date someone of another race mostly black
> I: Oh.
> R: I don't know, not because they're racist but because (.) just because it makes it a lot harder, you'll have lots of problems I guess, maybe uh it doesn't really matter, I mean if I wanted to I could (.) they're not gonna like disown me but
> I: Like for those who (.) like disapprove of like interracial marriage or sex or whatever I mean, what are some of the reasons that they might feel that way? Or like make an argument for their point of view?
> R: I mean I can understand why some people don't agree with it because you're coming from totally different (.) like culture, I guess
> I: Mm
> R: Which is (.) a lot of the values and (.) you know, like maybe that culture might be different from that culture=not all of them, but definitely some (.) and (.) it's (.) a lot more common I thi:nk, I'm not positive but to see black women single mothers than it is (.) and it's a pride thing too, like (.) black people, like when a guy has a kid and then it's like 'how many kids do you have?'
> I: Mm
> R: It's kind of like (.) °a pride thing°.
> I: Okay.

In addition to mentioning family members expressing disapproval of these relationships due to cultural differences, she appears to believe it herself, adding that the onus is on African Americans, who choose to remain separate from mainstream (white) culture. Note how she does add the semantic move "=not all of them, but definitely some" to avoid any dissent from the interviewer. Furthermore, she adds her own explanation for their self-segregation ("It's kind of like (.)°a pride thing°") under her breath as another attempt to avoid criticism.

Later in the interview Jane inserts a common storyline that the children of these relationships would suffer due to their interracial status:

U:m, I definitely have heard other people who (.) don't agree on interracial sex or marriage just because I said before that social problems and how you know having an interracial kid um can be hard on them like when they're growing up at school because they get teased or (.) because they're not one or the other, and just because (.) it's tense

Based on her utterances during the interview, Jane appears to have significant problems with interracial intimate relationships. There appears to have been much influence from her parents on this issue, though she deflects the responsibility for this division on black Americans. In her attempt to appear nonracist, she employs various discursive tricks such as semantic moves and impersonal pronouns to protect the image of both herself and her parents.

Validation of the White Racial Frame

Due to the misunderstandings and miscommunication, while failing to take any responsibility for the white racial order, the white racial frame continues to operate unabated, allowing the vicious cycle to continue. Many respondents, during their interviews, expressed deep emotions when recalling racial experiences. In the following excerpt, Mandy begins with rationalizing segregation as rational, while comparing it to gender segregation:

I've noticed that (.) people tend to stick together based on their background um but I've also noticed that a lot of the girls stuck together (.) on the hall versus like the boys were always stuck together with my floor

After I asked her why she thinks different racial groups tend to hang with another, she went through examples of the different things the groups did together, such as the example of black girls doing her hair. She then, however, recalled one black girl who caused tension in the dorm:

R: There was one situation where it was like a white girl and a black girl lived together, and (.) the black girl was from a very black community, everyone was black so, she (.) or she's from (.) maybe she was the only black girl in a white community so she had everything handed to her because (.) you know, she was that way and they didn't want her to like bring up race or anything, so she kind of like (.) slid by and didn't have to do anything and she just like (.) she's everything beca- 'oh, because I'm black,' it's this way and then she kind of brought those ideals here, and then had conflict with her white roommate because she thought that everyone should like (.) bow down to her or whatever.
I: Mhm.
R: Um, I know a lot of the black girls thought that there weren't many black people at our university, and they should've gone to a blacker? university?
I: Oh.
R: But (.) um, I thought we were pretty mixed here, considering like the ratio of like whites versus blacks in America and whites versus black (.) in America

that go to college? I thought we had a pretty (1.0) good ratio 'cause you can't increase that if they don't go to college.

In this passage, Mandy makes it unclear where she heard this story, suggesting she heard this from someone else (likely a white girl). She gives an implicit rationalization for segregation by depicting blacks as oversensitive and unreasonable, and then closes with a sincere fiction of the "integrated" campus.

Going further on the image Mandy portrayed above of one black girl as expecting everyone to "bow" before her, Penelope took a similar approach in recalling a friend's boyfriend:

R: Uh, I ended up living with her my sophomore year in a four-bedroom apartment with two other white girls and her, and uh she did have a boyfriend who (.) (laugh) we did not get along with the I guess we three white roommates did not get along with her boyfriend

I: Mm mhm

R: Who was (.) uh, you know, rude and (?) (laugh), a:nd uhm (.) just kind of disgusted me, he wasn't a [university] student, she was, he was a (.) [community college] student, but he would come and stay, and welcome himself in, and use our utilities and amenities, and not help pay, a:nd (.) was very rude to us and very unappreciative of us, and taking our space and our rent money basically 'cause he was living off of us, and uhm (.) it doesn't really answer black student on campus, but uhm it did create struggles between [black girl] and us because we could not (.) when we would try to confront her about it, that's where her very pride-driven African American attitude would come out, and make us look like well maybe we had some sort of racial discrimination towards him, when I by far have been discriminated in my past for being a Jew, and I would never ever in my life ever discriminate [against] someone, so it was taken out of context

This passage serves another example of how whites believe black folks stand up for each other, no matter what is going on. She equates "black pride" with (unfair) accusations of discrimination. Considering that he was an invited guest of a roommate, Penelope (while using the plural pronoun "we") acts as if he was invading "her" space and using "her" amenities. She also uses her status as a Jewish American to excuse herself from any charges of racism.

In a similar incident, Vincent mentions an example in which he shared an apartment with a Filipino student:

R: My freshman year I lived in an apartment, and me and my friend and one other guy=we didn't (.) he was never there, so we never saw him, but there was one other kid living there, and he was Filipino, and his three other friends that freeloaded off of us

I: Mhm.

R: And all three of them are black. They loved, you know, they would sleep on the couch downstairs or sleep on a chair, there were bunk beds in his room which didn't fit, but you know, he gave 'em one and they didn't pay rent or

didn't do anything (.) um, and there was one thing that happened, and me and my friend were away at spring break um that they burned our apartment
I: Oh, really?
R: Yeah, they burned our apartment. And we came back and we asked "what happened?" and he says uh "well, we got kinda rowdy, you know, not really paying attention," they were uh doin' some- they had some drug paraphernalia downstairs apparently, and then it just went from there (.) man! ((exasperated)) So me and my friend got into a (.) pretty large verbal argument with them over that so (.) we ended up movin'.

Similar to Mandy's previous excerpt, Vincent paints himself as a victim of blacks' irresponsibility and carelessness. His Filipino roommate's three black friends were "mooching" off of Vincent and his roommates, and then accidentally set fire to the apartment. This led to his resolution to move out.

Sometimes respondents expressed emotions that showed their antiblackness, even when respondents had said other things during the interview that were more antiracist. Despite some antiracist comments on racial privilege when shopping (see chapter 2), Xena made this comment about something she heard from another student in a different dorm:

R: I don't know if there was much tension there, but she would say a lot of times like at night they would kind of just like (.) trash the place, like throw garbage cans over, throw things at lights and I don't know what that had to do with, but she probably had more [tension] in hers.
I: Mhm. Well, they trashed the place? Like
R: I don't know if it'd be like they'd go out at night and come back and had been drinking, or what it was, but she said they kind of just acted like (.) animals at times (.) which is surprising 'cause if they're like athletes, but you know you feel like they would be a little more (1.0) ((avoid hangover for sport))

Xena does not specify the race of the students here, but the important point is that non-whiteness is equated with being animal-like. Meanwhile, she made the assumption that "they" were athletes. White students often assume that black students are beneficiaries of athletic or minority scholarships, which they use as fodder for the notion that blacks could not have attended university due to their intellect.

For some respondents, they openly expressed their fear of nonwhite Americans. For example, Amy spoke of her sister's apartment building:

R: [She] is living in an apartment right now, where there a lot of Mexicans, and if that was [me] personally, I would be scared for my life, because (.) they have a reputation? And I'm not saying that every Mexican is this way, but they've given themselves a bad reputation of stealing and um violence and stuff like that and (.) these people that live in their neighborhood aren't any exception, because they've been known to like hang out in the parking lot every hour of the night, sleep in their car out in the parking lot, there's like 15 people that live

in one apartment next to her that are all Mexicans and (.) um that would definitely be an issue for me, I'd make sure to lock my car all the time, always lock
my doors, um
I: Like how long has uh she lived there?
R: Um, she just moved there um a couple of months ago, I think.
I: Like has she told you of any like (.) experiences?
R: I don't think she really cares too much, there has been already, they um had
a little feud in the Mexican apartment next to hers where they said somebody
broke in and stole something=well, you have 15 people living there, it's probably one of the people living there that stole something from you, and (.) I'm
just glad it's not me living there=I don't think she has many issues with that
like she tends to um make friends with pretty much everybody and anybody, so
she doesn't really care too much (.) until she has an experience of her own,
probably.

Here, Amy insists that the stereotypes of Mexican Americans have been brought
upon themselves. Her failure to recognize the absurdity of these images facili-
tates the reproduction of the white racial frame.

Another example of white fears of nonwhites comes from Angie, who recalled this situation when traveling by car to see a friend who lived in a predominantly black community:

R: I was like 16 or 17 and um (.) one of my friends who pretty much lived in an
all-black community that was kind of like a poor part of town, and um, but it
was cheap to live there, so he had a place back there, and the first time I went
over there with a couple of my friends, like we were driving around trying to
find it and we turned down the wrong street that was a dead end, it was the next
street over, so we go down to the end and we turn around and come back, and
there wa:s a black family who was sitting outside their house, and the guy, um,
stood up as I as driving back towards the road and um, he walked out in the
middle of the street and the street was only one lane so I couldn't go around
him, and stood there with his hand behind his back.
I: Mhm
R: And (.) we were all like 'oh god, what's gonna happen,' like he was just like
looking at us like really threateningly, and he comes over and taps on the window and says "can you put down the window" and I'm like "yeah" and he
started yelling at us for like speeding down his street and like being disruptive
and we're like "we're lost, we're sorry, we're gonna go home but (.) thanks for
the help. That's great."

She suspected the black man of having something behind his back, and reports
feeling fear for her life.

Respondents often divided African Americans into two groups: good blacks
and bad blacks. The former group are those "well-adjusted" in that they intermingle with whites (and, more implicitly, do not rock the boat with charges of
discrimination; in other words, keeping it to themselves). Bad blacks, meanwhile, are drunk on "black pride" and (thus) cry racism whenever something
does not go their way. In an interesting passage along these lines, Penelope also

includes the issue of ethnic difference when making the differentiation in the workplace:

> R: I work at this pizza place, and there's an African American guy that works there who nobody likes, a:nd (laughs) this actually really applies to this as I think about, uhmm ((louder talk)) he is so rude to the girls, makes comments to us how we're white? How we're bitches? Stuff like this? We don't even talk to him. He is lazy? He is rude? He is unintelligent. A:nd he walks around, he never showers, he wears his <u>pick</u> in his hair, and we can't fire him, because that would be racial discrimination. So (.) he has this (.) you know, privilege where he can get by with keeping his job, where he should not, because he's so: rude and discriminatory towards everyone else, but we kno:w, I know that I talked to the managers who have hinted pretty much that they could never fire him, because if they did, he could come back and shoot back with racial discrimination
>
> I: Mhm.
>
> R: Now (.) ironically, there's one other black person that works there, who is a quiet, gentle black man (.) hippie, kind of peace-lovin' like reggae, he has like huge dreads he wears in a hat, doesn't associate with the other black guy at all, who actually can't stand him, it is so hilarious because they're the antithesis I think of the two black representations of the black people in society. [first guy's name], the asshole, is so: suppressed, I mean he makes comments about it, he's like 'you know, like you fuckin' white people,' like whatever and we're just like "shut up!" like we didn't say anything to you!' and then [second guy's name], who doesn't even speak, the guy's so quiet, I don't think I've ever heard more than one word out of him, and he's just this peaceful guy, and like just in his own world, like probably really high all the time, and (laughs) but uhm this happens every time I work, and it <u>pisses</u> me off, and it makes me SO ANGRY ((loud and aggravated)), like ((the first guy)) makes me so: angry me and three other girls have talked to the owner, and he's an ass! Like whatever, and I don't know what's going on with him=I think that the owner's afraid to fire him, because he could shoot back with racial discrimination, but uhm even though it's not that at <u>all</u>, but the point is, the ways he's rude and like make comments is all racially, it's all about racialness, I'm just like 'you're just getting' by, and getting' away with it 'cause you know you can,' and that (.) pisses me off. Everyday, I've requested not to work with this guy all the time, and it has nothing to do with the fact that he's black, it's just that stereotype, that black person, who just has to be so angry at everybody, like mhm god he is, he is an extreme of that type.

Note that in this extended invective the sincere fiction that leads to ambivalence: the supposed "free ride" blacks have at work since they can't be fired, though this is simply ridiculous. Furthermore, she apparently never questioned the accuracy of the manager's claims, while further blaming her black co-worker. She closes her emotional tirade with semantic move in attempt to save whatever face she thinks she has left. She seems to expect that the statement will make-up for her earlier comments.

Of all respondents, only Betty had an ongoing intimate relationship with a person of color, and she briefly spoke of the tensions she feels when interacting with whites:

> R: There was an instance where I was staying with my dad for the summer and my grandfather was coming for a visit and he asked me to take down my pictures (.) of my boyfriend, just because (.) we don't know how my grandfather would react, but we don't think it would be all that great.
> I: Right. Like how'd that make you fee(h)l?
> R: I was kinda having to hide a part of myself, but like (.) I'm someone who's like (.) mhm not trying to avoid conflict out of all costs, but like if there's something small and minor I can do that would accommodate somebody else and just avoid like the anger and frustration that it would cause, and (.) uh I'm gonna do it just 'cause (.) it takes so much energy out of a person to be angry and upset and you really don't want to hurt the ones you love, and even though like my grandfather by far is in the wrong (laugh) you know, but I'm not going to try and change his opinions, no. 'Cause I don't know how successful that would be.

Here, Betty provides a window into the tremendous barriers in U.S. society in black-white relationships, and the pain those barriers cause. At the same time, she mentions how difficult it is to complain to her grandfather for his prejudices, not to mention her father's apparent inability to confront it. To be effective as an antiracist, one must choose her battles and expend her resources carefully.[38]

Summary

In this chapter, I describe the contradictory nature of the way respondents recall interracial relationships, and the way they and others view such interactions. First, I provided an elaborate explanation as to why racial segregation continues in U.S. society: little beneficial contact between whites and groups of color fails to challenge the ambivalence and fear whites harbor of nonwhite Americans. Meanwhile, whites naturalize segregation in their discourse while minimizing the damage racism causes to its victims. Although some respondents came clean with the extent of segregation in their lives, most tried to sidestep the issue or downplay its significance. Some respondents based their integrated lives on the "virtual integration" of their media experiences, while others overexaggerated their numbers of black friends. Most respondents reported extensive tension in their interactions with people of color, and particularly with African Americans.

This tension is often a result of misunderstanding, which in turn leads to miscommunication between them and racial Others. They expect black Americans to undue the centuries of white racism, while stop acting "black," defined largely by the sample as scary, irresponsible, and mischievous. It is not the actions of people of color, but rather the interpretation of their behavior (often through stories and not personal experience) that ultimately legitimizes the white racial frame, and it is done through the generalization of an entire group's behavior and demeanor through the prism of one individual situation. Validating the white racial frame is not easily done for these whites, however. Thus, they utilize a series of linguistic moves such as hiding themselves by using plural pronouns and semantic moves to maintain face (though they are often unsuccessful). In the next chapter, I present the contradictions within the sample's discourse on programs designed to end racial inequities in educational and workplace opportunities.

Notes

1. Edward Glaeser, "Desegregation Is Unsung U.S. Success Story," *Bloomberg View*, www.bloomberg.com/news/2012-01-30/desegregation-is-an-unsung-u-s-success-story-edward-glaeser.html (accessed June 10, 2012). Glaeser wrote the original report with Jacob L. Vigdor from Duke University titled "THE END OF THE SEGREGATED CENTURY: Racial Separation in America's Neighborhoods, 1890-2010," *Manhattan Institute for Policy Research*, www.manhattan-institute.org/html/cr_66.html (accessed June 10, 2012).

2. Glaeser and Vigdor, "THE END OF THE SEGREGATED CENTURY."

3. Sam Roberts, "Segregation Curtailed in U.S. Cities, Study Finds," *New York Times*, www.nytimes.com/2010/01/31/us/Segregation-Curtailed-in-US-Cities-Study-Finds.html?pagewanted=all (accessed June 10, 2012).

4. For instance, in a "hard news" piece on the report from the *New York Times*, it concludes with various empirical facts cited by the report that, whether intended or not, seem to give legitimacy to the report, especially considering the cited examples of critics of the report earlier in the piece. Roberts, "Segregation Curtailed in U.S. Cities, Study Finds."

5. Michelle Alexander, "The Myth of Desegregation," *Time*, ideas.time.com/2012/02/03/the-myth-of-desegregation (accessed June 10, 2012).

6. Gary Orfield has done extensive work on the existence and consequences of resegregation in U.S. society. Examples include Gary Orfield, *Historic Reversals, Accelerating Resegregation, and the Need for New Integration Strategies* (Los Angeles: Civil Rights Project, UCLA, 2007) and Gary Orfield, *Schools More Separate: Consequences of a Decade of Resegregation* (Cambridge, MA: Civil Rights Project, Harvard University, 2002).

7. Feagin, Vera, and Batur, *White Racism*.

8. Feagin, *Systemic Racism*.

9. Allport, *The Nature of Prejudice*; Forbes, *Ethnic Conflict*; Christopher B. Smith, "Back and to the Future: The Intergroup Contact Hypothesis Revisted," *Sociological Inquiry* 64, no. 4 (November 1994): 438-455.

10. McKinney, *Being White*.

11. Thomas F. Pettigrew and Linda R. Tropp, "Does Intergroup Contact Reduce Prejudice? Recent Meta-Analytic Findings," in *Reducing Prejudice and Discrimination*, ed. Stuart Oskamp (Mahwah, NJ: Lawrence Erlbaum), 93-114.

12. Joe R. Feagin, *Racist America* (New York: Routledge, 2000), 132.

13. Allport, *The Nature of Prejudice*; Forbes, *Ethnic Conflict*.

14. Allport, *The Nature of Prejudice*, 263.

15. Michael Banton, *Race Relations* (London: Tavistock, 1967).

16. Mark P. Orbe and Tina M. Harris, *Interracial Communication: Theory into Practice* (Belmont, CA: Wadsworth, 2001), 265.

17. Mary R. Jackman and Marie Crane, "Some of My Best Friends Are Black: Interracial Friendship and Whites' Racial Attitudes," *Public Opinion Quarterly* 50, no. 4 (Winter 1986), 465.

18. Lee Sigleman and Susan Welch, "The Contact Hypothesis Revisited: Black-White Interaction and Positive Racial Attitudes," *Social Forces* 71, no. 3 (March 1993), 781-795.

19. Sigleman and Welch, "The Contact Hypothesis Revisited."

20. Smith, "Back and to the Future."

21. Jackman and Crane, "Some of My Best Friends Are Black."

22. James J. Dowd, "Prejudice and Proximity: An Analysis of Age Differences," *Research on Aging* 2, no. 1 (March 1980), 23.

23. Charles E. Case and Andrew M. Greeley, "Attitudes Toward Racial Equality," Humboldt Journal of Social Relations 16, no. 1 (Fall 1990), 67-94.

24. Hartigan, *Racial Situations*.

25. Pamela Perry, "White Means Never Having to Say You're Ethnic."

26. Joyce E. King, "Dysconscious Racism: Ideology, Identity, and the Miseducation of Teachers," *Journal of Negro Education* 60, no. 2 (Spring 1991): 133-146.

27. Bonilla-Silva, *White Supremacy*.

28. Frankenberg, *White Women, Race Matters*, 145.

29. Bonilla-Silva, *White Supremacy*.

30. Tom A. Guglielmo, "Rethinking Whiteness Historiography: The Case of Italians in Chicago, 1890-1945," in *White Out*, 49-61.

31. Allport, *The Nature of Prejudice*.

32. Leonard Steinhorn and Barbara Diggs-Brown, *By the Color of Our Skin: The Illusion of Integration and the Reality of Race* (New York: Plume, 1999).

33. Sut Jhally and Justin M. Lewis, *Enlightened Racism: The Cosby Show, Audiences, and the Myth of the American Dream* (Boulder, CO: Westview, 1992).

34. Jackman and Crane, "Some of My Best Friends Are Black."

35. John Hartigan, Jr., "Who Are These White People?: 'Rednecks,' 'Hillbillies,' and 'White Trash' as Marked Racial Subjects," in *White Out*, 95-122.

36. Charles Antaki, "Uses of Absurdity," in *Analyzing Race Talk*, 85-102.

37. Richard Buttny, "Multiple Voices in Talking Race."

38. Eileen O'Brien, "The Political Is Personal: The Influence of White Supremacy on White Antiracists' Personal Relationships," in *White Out*, 253-267.

Chapter 4
Products of the Retrogression

During the 2008 race for the nomination of the Democratic Party for President, Barack Obama appeared to have a big problem: gaining support from white, working-class voters who had (at least traditionally[1]) supported Democratic candidates over Republican ones, often in substantial numbers. Following the results from the primary in West Virginia, exit polling showed a significant number of whites who voted said race played a role in their decision.[2] This issue continued to receive attention from news outlets during the Obama presidency, and surfaced again when a convicted felon finished with 44 percent of the vote in the Kentucky primary four years later, further adding fuel to the fire.[3]

Political pundits and commentators have discussed this "problem" of the President for quite some time, arguing he should do more to court these voters. One course of action recommended was for Obama to embrace ending race-based preferences for affirmative action programs and replace them with class-based policies.[4] During one debate with Hillary Clinton in April 2008, Obama made some comments on affirmative action in which he seemed to suggest his support for ending race-based admissions policies at selective colleges and universities, replacing them with class-based policies. Commentators such as Richard Kahlenberg argued shortly thereafter[5] that Obama should continue in this vein, that it would help him win over the support of the so-called "Reagan Democrats" (a group of voters who, as polls had shown in their head-to-head match-ups with John McCain, neither of these Democrats would have won this group in the general election anyway[6]). As presented in his book from the mid-1990s, Kahlenberg posits that class-based affirmative action "would be colorblind but not blind to history" and "reinforce the common interests of working-class voters," while assisting Obama in his pursuit of the White House.[7] He continued to advocate this course of action as the Supreme Court deliberated over the case involving the University of Texas case.[8]

Unfortunately Kahlenberg and other proponents of ending race-based affirmative action fail to recognize the legacy of white racism and the continuing impact of the white racial frame in U.S. society. One simple reason of this is the fact that affirmative action benefits other groups, including veterans, persons with disabilities, and women, yet the focus is on race. The reality is that few students of color benefit from race-sensitive admissions policies at selective colleges and universities, so what we need is more transparency on what exactly affirmative action is, rather than mischaracterize what it does.[9] Kahlenberg and others also fail to account for precisely *why* we have race-based affirmative action policies to begin with, and argue that our society today is colorblind so we should end these policies. Some states have already moved in the direction Kahlenberg has wished for, and the results haven't been promising: following the passage of Prop 209 in California, for example, black enrollment at UCLA has dropped considerably.[10] A decline in black enrollment also occurred at the University of Texas, following then-Governor George W. Bush's "Texas 10 Percent Plan," as well as brother Jeb's similar "One Florida Plan" led to a decline in black enrollment at the University of Florida (though through recruitment efforts, black enrollment rebounded).[11] One reason why this has happened is the fact that the majority of poor people are white in this country, while applicants of highly selective and competitive colleges and universities are likely to come from middle class families, not poor ones.[12]

We need to understand why race-based affirmative action remains necessary in dealing with racial inequality and misunderstanding. As Bowen and Bok point out, whites need contact with students of color in order to prepare for interactions within an increasingly globalized society.[13] Furthermore, one must ask why Obama is encouraged to express support for policies that would likely undermine the interests of African Americans, when other (white) politicians are not asked to do the same when it comes to opposing policies that further white interests. Finally, while President Obama's daughters may indeed be in a privileged position in terms of socioeconomic status, they remain black in U.S. society, and race can operate independently.[14] In addition to future employers, will his daughters be viewed as raceless beings by police officers, judges, teachers, or salespeople due to their more favorable socioeconomic status?

Political expedience should not be the reason to do away with race-sensitive programs and policies. That said, why are there those who, despite acknowledging the need for some affirmative action policies, seem content to do away with race-based policies, despite evidence that race remains a barrier for people of color in U.S. society? The war being waged against "affirmative action" in this society is one reason I believe we are in a time of *retrogression*: i.e., a change to a less complex or primitive state, or to a process of deterioration.[15] This process has emerged in U.S. society regarding race relations: after making some movements towards achieving racial equality and justice, we are now witnessing a reactionary movement against that progress. In this chapter, I highlight the ways that whites in this sample paint themselves as victims of "reverse racism" while questioning the claims of nonwhite Americans that they face injustices. First, I explore the ways in which respondents oppose policies designated to alleviate past racial injustices (including their comments on reparations). Second, I investigate the way the sample comes to see itself as victims of the "quest" for diversity. Finally, I shed some light on how they will likely reproduce the racist social order as potential employers in the future. Similar to earlier chapters, I expose the various strategies respondents use along the way to maintain face while expressing their hostilities toward attempts to achieve a more just and free society.

What Losses?

How do white Americans claim to support racial equality while opposing actions to end affirmative action for whites? I this section, I explore in detail the various sincere fictions employed by the whites in this sample that assist them in their claims that racism is no longer a problem for African Americans. They do this in three primary ways: the first method is utilizing delusions of grandeur to oppose policies to deal with systemic racism. I introduce three major storylines they use to achieve this end: (1) the past is the past, (2) we can't stop racism anyway, and (3) if only we could wish it away. The second sincere fiction I examine is respondents' atomistic view of racism; i.e., racism is merely the product of a few bad apples. The third way respondents deal with the contradiction is by blaming blacks for their problems. Sincere fictions like these project feelings of ambivalence and even hostility towards programs and policies enacted to deal with the legacy of white racism in U.S. society, while simultaneously reinforcing privileges for white Americans.

Delusions of Grandeur

Bonilla-Silva argues that "all ideological formations produce common stories that become part of the racial folklore and thus are shared, used, and believed by members of the dominant race."[16] With the little experience they have in discussing racial matters with black Americans, whites in the sample usually do not grasp the extent and consequences of systemic racism in our society. In addition, their responses during the interviews suggest that they are delusional on these matters. In this section, I document these delusions, communicated through various storylines. First, I examine their storyline "the past is the past," a common line when discussing racial privilege.

The Past is the Past
Respondents utilize this storyline to balance their support for racial equality in an abstract sense, but oppose the implementation of programs to achieve racial equality. The primary delusion that appears here is the myth that white racism is

no longer a problem in U.S. society. When responding to the statement "The government should address the losses of certain racial groups who have struggled due to racial discrimination," Elizabeth had this to say:

> Um (1.0) yeah, I think they should definitely like recognize like (.) what happened in the past, but I'm not sure that necessarily people now should be compensated for like (.) monetarily at least for like what happened to people that they didn't even know that were from (.) years and years and years and years ago, but I think it should definitely be like made aware because it's important to know what happened in the past and, so like that kind of thing doesn't happen again 'cause it's not good.

In her response, Elizabeth inserts a semantic move: first, she states that people should be aware of the racial injustices of the past; still, she argues that there should be no monetary compensation for those losses. Furthermore, she apparently has no recognition of the racial discrimination of the present day. She concludes with a resolution that is incapable of dealing with the problem; that is, the need to alter the racialized social system.

Harriet takes the delusion one step further, arguing that attempting to deal with the racial injustices of the past (and present) will only cause further racial animosity:

> R: Racial discrimination's just something that's just trapped in our history and I don't know necessarily that they should be compensated for it? Just because I'm not sure what you could do (.) um (.) to address that without having (1.0) about like separating society even more because if they, if the government did try to compensate (.) I don't know, um (.) any specific race or ethnicity or whatever, I think it would (.) another race would probably get offended
> I: Oh
> R: And that (.) maybe (.) everything that people have done to integrate it, to like today's time it might (.) separate it even more.

In this exchange, Harriet downplays the significance of race, claiming to be "just trapped in our history." An emerging contradiction when connected to Elizabeth's comments is the notion that we should educate people about racial inequality, but not compensate those harmed by past injustices due to increasing animosity between racial groups. But wouldn't a rigorous education about the injustices endured by African Americans increase understanding, and thus support, for reparations or other programs to right the wrongs of the past?

A final excerpt from the interviews on this storyline comes from Frank, who expresses a similar disapproval for compensation:

> As far as the second one umm (2.0) I don't know if now the government should give specific um (3.0) be more generous with racial groups who have suffered in the past, I don't know if that would be the right thing to do really, I don't know if that I mean can even solve what's happened in the past but, um, I guess

the best thing they can do is just to make sure that (.) equality is more (1.0) up-
held now than it ever has been.

Many whites argue against affirmative action, reparations, or other programs
meant to end racial privilege for white Americans due to the statute of limitations, or the notion that if a certain time period has passed following the oppressive conditions, then those who committed the actions cannot be held liable.
This kind of thinking ignores the cumulative impact of white racism in that
white families have accumulated wealth over the years at the expense of African
Americans and other nonwhites. Another point whites fail to understand when
utilizing this storyline is the reality that white leaders denied black Americans
their just due. And lastly, respondents who used this storyline conveniently forget the current discrimination that nonwhite Americans face today.

Can't Stop It Anyway
Another delusion expressed by respondents was the notion that racism exists and
there is nothing we can do to stop it. This myth provides whites a method of
impression management in that they can oppose "affirmative action" programs
without sounding prejudiced; i.e., overtly legitimizing the racist social order. For
example, Dina first tried to install the "past is the past" storyline, but I referred
to the lack of equal opportunities in education or employment today. She responded this way:

> R: Okay. Umm (.) I think it's really hard to prove that there's like (1.0) like if
> (2.0) for the housing example I think it's really hard to prove that there's like
> racial discrimination like whether there was or there wasn't I think the long
> term is really hard to like (.) say that that's definitely due to discrimination and,
> due to just a different factor? Even if the person is, trying to discriminate
> [against] another?
> I: Okay.
> R: I don't (.) really think that there's anything the (.) government can really do
> about it?
> I: Okay.
> R: Because, it's, there, I mean there might be so many situations I don't know
> how they would want to deal with that, and if there was something really major
> that ((unintelligible; trails off))

It is intriguing how she thinks the government should not be involved in eliminating racism because it is too *large* of a task. Xena takes a similar approach to
this issue:

> I think it would be very hard to really enforce like with a business, 'cause you
> can't go around to every single employee, you know, like every single business
> and make sure their manager is enforcing every single employee, but I think
> there should definitely be like you know laws if there's like (.) if there you

know something really discriminatory happens, and that person feels really you know insulted or humiliated, then that shouldn't be acceptable, but I think (.) in the sense of businesses, it would be hard for the government- maybe more of a local government, but (.) I think it would be kinda hard to enforce, 'cause you can't have someone there at all times, and things are gonna obviously happen that aren't supposed to, you know? Just because that's the way people think and that's their opinion, it's hard to (.) you can say as much as you want to some-one, but (.) you really have to have them experience like a real-life situation to really change their perception and their attitude (.) but, I think it should defi-nitely be a concern, if they have a solution, you know, if they have a way of (.) making things better for racial groups, then definitely (.) because our country is so mixed, and it's just gonna get more so, I mean especially here in [state], you know? And I think maybe it should be more of like a state government thing, because some states are still, you know, northern states are very integrated, but I think it's important for where it's needed.

Discrimination by businesses needs to be documented via auditing programs similar to catching storeowners who sell cigarettes to minors. When it comes to fighting discrimination, whites magnify the potential drawbacks of actions im-plemented to do something about it (e.g., it's too expensive, racism is not a problem anymore, etc.). When stopping other crimes, whites do not talk about how they cannot stop everyone, whether dealing with murders, rapes, etc. (some of which are race-related). The "Can't Stop It Anyway" storyline aids whites into taking a nihilistic approach towards stopping racism, which produces am-bivalence towards dealing with racism.

Wish It Away

Another delusion expressed in the interviews was that if only they could wish racism away, then society would be better off. This is a common myth utilized within the repertoire of color-blindness. If only we Americans started ignoring our racial differences, racism would cease to exist. In the following passage, Frank defended the value of color-blindness:

> R: Um, I definitely agree unfortunately that people do and like employers hire based on certain things or=
> I: =Sure.
> R: Like um (1.0) people aren't (.) color-blind, unfortunately, and so people are hired depending on things like that and not just employment but also (.) just judgment too.
> I: Do you think that's a good value to have, um, color-blindness, like for people to be color-blind?
> R: Uh yeah, I definitely do because (.) 'cause [then] everyone would have a fair shot, certain people with advantages and certain disadvantages.

Frank seems convinced that only if people failed to recognize color differences, then the systematic processes of discrimination would disappear. The problem with this approach is that it allows whites to evade the structural reality of systemic racism and therefore "preserves the power structure inherent in essentialist racism."[17]

In the next segment, Linda argues that the government should not have to enforce anti-discrimination measures, while downplaying the significance of racism:

> R: I don't know like the extent↑ to that, like I don't know if I like agree with affirmative action and everything but like I just (.) if there were a way for people to like <u>not</u> be (.) like and (.) I know it's like (.) a bit of a like fantasy statement like if no one could be like racist but I don't know
> I: Right.
> R: Like the government shouldn't have to.
> I: Like what is affirmative action to you?
> R: Like their preferential treatment of (.) like minorities just because (.) like to like make up for the things in the past that have (.) caused them like harm and stuff.

In Linda's response, she delivers the "fantasy" buffer statement prior to stating her disapproval of government action towards racial discrimination. This serves her as a face maintenance strategy, while allowing her to dismiss such actions without sounding prejudiced.

One respondent offered an interesting explanation for opposition for government intervention in eliminating systemic racism: people will do it naturally. When discussing the issue of compensating groups who have lost out on opportunities, Zachary emits a smudge of social Darwinism in the process:

> I don't think it's really the government's place to address losses of certain racial groups? Who struggle due to racial discrimination because (.) I think that (.) I believe in just kinda like in just like people will weed themselves out if- and not like in a manner in which like there'll be like this elite race, but people will get along however they get along and that it's not nec- the government's responsibility is to care for society as a whole as opposed to starting to keep people here and you know, 'cause I feel that integration happens naturally, so you know, sooner or later it's just a big blend, so there's no one you know one race should be (.) I think it [the government's role] should be a very reserved role. I think there should be some role, but it shouldn't be you know a constant hands-on process where they're trying to (.) you know, rebir- no, rebirth is a bad word, but like you know trying to grow [the] Hispanic population in Ohio or like grow the African American population in Montana, I don't think it should be sectored off like that, I think that it just naturally will take care of itself over time, I think that as you can see since like the United States was founded, you know, slowly integration has occurred, and you know there are times where there are some issues, but (.) do they really need to step in constantly? I don't think so.

Similar to Linda, Zachary does not think the government should be involved in equalizing U.S. society, though he does so in a very gingerly, even ambiguous way (e.g., "I think there should be some role, but it shouldn't be you know a constant hands-on process"). He also makes use of the naturalization frame, which was not as commonplace in these repertoires. Given the centuries of white-enforced segregation and supremacy in U.S. institutions, it is quite unlikely that equal opportunity will exist without some social engineering. Furthermore, in an attempt to bolster his argument, he uses absurdity ("trying to grow [the] Hispanic population in Ohio or like grow the African American population in Montana") to make his point that the government is only making things worse.

Atomistic View of Racism

People generally accept the notion that Americans celebrate the value of individualism, and that we live in an individualistic society. When coming across the race discourse of white Americans, people might presume that whites' tendency to present an individualized understanding of racism reflects the sociocultural system they live in, but this would be a mistake. As I mentioned in the opening chapter, when discussing racial matters that involve the racist actions of white Americans, whites take an atomistic approach; however, when discussing the actions of black Americans, they often use the acts of an individual to generalize for the entire group. The tendency to see racism as atomistic (not structural) is the second sincere fiction I introduce in this section.

One way to uphold the delusion of an egalitarian society is that respondents struggle to recall any particular instances in which they profited in some meaningful way due to their whiteness. Ursela, for example, responded to the issue of paying people back for losses due to racial discrimination:

R: Um well, obviously (.) I feel really cliché saying this obviously, whi:te people (.) definitely have the advantage, especially in the U.S.? u::m (.) as far as like personal experiences, I don't (???) Umm, oh my god (laugh), what it is (.) alright, if you're black you get into school easier, what is it ca(h)lled?
I: Oh↑, u:m
R: I can't think of the stupid term!
I: You mean, like affirmative action?
R: Yes: Thank you, wow. I feel like a complete idiot. Affirmative action, I don't believe in that, and I don't (.) I don't think that um you know, people that were (.) or like, are descendants of people that were enslaved should like (.) you know, get [?] money for that or whatever
I: Mhm.
R: Um (.) but they're definitely (.) everything should be equal, um (.) I really don't have like a personal situation where I can really relate that to my life (.) um (.) I'm sure things would be different for me, though, if I wasn't (.) differ-

ent color, of course, I definitely would have (.) have different friends, um (.) just because [?] tend to stick together, you know.

A lot just went on here: first, she begins with a presumably antiracist statement by insisting whites have an advantage over blacks. However, she then denounces affirmative action, and inserts an "insurance statement" that all should be equal to maintain face. Moreover, I inserted "[?]" in the script to show that she omitted the pronoun for the statement naturalizing racial segregation. Thus, it is problematic to classify different kinds of white speakers (e.g., race-cognizant, essentialist, etc.) since they all use the same techniques, so Frankenberg failed to acknowledge the structural nature of the problem.[18] The reality is that most white Americans engage in a discourse that fails to challenge the racialized social system.

In the next passage, Troy evokes the issue of reparations and inserts the common storyline "I didn't own any slaves,"[19] failing to recognize the structural nature of racism in U.S. society:

R: Well, as far as like reparations go like (.) nobody from my family ever owned slaves like (laughs) we came over pretty recently, you know Italian and German um never had any big plantation so you know uh and you know of course the people today, they never owned slaves um you know maybe they're some older people now that experienced stuff back in the '60s and '50s that were (.) pretty brutal but (.) you know, I don't see how the government should take money from everybody in society, especially when my family and I have done nothing to (.)
I: What role if any should the government have in dealing with racism?
R: Well act- I think they should pretty much you know it sounds kind of bad but just leave it alone you know, I think it's just something that society just has to work out for itself um (.) I think the more you know of course, when you bring stuff up in the government everything is political now so (.) you know, really you're just (.) I don't know, I kind of see it as providing more racial division when the government gets involved and you know saying "all right, we're gonna do this for blacks, this for whites," actually that's causing more problems.
I: Sure. So if not the government then where else or who else should be (.) taking on that responsibility=
R: =I mean, everybody should take it on for themselves, I guess. You know, I don't see how should force anybody to do that, um (.) you know, everybody has their opinions um (.) I don't really think it's necessary to (.) make somebody do that but you know it's the right thing to do so you'd hope society would do that but of course these days you know we like get a whole lot of that so (.)

Troy opposes reparations for slavery because he argues it would not be fair for white Americans who did not own slaves to pay for past injustices. He fails to realize that whites have benefited from unjust enrichment, regardless of whether or not they were slave owners (e.g., working-class whites benefited in that they were not in shackles).[20] Even when he acknowledged injustices experienced by "older people" still with us, he dismissed the government getting involved due to increasing more racial antipathy (though notice how his use of reported speech "all right, we're gonna do this for blacks, this for whites," he included "whites" here to suggest that everyone would benefit from the governmental inaction). He reduces racism to mere "opinions" and apparently thinks no one can be forced to respect fellow Americans' civil rights, which among them include compensation for unjust impoverishment.

Another respondent who explicitly brought up the issue of slavery was Cynthia. She took the argument against reparations a step further than Troy in that she feels African Americans are now too privileged for society's "bleeding heart" towards the injustices committed against them:

> R: In the past, I think (.) bring up the issue of slavery, I think it should be addressed? But in terms of (.) mhm over like o- making such a big deal about it? In terms of them being overprivileged now because of it? I don't really think it should be a factor? (.) I tend to look at it as it's in the past, and I mean it's terrible, and it was wrong, but I think we shouldn't dwell on the past in terms of racial issues, that we should just the best thing is to move forward and just improve upon it instead of bringing it up and not have such a socially strong issue.
> I: Okay. Like whose responsibility do you think it should be to um deal with racism, try to eliminate it, or deal with it?
> R: Um, I think each person actually on an individual basis, um I think the generation now growing up is more open to it and more accepting of different races, and I think [as] this generation esp. grows older and they have children, they'll open their children's eyes to more being obsessed or not obsessed but uh accepting of racism (.) than earlier generations, so I think it's mainly parents should in each person on an individual basis, and also the government, you know, whether it be through I don't know what kinds of means but should definitely step up and make sure everyone is accepting of other people.

Notice how she made her claims that black Americans are unreasonable and "overprivileged" with the rising intonation following the statements, as a device to invite opposition from me if I disapproved of them. An important contradiction here is that we should address the impact of slavery, but we should not talk about it too much, or make too much of it. Ultimately, her first claim that we should address the issue is a prop for face maintenance, since she later claims we should move on and forget it happened. Similar to the others in this section, she concludes with an atomistic view of racism, inserting the myth that people are getting more open-minded with every generation, and government action will only inhibit the evolutionary trend.

It's Their Problem

Besides evoking the delusions of how to eliminate discrimination and presenting an atomistic view of racism, respondents also turn to a common theme throughout much of the interview discourse: blacks are to blame for their problems. Whites commonly project racial motivations onto blacks as a way to protect themselves and avoid responsibility for social ills such as segregation.[21] They use this myth to dismiss government action to eliminate racism as a waste of resources. Connected to their atomistic view of racism, they implicitly suggest that blacks have deficient personalities and cannot get along with whites. Furthermore, they segregate themselves from society. For instance, when responding to the statement that some groups benefit from their racial privilege, Angie responded this way:

R: I don't think so. I think it's just basically like our past, which makes
I: Like what, maybe some things about our past?
R: Um, I guess that everything's traditionally white I guess back when (.) America was founded and stuff it just (.) white males who were like the ((unintelligible)) and everything
I: Right.
R: And (.) a lot of people who still see that as like bad.
I: Okay.
R: I think a lot of the barriers are self-imposed. They don't feel like they can break free.

In her statement, Angie evokes the "past is the past" storyline and downplays the significance of the historical reality ("...and everything"). Her comment "And (.) a lot of people who still see that as like bad" is especially intriguing; so slavery should be seen as something good? She fails to understand the links between the past and present, suggesting that "they" (notice how few respondents say "black" unless under their breath) are keeping themselves from prosperity.

Later in her interview, Angie provided more insight into her thoughts on self-imposed barriers, while including a classic absurdity statement:

R: Um, I don't know I guess part of it's the government's responsibility but I think past of it is also just like social responsibility in that we should adjust the way we behave but (.) I don't know like I really↑ (.) don't see racism as that big a problem except in the fact that people of minorities like seem to perpetuate it like separate themselves from us too.
I: Why do you think like, all minorities or specific minorities [(.) separate themselves.
R: [Um mhm↑
I mean like when you walk around campus you always see like people hanging out with their own (.) like racial group and you don't see very much like (.) interaction between them and

I: Right.

R: You have like 20 million like black fraternities and sororities that are like specifically for black people and there's nothing really that's like (.) they're like "come join us."

I: Why do you think that? Do you have any thoughts on why that happens?

R: Um, I guess they want to like (1.0) I don't know, just kind of give themselves like a sense of pride, maybe? But (.) um, I guess it goes both ways like maybe if they'd <u>try</u> and be involved with each other (.) I guess it's just the separation that just everyone kind of puts upon themselves.

In this passage, Angie thinks racism is only a problem because African Americans see it as such; hence, if only they pretended white racism was nonexistent, then racial problems would cease to exist. She includes the absurdity statement "you have like 20 million like black fraternities and sororities" to exaggerate the opportunities on campus for black Americans to participate in campus activities, much like women participate in women's organizations. She fails to recognize the fact that blacks do not interact with whites because they do not feel welcome in predominantly white spaces.[22] She finishes with an attempt to make it sound more even-handed, however, in that "everyone" tends to stick to one's own group, evoking the naturalization frame, which also serves as a face-saving strategy.

When I asked her if privileges existed in our society based on racial identity, Penelope had this to say:

I swear to God, I'm not like racial in any sense, uhm but I guess stereotypically? Uh the Af- uh some African Americans tend to fall in the last fortunate category or whatever? And I know [the university] reaches out to them to give them scholarships to come here and what not to make it more (.) racially equal around here, but uhm I do think that (.) a lot of them are kind of taking advantage of what they're getting here, because I <u>don't</u> think some of them take it as seriously where I think some of them really do actually, so there's two sides to that. I think some of them are very appreciative of what they have, and they take complete advantage of their education here, while I think others kind of get by, uhm they have their scholarships as excuses, and they're just I guess lucky enough to be able to go to a major university, uhm where I don't know if they've really had (.) even the best like performance in their studies, maybe in high school or beforehand, I think that it's like that here, somewhat, and I think that many of the uhm racial groups kind of do get more privileges, I think they're kind of like (.) they get by with a lot of things, where a lot of us who busted our asses who got into this [university] because we're white, uhm we don't really get as much, I think there's a lot more leniency towards them, just to keep [university] racially equal.

Similar to the "good black, bad black" storyline presented in the previous chapter, Penelope argues that black students have unfair privileges today, all in the name of "diversity." She claims that black Americans are "stereotypically" in the least privileged category, as if it would not be true if we did not think that way. Toward the end of her tirade, she expresses her discontent for the folklore that blacks "get a free ride" at the expense of whites like herself "who busted our asses" to attend the university. She expects African Americans to pat white folks on the back for their generosity, though they have received what rightly belonged to them in the first place.

The last example is from Amy, who delivers the contradiction that, on one hand, racism is less significant than at any point in our history, while combining that with the defeatist approach to eliminating it entirely. This view of systemic racism, in that it's been taken care of while we cannot stop it, provides whites a way to weasel out of accepting the need for aggressive affirmative action, depending on the context. She also blames problems black Americans have today on themselves:

> I don't know how much the government really has to do with that. I mean, blacks have the right to vote, as do women, they've given them that, uh (.) again, they kind of do it to themselves, I mean they're- they're the ones that are taking up all the welfare and (.) using all the food stamps and like (.) doing stuff like that, and yet they still are allowed to go out and have ten kids and like [live] on welfare, and I think the government's already done stuff to help them out, they say that it's helped everybody out, but they're the ones taking the most advantage of it or benefiting from it the most, um (.) but I really don't think that it's ever really gonna go away, I think that it's maybe better than it ever has been, but it's definitely still there, like racism is still there, we're segregated to a certain degree (.) um, yeah our schools may be integrated, and jobs may be integrated and stuff like that, but there's still obvious segregation, I mean certain people ruin it for the rest of them and that's really sad because everybody else is ((unintelligible)), but that's why (.) I mean, you can't judge somebody just by looking at them, you really have to talk to them first, um and it's hard to approach somebody when they have su(h)ch a bad reputation, it's just like [a] vicious cycle.

Looking back at her comments toward her neighbors in chapter 3, did she talk to them before placing judgment (i.e., fearing for her safety)? Still, although she submits a classic color-blind statement about judging people, she still implicitly blames blacks or other nonwhites for having "su(h)ch a bad reputation." She adds an absurdity statement "they still are allowed to go out and have ten kids" in a pathetic attempt to validate her argument. The saddest thing about these statements is that she speaks of a vicious cycle, but places the onus on black Americans, while inserting several of the myths whites use to perpetuate antiblack stereotypes (e.g., "taking up all the welfare and using all the food stamps"), and thus the white racial frame. This frame, in turn, produces defeatism towards white racism and disapproval towards the programs intended to deal with the legacy of white racism.

Delusions of Disadvantage

When discussing racial privilege, whites often mention how nonwhite Americans have traditionally been at a disadvantage in landing a job or an education. However, this research shows that whites in this sample are ambivalent, and even hostile, to any programs and policies intended to deal with those past and present injustices. How do whites come to terms with this inherent contradiction, in that they claim to oppose discrimination yet resist the very policies needed to alleviate the situation? They do this by inserting a sincere fiction into the equation as an antithesis: that blacks and other nonwhites also discriminate against white Americans. Therefore, in their synthesis of the discrimination issue, they naturalize the phenomenon, which in turn leads to their ambivalent feelings and defeatism about ending it. Furthermore, they come to the conclusion that any actions intended to alleviate racial inequities in social institutions like colleges (an issue they have experienced) and in the workplace (another issue most have yet to experience) actually put whites at an unfair disadvantage. They believe that what they generally refer to as "affirmative action" is not the "American Way."

Thus, the fundamental contradiction is that respondents express disapproval of racial discrimination and even agree that it remains a problem in our society today, yet are unwilling to adopt and enforce the laws needed to do anything about it or even downplay the problem when forced to do anything to deal with it. In this section, I focus on their responses to the statement "Some people have certain advantages, based on their racial identity, that others don't have in this society," and how they believe that attempts to equal the playing field has put white Americans at a disadvantage. First, I explore how respondents feel they are sacrificial lambs in the social quest for diversity. Second, I investigate the retrogressive backlash towards the values of the Civil Rights Movement (while destroying any thoughts that young whites today are more liberal than their parents). Third, I inspect the clash between two allegedly contradictory values, diversity and individualism, and how, at least concerning this particular issue, respondents choose the latter over the former.

Sacrificed in the Name of Diversity

Sometimes respondents are ambiguous in their responses to the statements during the interviews; Elizabeth, for example, read both statements on the first slip of paper before responding. She had this to say regarding racial privilege in U.S. society:

> R: I'd say just you know in, like even applying to colleges it's definitely like a prevalent thing that they make sure that they find out like what your race is like all that kind of stuff (.) I don't know, I think that makes a difference, um, may-

be like (.) not even for the better, to be like white↑ for that reason? Just because I know that like diversity is such a big deal on campus

I: Okay

R: So, I don't know.

I: Um what do you think about the president [of university] talking about (.) the importance of diversity on campus, you know, to be that top ten research university

R: Um mhm.

I: Do you think he's right about that?

R: Well I think diversity's definitely a good thing but I don't think they should (.) like, affirmative action I don't really think it's a good thing (.) 'cause it kind of limits the ability=like if you are (.) stronger than, than somebody else in applying to the school you should get in, it shouldn't be based on (.) all that other kind of stuff, but I think once you're like in the school like, everyone should have an equal opportunity to participate in things so I think that diversity is a good thing.

Throughout her response, Elizabeth tiptoes around the issue of racial privilege and diversity, epitomizing the tightrope act whites walk when they claim they are at a disadvantage relative to nonwhite Americans. When asking her about the University President's recent remarks concerning the importance of embracing diversity in order to become a high-ranking research institution, she inserts a semantic move to stage support for diversity but oppose any actions needed to achieve it. She completes the passage with a color-blind statement, insisting that the best way to achieve diversity is to give everyone an equal chance. If that is the case, then why was the Civil Rights Movement necessary in the first place?

Participants in this study commonly evoked the issue of listing your race on university admission applications, and felt that their racial identity put them at a disadvantage. In the following segment, Troy employs an atomistic view of racism when implicitly addressing white racism before quickly shifting to white disadvantage in higher education:

R: Yeah, to a certain degree, yeah, I mean (.) of course there's always a few people that have (.) racist opinions, and you're going to apply for jobs and (.) maybe even black or white would help you in that situation, um also it you know it might benefit you to be a minority, especially if you're ah applying to colleges these days

I: Sure

R: You know you're more able to get uh scholarships, you're more likely to be looked at, you know

I: Yeah

R: Just because people want to diversify their college environments right now.

First, Troy downplays the significance of a few "people" (here he implicitly means white people) who are prejudiced, and tries to make the argument that due to scholarship opportunities for nonwhite Americans, whites are now being

left behind. It is worth noting that these white respondents, with a few exceptions, know better than to actually believe that blacks oppress whites in certain
ways; instead, they cite government policies and programs that deal with these
issues.

A common theme from these interviews was that whiteness has become a
liability, not a privilege. In the next excerpt, Davis inserts the "white man's burden" storyline, or the notion that whites are fatigued due to their encumbrance of
whiteness:

> A lot of the problems we see nowadays like you see the actual general wealth
> people have, like [people] in power make a lot of money, but like the majority
> of the wealth? In today's society is generally like the upper-white like the
> WASPs you would say basically, so about the advantages of whiteness, uhm
> you see a lot of people stressed to have whiteness like as let's say like a black
> person stereotypically acts like ghetto: you know, they're all thuggin', but like
> they won't act white, and it's not seen as a norm to act normal, it's to act as a
> white person would, I can relate to one of my friends who's actually multira-
> cial, and she's half black, half white, but she totally hates the whole fact that
> she had black in her because she assumes that being black means being like you
> know this ((unintelligible)) so she acts white, when really it's just acting (.)
> normal

In this reply, Davis uses his knowledge of the wealth distribution of U.S. society
as a defense mechanism for white Americans. This serves as another instance in
which whites fail to recognize the unjust enrichment of all white Americans at
the expense of blacks and other nonwhite Americans. Furthermore, he implies
that acting white is acting normally, and thus acting black is acting abnormally.

Continuing in a similar vein of the "white man's burden," Kaitlin acknowledges white racism of the past but does not believe contemporary whites should
"suffer" for the sins of their ancestors:

> What do I think=I think that (.) um what happened was in the past and that we
> shouldn't be punished for what like our ancestors did and we shouldn't be de-
> nied spots in colleges because (.) colleges have to meet like racial quotas and
> stuff like that. I just think like (.) I just think it shouldn't be on there at all, like I
> don't think it should be considered, like if it wasn't on there then there
> wouldn't be discrimination if no one knew (.) what race they were, like whether
> (.) getting into college or (.) getting a job or whatever.

Kaitlin tries to come across as believing that discrimination would end if only
we did not have to record our race on admissions applications. She also registers
the common reference to "affirmative action" as "racial quotas," which have
been illegal since the Bakke decision.[23]

In the last example for this section, Ursela's response personifies the structured incoherence in this discourse, and the difficulty in understanding exactly
where they stand on these issues. This was her response to my question if affirmative action has been successful:

I mean, I just don't (.) I don't think it's fair to you know the majority or whatever. I just feel like people should be admitted to wherever because of you know how they did in school (.) but I understand also that like people are you know since kindergarten, put on like a track game, and they automatically fall behind, as soon as their first like standardized test, or whatever, you know, so I agree with that also, but that's just a hard problem to solve, I don't know, I feel like affirmative action's just the way, the wrong way to go about solving it (.) 'cause groups, they create more hostilities whereas, you know, different races too so (.)

In this excerpt, Ursela emits an example of tracking in grade schools that puts nonwhite students at a disadvantage. Despite this knowledge of systemic racism in action, she takes a defeatist attitude towards it: first, she provides a resolution that affirmative action is the wrong way to go about the problem, and then rationalizes the resolution (affirmative action creates more hostilities). She then completes her statements with some incoherence, which I argue is one part common in WRD since they do not talk about these issues very often and another part deliberate attempts to save face when they fear they have said something that makes them look prejudiced.

Backlash towards Civil Rights

One of the primary components of the retrogression is the backlash towards the practices implemented during the Civil Rights Movement. White Americans cannot explicitly state their opposition to the Movement, however; thus, they cherry-pick one-liners of the Movement (e.g., Dr. King's "I Have a Dream" speech) and use them to effectively distort the real intentions of the Movement, such as payback for past injustices.

Vincent was one respondent who mentioned that past generations of whites had benefited from white racism, but today blacks have the upper hand. He, like so many other whites, fails to understand the value of policies like race-sensitive admissions of colleges and universities:

Well, uh (.) like I can think of recent, recent past like a couple of years ago, like I wasn't (.) when I applied for college and for scholarships and stuff, I was only given a very short list of what I could do, you know, because of what my parents made and that. But then one of my friends who goes to [state university in a neighboring state] and he's a, he's a black kid, and he's really smart too, he deserved to get in there. He was getting this list, like pages upon pages of scholarships he could receive. Wow↑, that's a lot of free money you're getting! So that was one incident that (.) I saw that he was getting a lot advantages, so (.) which I was cool with it.

Although Vincent apparently did not have a problem with the scholarships his black friend could apply for, many whites feel it is unfair (perhaps his approval was in part due to the relationship he had with him). His statement "Wow↑, that's a lot of free money you're getting!" could have been expressing his displeasure of the opportunities available to his friend, but it is hard to say.

Another interesting theme indicative of the retrogression is the notion that black Americans deserve some concessions for systemic racism, but they should not reap the rewards. It seems as if these whites just cannot stand to see blacks "invading" historically white social spaces and enjoying a higher standard of living because of an increase in social integration (at least in colleges and universities). Mandy's comments on racial privilege underscores this point:

> R: I had a roommate one summer? Who just started [university] it was this summer and she (.) it seemed very apparent that she got in because of affirmative action she seemed like she (.) if she had those same credentials and same knowledge she and she was white (.) she wouldn't even be considered to come to this university?
> I: Mhm.
> R: So I understand affirmative action and (.) um I'm all for it but then on the other hand (.) I don't know if she should get in and have a full ride just because she's black like if they want equal rights (.) then (.) they should get in on their own credentials just
> I: Mhm.
> R: I guess I find it also with women like we say we want equal rights and we want to get paid the same and stuff (.) but on the other hand we have to take the downfall too you know we need to- [you] can't just reap the benefits.

Like so many others on the issue of racial privilege, Mandy just does not make sense with her semantic move in that she supports affirmative action but then disapproves of what it produces. Young whites simply do not understand the need for affirmative action in the first place. She also interjects gender to make her point, though she gives it up and states her resolution "[you] can't just reap the benefits."

In a particularly incoherent passage, Casey disapproves of reparations, though initially stating his support for governmental intervention in dealing with racism:

> Um, yeah, I think- yeah, they should like address that and ahh make it more, more open to like how it's wrong, like uh I guess it's easier for them to write about it now than it is to like talk about it, it's always easier to do that sometimes. But I think it should be addressed that, like you're not gonna [have] too many (liars?) like, from the south or someplace and then say that what we did back then was wrong, but I think you shouldn't uh I guess I don't know his personal opinion er (1.0) er what you think but I think that uh there shouldn't be (2.0) you kn- reparations for what they've endured ((trails off; unintelligible)).

In his statement, he makes an appeal to the recipient as he has difficulty stating his opposition for reparations. This example exemplifies the limitations in paper-and-pencil questionnaires that utlilize closed-ended questions because his initial answer on this issue would have been supportive.

Diversity and Individualism

In the interviews, respondents usually support the need for and importance of diversity. However, when discussing admissions policies to colleges and universities, diversity takes a back seat to the value of individualism. Moreover, they often evoke the codeword of "credentials" to defend the bastions of historically white institutions. As long as the issue is relevant to their time and space, they will oppose actions designated to end affirmative action for white Americans.

Respondents often display interesting methods to prove their point that race-sensitive admissions policies are the wrong way to go. Linda, for example, claims that her nonwhite friends disapproved of the practice as well as she:

> Umm for the first one, I think it's somewhat true obviously like (.) getting into school like (.) I know a lot of (.) umm, my friends who were like minorities I think probably like (.) even they thought that they have more of an advantage just because of that and like- I mean to still be like smart and like have good grades but just like that kind of like helped them out and then (.) like I know some people who didn't get in (1.0) like and then but- would have better grades than that

Similar to other excerpts in this chapter, Linda is very careful in expressing her opposition to race-sensitive admissions policies, including a reinforcement strategy with her claim that her black "friends" thought it is wrong and also through "evidence" that is impossible to verify (i.e., if any whites she knew got turned down despite higher grades—which isn't the only thing schools look at).

Meanwhile, in a similar vein of the delusions of grandeur earlier in the chapter, Kaitlin blames the social hierarchy, which situates white men on top, on bad luck:

> Um (2.0) I think that people...in like higher positions are white Americans like (.) white men but um (2.0) I'm (sighs) I don't know, like I do think that's true? but (.) (sighs) I don't know I kind of think it's (.) just like unlucky like I (.) I'm one who thinks that like you should make your own way in life and I don't think you should have people help you and (.) so, I definitely think there are like advantages but (.) I don't know.

She completes her statement with considerable ambivalence towards the issue, suggesting that she simply does not consider this issue in any meaningful way.

In the next passage, George brought up the issue of slavery as well as the false imprisonment of Japanese Americans during World War Two, and still concluded that individual "qualifications" are more important in admissions, though stating so with some ambivalence:

R: As far as the government addressing losses of certain racial groups uh due to racial discrimination anywhere from uh the south, back in the antebellum south and um slavery or, anywhere from world war two when the Japanese were discriminated uh I think that's very important that the government should uh address these losses.

I: Sure. Um, like what kinds of ways can (.) well, the government, or even more generally society, um, address like (.) uh (.) you know how to address that?

R: Um, I think (.) anything from uh (1.0) well, it's not so much that (.) like it's even affecting them today, and so anything from uh (.) anything from trying to help them out with SAT scores or (.) or uh (1.0) just uh trying to (.) uh, like uh, when they relocated the Japanese away from their homes, I think that they could of tried to help them get into homes again, well like the government should intervene in that [aspect so

I: [Mm.   Okay. Like as far as like (.) education you know, like getting into colleges and universities, like do you think having like race-sensitive kinds of like (.) I mean, like affirmative action kinds of things like policies and what not, as far as admissions policies like do you think those are a good idea?

R: I think it's a good idea to some extent. Uh, sometimes it goes a little too far uh (.) with affirmative action like uh (.) I think it's a good idea to have to try to eliminate too much discrimination, but then again, it could hinder some people who are more qualified to get the position. I think qualifications should be the most important standard, and uh (.) then (.) yeah, it- I don't know, that it-huh hu(h)h it's kind of hard to explain, 'cause [of] some people that come from disadvantaged backgrounds.

Despite his support for assisting Japanese Americans to relocate to new homes after internment, when asked about an issue pertinent to his own experience today, he shifts 180 degrees and takes the individualism route, stating that affirmative action goes too far and that "qualifications" should be the most important factor. His ambivalent statement at the end could be legitimate, or merely another face-saving mechanism.

Sometimes even personal experiences in which whites recognize racial discrimination do not facilitate understanding for the need for aggressive affirmative action. In the following excerpt, Yannie recalled the discrimination in the grocery store he worked in, yet resembled the comments made by others in the sample:

Well, I already mentioned that at times there's certain individuals who will lose like a spot like a job or admission to a university because of their race, and I think when that happens, it's kind of an issue, but (.) um (1.0) how should the government act? (.) obviously, there's an issue where they're not hiring people based on race, the government should jump in and like enforce racial equality, and that's why we have equal opportunity employers? And I think it works for the most part? But I actually work at [grocery store], and there are very, very few black individuals who work there, and if they are, they definitely don't make it beyond departmental management? So (.) in those instances it really seems like the government should jump in, but by the same token, um (.) public is trying to make it more racially equal, because there was issues with uh gender stratification and racial stratification? And one of my friends isn't able to get promoted because he's not a Hispanic female because they [have] to meet a quota even though they can't have them? So the government should jump in a certain point? But when it gets too far, then (.) like its very hard to describe, there's a very thin line between too much and too little, so I guess everyone should [jump?] in when it's obviously an issue, and when people make a valid complaint about it?

Yannie's example of meeting a "quota" by promoting "a Hispanic female" is hard to believe, and is likely another absurdity statement to provide support for his argument. As an issue gets more personal to whites, they increasingly disapprove of the action. Similar to stating support for intermarriage in the abstract and later saying "as long as it's not my son or daughter," respondents support the abstract value of diversity and the need for affirmative action, but when it affects them or white friends of theirs, their support diminishes.

Future Enforcers of the Status Quo

Up to this point in the chapter, I have presented evidence of the sample's extensive disapproval to issues relevant to them today; namely, race-sensitive admissions policies of colleges and universities. But how will these young white folks act in the "real" world after they graduate and enter the workforce? As future managers or employers, how will they make decisions in employment matters? I address this issue in the following section.

ABZ Company Hybrid

To explore this issue, I asked respondents what I refer to as the "ABZ Company Hybrid" question, a question inspired by Bonilla-Silva and Forman.[24] One limitation with the original, however, is that it asked respondents to reply to a hypothetical situation involving a third party (the "ABZ Company"). Although one could conclude indirectly how respondents would act in the situation personally, they could say one thing in an abstract sense and then something else when the issue is personalized. Thus, I personalized the question like the following I asked Jane:

> Imagine you were like a boss or a business owner, and you were looking to hire
> a new manager to help run your company, and um you know you have your ap-
> plicants come in for interviews and eventually after interviews, follow-up in-
> terviews and other things you know and if you broke it down to two finalists (.)
> and you know you looked at both of them, you know everything from personal-
> ity and work experience and you know (.) educational background and every-
> thing else I mean you pretty much felt that either one would yeah, pretty much
> be a great addition you know to the team. Um, you know, one happened you
> know to be Caucasian or white and the other happened to be African American
> like, which would you choose in that situation?

In an earlier study, I asked a similar question to the sample of this study. The
statement for that study was "If I were an employer, and two equally qualified
applicants, one white and one black, applied for the same position, I would be
more likely to hire the black applicant." I found that respondents found multiple
ways to evade the question, including the type of position available to the applicants. In fact, in one exchange I encountered the following:

> R: What are, like are these applicants for, like is this just for minimum wage
> jobs?
> I: Oh, uh (.) I mean, it really could be anything. It could be minimum wage, or
> it could be a professional or managerial position, like supervisor or something,
> I mean a, pretty much anything.
> R: 'Cause um, I don't know, like a professional position once you've gotten
> that far, you've certainly made it, um, the job isn't gonna like, make or break
> you whether you get it, but some people on minimum wage jobs they really,
> need that. I guess for a minimum wage job I would probably hire the black ap-
> plicant, but for the professional job it really wouldn't matter, based on race.
> I: What do you think you would do if it were a professional job?
> R: Um (.) I wouldn't be more likely to hire either one (.) based on race.

In this passage, the respondent appears to be support the protection of high-wage
and status jobs for white Americans. To avoid this problem in the current study,
I inserted "manager" into the hypothetical job search.

I asked about two-thirds of the sample this question. Several important
themes emerge from their replies, which I present in this section. First, respondents have a difficult time imagining a black candidate being equal to a white
applicant. Second, they often attempt to avoid answering the question altogether.
Third, some study participants actually come clean and admit they would choose
the white applicant. Finally, a few women in the sample interject gender in their
responses as to cloud the issue.

And They're Equal?

Some respondents just could not accept the hypothetical notion that a black job
applicant could possibly be equal to a white applicant, at least not from their

perspectives. After trying to evade the issue with a classic color-blind statement, Jane replied this way:

> R: I would choose entirely based on who I thought was better for the job not at all on skin color because (.) a white person can do those kinds of jobs that a black person can do
> I: Right.
> R: And maybe- it doesn't matter what color your skin is.
> I: Right. Well if you happened to be in that situation where (.) everything from personality to you know their you know they've got work experience they've got whatever degrees you were looking for, and you know, for the most part either one would do fine, I mean either one would do a great job u:m (1.0) what would you do?
> R: I guess I'd have to go with my gut instincts and you know hope that I wouldn't be choosing somebody on the color of their skin
> I: Mm
> R: But (.) I would definitely try to assess both of them and (.) pick which one I think would be better.

Like many others, she misses the point that in the hypothetical situation she had already considered them to be equal. Thus, it appears that they have a hard time accepting the possibility that the situation would ever happen—in that a black job candidate could be equal to a white candidate in "qualifications" for a job. Another discursive trick that emerges from this exchange is her reversal of "white" and "black" when insisting the applicants are capable of doing the same work. This trick performs two important tasks: first, it shields her from any doubt that a black candidate could not perform equally to a white applicant; and second, it implicitly implies the burden of whiteness in contemporary society.

When answering this question, respondents often mention the importance of the candidates' personality in making their decision. In an interesting response, Linda replied to the Hybrid question this way:

> R: Umm, it would probably be like if I had like interviews like whichever one I got along better with kind of you know like (.) personality-wise
> I: Well, I mean th- the idea that if you know everything from personality to you know um work experience you know academic achievements and all kinds of things I mean if you pretty much saw them on an equal footing like (.) like how would you know like handle that situation?
> R: Umm (.) I don't know. (3.0) I don- like if I had two people that were exactly the same (.) I don't know how I would like go about hiring, so (2.0)
> I: I mean at least that the same in that you know the idea that either one could d:o=
> R: =the same thi-=
> I: =Right.
> R: Yeah. Like one would[n't] do a better job than the other one?

I: Right. I mean *for the most part* they- you think that they would both do fine, you know.

R: Yeah. Well I wouldn't like hire the white one like because (.) 'cause I like white people better and I wouldn't hire like the black- the black one because I like black people better, like I think I should have more like diversity in my business but like (.) so I wouldn't hire based on that, if that's what you're °trying to get at.°

She gets creative in her attempt to dodge the issue of race, and my own attempt to probe and force her to make a decision. When she does get around to answering the question, she refuses to accept the possibility that she would hire the black applicant to increase diversity in her company. It might shed light on her response here that on the survey she answered "not very important" to the statement "college administration officials should stress racial diversity for a quality education" and "very important" for the statement "employers should be able to hire whomever they want for a job, regardless of race" (Table 4.1 provides the sample averages to these questions). Along the same lines, Troy responded this way:

Oh man, that's really difficult, I would really have to sit down and find some kind of flaw with one of them. You know 'cause (.) sure, if they're both qualified and all, I really don't wanna pick somebody you know, pick the black guy just because you know it'd help even things out or pick the white guy because he's white I just (.) I'd really have to sit down and see like you know (.) when you really boil it down, they can't be exactly equal, there's gotta be someone that'd have a little better quality, so I'd just take extra time to try and find that (.) I really don't think I could base it on race.

Notice how he would not want to hire the black candidate "just" to increase diversity in the workplace.

Avoidance

Respondents commonly tried to avoid the issue of race altogether. How can white folks expect to deal with real-life situations when they have never thought about them, and avoid thinking about it when the situation presents itself? A few in the sample said they would choose the black applicant, though usually for the wrong reasons. Rather than choosing the black applicant to make-up for past injustices, respondents would cite examples such as society's demands for that choice, like Elizabeth:

Um (.) well, I don't think it would really like, I don't know, I think probably just because of the way that our society works like I would (.) be more inclined to choose the black person? Just because (.) that's the way that like the public's gonna perceive it, like if you have someone higher from the company like, like

I know this is the case with my mother's company 'cause she umm there's a female that runs the office? And so that allows them to get more grants from the government like to do things just because it's a woman like, it's stupid↑, but that's just the way it works so I think I would be more inclined to choose the black person? For absolutely no reason other than (.) just because that's the way the rest of society, but to me it wouldn't matter either way.

In this response, Elizabeth claims she would choose the black applicant, although she does not understand why it would be a good decision. Instead, she thinks that type of action is "stupid↑" but is "just the way it works" in society today.

Table 4.1   Questionnaire Results for Attitudes towards Race-Sensitive Policies

Question	Mean
College administration officials should stress racial diversity for a quality education.	3.03
Employers should be able to hire whomever they want for a job, regardless of race.	3.27

In the next example, Harriet refuses to entertain the possibility that she would make a decision in which race was involved:

In that situation I probably wouldn't look at race, and I would just (.) go with the applicant that seems to be more qualified=I know that (.) there's gotta be somewhere in their application that someone's probably strong- a little bit stronger than the other one but race- no, would definitely not be like a factor in my decision.

Unfortunately, I did not probe Harriet following her reply, in which she cannot imagine two equal candidates. In an exchange when I did probe an evasive respondent, Irene took a similar approach:

R: Whoever's most qualified or if I've had more recommendations or if I know someone, [someone like a friend or

I: [Sure, well, I mean, the, the notion that if they are, I mean if you
come to see them as, you kn—I mean, either way, they have good recommendations, they're, you know, [they're both stellar applicants
R: [It would just depend on who I talk to, if
people know them, if, it has nothing to do with, if anything I would draw from
a hat, if, if they were so equal which, that doesn't happen, I mean I'm sure I
(1.0) people know one person more than the other I'll find out, about their history, who kn—who's worked with 'em before, who knows them and just pick
that person.

For whatever reasons, respondents are unwilling to answer the question directly,
and cannot accept the fact that candidates are equal. She does add, however
(with sufficient probing this time), that she would "draw from a hat" if they
were indeed equal.

Despite their evasiveness, there were some interesting things they mentioned about what they would look for as "tie-breakers." They included "personality," "speaking skills," the way candidates dressed for the interview, and so on.
Given the pervasive racial segregation experienced in their lives, coupled with
their possession of the white racial frame, is it any wonder that whites would be
more likely to choose the white applicant in this situation, unless they were under pressure to do otherwise? In the following passage, Zachary adds another
"tie-breaker" to make his decision:

> I think that most people will go on personal experience, I think like if some-
> one's had a horrible experience with some, you know, white guy that hired as
> their vice president of their company, they might be looking for a change, and
> vice versa, or I think personal experience has a lot to do with it

This is a ludicrous example in the idea that employers would generalize for all
white males in this situation; this is merely another evasive tactic. Still, this response suggests that employers may well base their decisions on a personal experience with a black employee, generalizing then for the entire group of black
applicants in future hiring decisions.

One bright spot among the onslaught of evasiveness and misunderstanding
is from Vincent:

> Like, is their experience completely the same? Everything is (.) what you could
> do, which actually might work out is I would (.) I would hire the black person,
> because this white person has the same credentials as this person that can go
> next door, and be easily offered or given another job, so let's go ahead and get
> him in here, give him the job, give him the leg-up, and then bang shoot him
> over there, and then he's got his, so I think that could work out that way, but (.)
> I don't know, if this was the last job on the planet, then (laugh)

Sadly, Vincent is the only respondent to answer this way, though note that his
last statement still suggests overwhelming opposition to hiring the black applicant in this situation (i.e., the suspicion in the black employee's abilities relative

to a white). Nonetheless, he is right on target regarding the opportunities whites have elsewhere, and that choosing the black would not be "racist."

Coming Clean

Sometimes respondents admitted that they would choose the white applicant in this hypothetical situation. For example, George blames the decision on his "upbringing":

> Uh if they were both equal, equally put in place, I don't know, I fear that (.) just from my upbringing that I might be more comfortable with the Caucasian, I fear that might happen but (.) if that's not the case, I don't know, it'd b(h)e a really hard decision too, so (.)

Note his bailout tagged on the end of his statement ("it'd b(h)e a really hard decision too") after catching himself for being a little too sincere, and then his "move" to get me to enter the conversation to bail him out ("so (.) so"), and I fell into his trap. Cynthia also was more direct and honest about her decision, once I controlled for gender:

> I: Like say you know you were that employer in that situation and maybe it was like say one black male and one white male, like how do you think you would maybe deal with that if like um like if they were just two men, like how would you deal with that?
> R: Mhm (3.0) I don't know (laughs). I mean, I definitely think race would be a factor, I definitely would, as far as to say I would choose the white man over the black man I mean I really don't know, I would probably say I would lean towards the white man? Just because it just seems (.) I think kind of like in society we see white men being more dominant, always having the powerful position, and that kind of relays to the person picking someone to be an employee you know? I probably would lean more towards the white person, to be honest. And I would definitely base it on other factors as well.

Once gender is controlled for, she admits race would be a factor. However, note how she saw that recognizing race is negative, in that doing so is equated with racism. Also note how she makes the admittance rather gingerly, with the "probably hire" and rising intonation at the end of the utterance. She also adds the final statement as a face-saving mechanism as well.

A more implicit example of choosing the white candidate came from Samantha:

> R: Like the qualifications would be the same?
> I: Yeah, basically.

R: Like I would <u>hope</u> I wouldn't be racist, but I also understand that you (.) you get attracted to people that are more like you, and if everything else is exactly the same, I don't know how else you would distinguish who (.)
I: Mhm
R: I mean, it's almost like (.) I would hope it would not be that way? But I understand also it's perfectly human for people to (.) cling to something that's (.) like them (.)

Similar to Cynthia's excerpt earlier, she equates "racism" with making a decision in which race was a factor. However, she completes the semantic move with utilizing the naturalization frame, in which people tend to like those like themselves. To be safe, she adds a face-saving statement ("it's almost like (.) I would hope it would not be that way?") to avoid criticism.

The most essentialistic view of the respondents came from Amy, who rationalized hiring discrimination:

R: I don't know, I'm not exactly sure what you're asking.
I: Well, if you think like an employer should take history into account as far as like (.) um that traditionally, like these underrepresented groups, like they've been getting denied, um
R: Yeah, I think it's important to (.) I mean, you don't want history to repeat itself, well in most cases you don't want history to repeat itself, so I think it's a good idea to look back on that, but um you also have to look at I mean why it happened like that in history, and maybe there's good reason why it happened like that and so maybe things should just be traditional and keep going the way they were, it's worked out so far, or (.)

It is worth noting that this response was exceptional; most chose to follow along the lines of color-blindness.

Interjection

A few female respondents used a particular method to evade the Hybrid question: interjecting gender into the equation. Rather than using gender to see the commonalities in discrimination, they often failed to make the connection (as Amy did). For example, Kaitlin responded this way:

R: I guess I would ask this question but are they the same sex? (.) 'cause I would probably hire the woman ((laughs))
I: Oh↑, okay. Yeah↑, I mean (2.0) you know, that could be the case I mean do you think that might be a situation in which you would go with the woman?
R: Oh, definitely. Probably. If they were the exact same qualifications 'cause I think (.) women have more trouble getting in higher positions so (.) I would definitely choose a woman
I: Sure

R: I don't really know about race. I don't think that would really matter if they were both (.) equally qualified, I don't know if I would make the decision other than pulling the name out of a hat or something probably (laughs)
I: Like you think it's like (.) more difficult for a woman regardless of race like to get like that higher job than
R: Yeah
I: Like say for a black male or Hispanic male or (.)
R: Well (.) I think maybe a white woman (.) might have it a little easier just because of her skin color 'cause I don't- I'm just getting this all from my sociology class but just saying they hire people that look the most like them. and (.) like 'cause they see them in their position? (.) and so (.) I don't know (.) yeah, I think that (2.0) (laugh)

Kaitlin said she would draw a name out of a hat to make the decision, despite claiming she would hire a woman candidate due to difficulties in getting high positions due to discrimination. Even worse, she evokes the naturalization frame, suggesting she may well choose the white applicant. Cynthia spoke in a similar way:

If I saw (.) a woman candidate over a man candidate, and they're both equally (.) they had equal credentials, I personally would probably pick the woman candidate, even just I probably would take into account you know just the struggle of woman on general, and even it was say the race issue of um (.) like if you were saying like an employer was like a white woman or a black woman, and [the] employer was white, I think they would choose maybe the white woman, just because they identify with her more (.) I think it's kind of conflicting actually, like it depends upon (.) the person? You know? Like a lot of people tend to pick people that are closely related to them, you know, same shirt, same characteristics, you know, and then other people might take into account losses, like "oh, well women have struggled more, especially black women," so they might feel more (.) not obligated, but more willing to hire them over someone else with the same credentials, or even they may want to diversify, you know, their workplace.

Note her appeal to the recipient ("it depends upon (.) the person? You know?") as a method to ensure my approval. She completes her statement with the alleged pressure whites feel to diversify.

Summary

In this chapter, I explored the myriad contradictions that exist with WRD when discussing policies and programs designed to achieve racial justice (e.g. race-sensitive admissions policies of colleges and universities). Despite the sample's ignorance of the social realities due to extensive separation from black Americans, they have rather sophisticated techniques to protect white privilege. First, they question the losses of black Americans in contemporary U.S. society, and utilize various myths to make their case against providing compensation to those victimized by racial injustice. Although they recognize injustices of the past, they refuse to see them connected to present social reality. They blame white racism on a few bad apples, while they blame blacks for their problems today. Furthermore, they feel white Americans are now disadvantaged due to the social quest for diversity. A key component of the retrogression we face is the backlash (however cloaked) against the Civil Rights Movement. Respondents charge that the quest for diversity violates our value of individualism. Finally, these young whites will likely reinforce systemic racism by choosing white candidates over black candidates for employment opportunities.

Notes

1. Thomas Edsall had a good blog on this phenomenon. Thomas B. Edsall, "White-Working Chaos," *New York Times*, June, 25, 2012. Available online at campaignstops.blogs.nytimes.com/2012/06/25/white-working-chaos (accessed June 27, 2012).

2. Twenty-one percent of whites who voted in the primary said that the race of the candidate was important to them, and they supported Clinton over Obama by a margin of 84 to 9. Results of the primary and exit polling is available at www.cnn.com/ELEC-TION/2008/primaries/results/epolls/#WVDEM.

3. Examples include Sean Trende, "Why Tuesday's Democratic Primaries Matter." *RealClearPolitics*, May 24, 2012. http://www.realclearpolitics.com/articles/2012/05/24/why_tuesdays_democratic_primaries_matter_114256.html.

4. Richard D. Kahlenberg, *The Remedy: Class, Race, and Affirmative Action*. New York: Basic Books, 1996. Also see Richard D. Kahlenberg, "What Obama Should Say About the Texas Affirmative Action Case." *Slate*, 2/21/12. Online at www.slate.com/articles/news_and_politics/jurisprudence/2012/02/fisher_v_texas_how_obama_should_talk_about_affirmative_action.single.html.

5. Richard D. Kahlenberg, "Barack Obama and Affirmative Action." *Inside Higher Ed*, May 12, 2008. Online at insidehighered.com/views/2008/05/12/kahlenberg.

6. Polls had shown in their head-to-head match-ups with John McCain, neither of these Democrats would have won this group in the general election anyway. The slightly better position for Clinton was due to her stronger numbers among white women. See http://www.gallup.com/poll/107416/Obama-Faces-Uphill-Climb-vs-McCain-Among-White-Voters.aspx for an analysis. Joe R. Feagin had a bog on this at http://www.racismreview.com/blog/2008/05/28/clintons-main-strength-not-working-class-whites.

7. Kahlenberg, *The Remedy*.

8. Richard D. Kahlenberg, "The Achilles Heel of Affirmative Action." *Chronicle of Higher Education*, 10/11/2012. http://chronicle.com/blogs/conversation/2012/10/11/the-achilles-heel-of-affirmative-action.

9. William G. Bowen and Derek Bok, *The Shape of the River: Long-Term Consequences of Considering Race in College and University Admissions*. Princeton, NJ: Princeton University Press, 1998.

10. Elaine Korry, "Black Student Enrollment at UCLA Plunges." *National Public Radio*, 7/24/2006. www.npr.org/templates/story/story.php?storyId=5563891

11. Peter Schmidt, "Bans on Affirmative Action Help Asian Americans, Not Whites, Report Says." *Chronicle of Higher Education*, January 20, 2008. www. chronicle.com/daily/2008/01/1424n.htm.

12. Thomas J. Kane, "Racial and Ethnic Preferences in College Admission," in *The Black-White Test Score Gap*, ed. Christopher Jencks and Meredith Phillips (Washington, D.C.: Brookings Institution, 1998).

13. Bowen and Bok, *Shape of the River*, 279-280.

14. Marianne Bertrand and Sendhil Mullainathan, "Are Emily and Greg More Employable Than Lakisha and Jamal? A Field Experiment on Labor Market Discrimination," *American Economic Review* 94, no. 4 (September 2004), 991-1013.

15. For example, one source defines retrogression as "the act or process of deteriorating or declining" or "a return to a less complex or more primitive state or stage." Found in The American Heritage Collegiate Dictionary, 3rd Edition. Boston: Houghton Mifflin, 1993.

16. Bonilla-Silva, *White Supremacy and Racism*, 157.

17. Frankenberg, *White Women, Race Matters*, 147.

18. Frankenberg, *White Women, Race Matters*.

19. Bonilla-Silva, *White Supremacy and Racism*, 158-159.

20. Feagin, *Racist America* and *Systemic Racism*.

21. Sam Keen, *Faces of the Enemy: Reflections of the Hostile Imagination*. New York: Harper and Row, 1986.

22. Beverly D. Tatum, *Why Are All the Black Kids Sitting in the Back of the Cafeteria?: And Other Conversations about Race* (Revised Edition). New York: Basic Books, 1993.

23. This point was made clear in Richard Delgado and Jean Stefancic, *Critical Race Theory: An Introduction*. New York: New York University Press, 2001. Quotas are extremely rare and are reserved for only the most egregious instances of deeply-rooted discriminatory practices (Matthew Desmond and Mustafa Emirbayer, *Racial Domination, Racial Progress: The Sociology of Race in America*, New York: McGraw-Hill, 2010, 194).

24. In the original question, they asked respondents to agree with the decision of ABZ Company to choose a black job applicant over a white due to its workforce being 97 percent white and are concerned about the lack of diversity. See Bonilla-Silva and Forman, "I Am Not a Racist, But..."

Chapter 5
Defending White Supremacy

Following the inauguration of Barack Obama, some people began to dispute the new President's country of birth. These individuals came to be known as "birthers," and part of the more general "birther movement," or those who believe that President Obama was not born in the United States. Despite general dismissal of their conspiracy theory, their voices were given ample coverage by the news media. For reasons political or otherwise, elected officials and others began to express sympathy or even outright support with the birthers. This fiasco reached a tipping point of absurdity in 2011, when casino tycoon Donald Trump who, while flirting with a possible run for the presidency, demanded that the President release his birth certificate and claimed to have dispatched a team to Hawaii to investigate the matter. Shortly thereafter, President Obama released his birth certificate in an attempt to put the matter to rest.

When analyzing Obama's first term as President, one question worth asking is whether his administration has been scrutinized differently than others before it. Certainly, the Clintons faced vicious attacks during their time in the White House, attacks that ultimately culminated in his impeachment.[1] However, there was a critical qualitative difference between the attacks on the Clintons and those levied towards President Obama by the birthers: while Bill Clinton was seen as a traitor or adulterer, Obama is perceived of as counterfeit, a Manchurian candidate. It is folly to believe that Obama's ethno-racial history has had nothing to do with these allegations. Furthermore, both the individuals involved with (or at least sympathetic to) the birther movement and the spotlight awarded them by the news media are disturbing in and of themselves. Why have media outlets been more than willing to provide a platform for such blatantly racist propaganda?

While the reasons for this media coverage of the birthers is multi-faceted,[2] one important reason is something I give attention to in this chapter: that white Americans, while dismissive of supremacist discourse in general, are willing to provide a microphone for those who espouse white supremacist views, whether they agree with such views or not. Are they not aware of the dangers of such views, even while simultaneously running "search and destroy" missions on other hate speech that might lead to violence against whites or groups whites support or commonly associate with? In this chapter, I explore the contradictions prevalent in the sample's discourse when speaking about racism and white supremacy, and how respondents, through their discursive antics, implicitly defend white supremacists and their organizations. They defend white supremacy in three ways: first, they downplay the significance of their activities. They dismiss white supremacists as ignorant fools whom no one takes seriously. They also believe that anyone is capable of such actions. Respondents ultimately project ambivalence towards the activities of white supremacists. Second, I present ways that study participants are more likely to defend the "free speech" of white supremacists than that of black Americans. They compare the speech of white supremacists with that of individual black Americans, and lack the understanding of the stark differences between the two. Third, I examine the ways that respondents express ambivalence towards racist jokes and even engage in racist joking.

Downplaying the Significance of White Supremacy

In this section, I analyze the fundamental contradiction regarding respondents' views toward white supremacists and their organizations: They express disapproval of white supremacists but lack an understanding of the danger they and their organizations pose to members of U.S. society. For the most part, the sample dismisses the threat of white supremacy, due to their experience living in communities insulated from communities affected by their activities, both past and present. Meanwhile, respondents speak of nonwhite supremacists to further dilute the significance of white supremacists and their organizations. Using a typical color-blind method, they equate race with racism, and naturalize supremacist activities. Finally, while initially presenting an antiracist image by labeling white supremacists as a "serious problem," they are ambivalent about that presence.

Serious Yet Ridiculous

It is interesting to think of the massive quantity of resources spent on the destruction of an individual terrorist organization, Al-Queda, and the space it occupies in the minds of Americans, while terrorist organizations such as the Ku Klux Klan receive much less attention and little public outcry for their activities. Despite causing more harm and destruction than foreign organizations, these domestic terrorist groups receive little coverage by the news media. In fact, much of the attention directed towards these groups is trivialized and dismissed as an impotent force in our society. In this study, the responses of those inter-viewed underscore this point.

Respondents present a contradiction when they say white supremacists and their organizations are "a serious problem," yet dismiss them as irrelevant due to presumed low numbers and significance, and limited to particular areas of the country (i.e., the south). For example, Frank initially agreed that white suprema-cist groups were a serious problem, but said they were not as much of a problem now as in the past, though adding a semantic move that "there are definitely still organizations around, especially in the south." While discussing the role white-ness has played in his life, Troy replied this way:

R: U:m (.) yea:h it's not really a whole lot because you know (.) I don't know, maybe it's a little different here in the south but I grew up up north and
I: Right.
R: You know it's (.) you know, of course there's racism everywhere but it's not really in your face up there

This contradiction occurred throughout the interviews, in that respondents acknowledge that racism is a factor "everywhere," yet whiteness has not been a factor in their own lives. Specifically regarding the presence of white suprema-cy, many participants describe the phenomenon as being a few "bad apples" who live somewhere "far away," or somewhere in the south.

How can a social phenomenon be a serious matter when it is ridiculous at the same time? Zachary comments on white supremacists this way:

I: Do you think white supremacists are a problem?
R: I think white supremacy is ridiculous. I have a serious problem with it, be-cause it's not only uh it deals racially and religiously, and uh I just think that it's uncalled for? And I think that people can have their own feelings and their own opinion, but I don't think it should exist (.) in our society at all.

Unfortunately, few respondents explicitly state that these organizations should not exist in our society, yet Zachary, like so many others, downplayed the dan-ger these groups pose. He evaded my question entirely (in that he has a problem with white supremacists, rather than whether or not they are a problem). Later in the interview, when making his argument that racism was decreasing in our so-ciety, he remarks "I don't think that it's this (.) large pro- I mean, it's a signifi-cant problem, but not as big=" before I cut him off.

Respondents apparently find it necessary to consider white supremacy a "significant problem" in our society, though they generally think they are in the shadows and soundly rejected by the majority of white Americans. In fact, Amy responded this way:

R: Are there still white supremacists?
I: Sure. ((Recent story about neo-Nazis on CNN about freedom of speech))

R: I think, I wouldn't necessarily say that white supremacists are (.) a serious problem? because there's really not that many of them that I know of that are really causing that many problems, however I think that, I don't know how to say this, I'm biased but I just think those groups are just ridiculous, and when a group is made up on the basis of hating somebody else, I think that's terrible

In this excerpt, she questions whether white supremacists even exist anymore. When I provide an instance of white supremacy from a news story, she dismisses their presence. In doing this, she utilizes discursive moves such as the rhetorical strategy of apparent disagreement, with rising intonation when making the statement "I wouldn't necessarily say that white supremacists are (.) a serious problem?" This suggests her uncertainty about my own response as well as the presence of these groups in society. Her semantic move "I'm biased but I just think those groups are just ridiculous" is especially intriguing in that she appears afraid to criticize these groups, as if I or anyone else would think otherwise.

Anyone Is Capable

Besides their dismissal of white supremacy, respondents overwhelmingly agree that anyone is capable of racism, based on their assumption of equating "racism" with "prejudice." In fact, due to their view of themselves as raceless beings (see chapter 2), any acknowledgement of race is equated with racism. It enables them to naturalize supremacy and racism. As we will see, this method allows them to express ambivalence towards racism in society.

Race Equated with Racism
Due to respondents' color-blindness, they often evade the issue of race. When they did talk about race, they often viewed it negatively in and of itself. In fact, they sometimes equated race with racism. For example, Cynthia recalls "many instances" of racist jokes in newspapers and the Internet, and added "I don't think race is increasing, like I said before, but it definitely still is you know relevant today, and people will make jokes and stuff like that." Perhaps this was a transcription error on my part, or that she meant to say "racism." Still, when upholding the tenants of color-blindness, respondents view race as bad (e.g., racist) in and of itself. In addition, Quilla agrees that anyone is capable of racism:

Yeah, I think anyone is capable of being racist, just because uhm (2.0) I don't know, I think just the way things are portrayed like through t.v. and just there's a huge emphasis, like there's white shows and there's black shows, like it's just like wherever you look, things are kind of (.) um I guess separated, even if they don't mean to be.

She equates racism with race based on television programming that portrays different races.

Meanwhile, Harriet reduces racism to "personal opinion." When I asked her what she would tell her children what racism was, she responds this way:

R: Um, I would probably just tell them that um (.) it's when you think that your race is superior to any other (.) race, and that you have negative (.) um, you negatively think I guess about (.)
I: Like uh, generalize (.) or stereotype=
R: Yeah, stereotype other races (1.0) and have a negative outlook on those races.

In this excerpt, Harriet reduces racism to hating people, and fails to distinguish individual prejudice from institutional discrimination. I enjoy asking respondents this question because it gives us a clue how these young whites will respond to their children's questions of race in U.S. society. Questions like these provide us evidence that whites pass on their atomistic view of racism onto their children, as they do the white racist frame.

In the next excerpt, Casey appears to recognize the importance of one's social location in being "racist"—that is, having the power to discriminate against people of a different race—but is incoherent and ultimately follows the familiar line of reducing racism to a state of mind:

I guess anyone is capable of being a racist but I mean I also think it's harder like, how you're like, like uh, sociological location, and how you're (.) brought up, that you're like, you're (stressing?) it in your mind from your parents because some parents will um put that in there.

In his remarks, he apparently tries to say that it is more difficult to practice racism but cannot state it clearly. However, he concludes that racism is something inside someone; something one possesses. Many whites view racism this way, in that it is a state of being or a condition. The reality is that racism is a set of practices against members of another racial identity; it is a process.[3] Not anyone can be racist, regardless of individual desire; racism can only be exercised with power.

Naturalizing Supremacy

A poor conceptualization allows respondents to believe that since all people are capable of racism, it is something natural. Since all people are at least a little ethnocentric, everyone is a little racist. For example, Amy declares during her interview that "everybody [has] at least one percent racism in them, because that's just how we were taught by teachers and by our parents, that's just (.) the society that we grew up in." Meanwhile, Troy reduces racism to a product of human nature:

It's just sort of human nature, I think, to classify things with (.) you group things together and (.) you know it's (.) you know, I think pretty much everybody is to a small extent u:h (.) you know some kind of notions like (.) you know, if you're walking through a dark neighborhood at night and (.) see a group of a couple of white kids walking past you, you know, you wouldn't think much but (.) you know, if you had some (.) thugged-out black guys walking out, you might be a little cautious, so (.) technically I guess that would be racist, but (.) you know, it's not something that really (.) hold against anybody, um (.) you know, it's just (.) preconceived notions I mean that people [have] (.) you know, as long as it's not (.) you know, the biggest I really hate is just like you know (.) you could have preconceived notions about a person, but I don't want anybody to form an opinion on them automatically before even talking to them (.) uh, because you know (.) it sounds kind of cliché but don't judge a book by its cover um (.) it's you know some of the nicest people in the world you meet, and you're (.) kinda maybe put off at first based on past experiences with people who look like that uh so (.) you know, as long as you get to know somebody before forming an opinion on them, you know, whatever that opinion is, go for it.

In this excerpt, Troy contradicts himself by his color-blind rhetoric (e.g., "don't judge a book by its cover") with his own apparent judgments of "thugged-out black guys." Thus, his naturalization of racism serves as a face-saving mechanism, as an excuse for his own negative images of young black men. Of course, paper-and-pencil questionnaires could not get to this information in the first place.

In the next excerpt, Kaitlin also conceptualizes racism as something we are stuck with forever, although she thinks it is decreasing in our society:

R: Umm I think it's decreasing I think I honestly think it'll always be around (.) I don't think it's ever gonna totally go away 'cause there's always gonna be people that pass on, like white supremacists, they're gonna pass it on to their kids and (.) when you're raised a certain way, it's kind of hard to get away from it, so (.) I think it'll always be here, but I definitely think it's you know diminishing it, diminishing a lot.
I: Do you think that you know (.) we in society I mean whether it's the government or schools or you know whoever I mean do you think we're doing enough like to address like well to try to stop it or (.) racism or (.)
R: Umm (2.0) I don't even know if they're doing anything
I: Mhm
R: I don't really know- I mean, I definitely think that (.) they need to try to erase it like the stupid commercials about um like giving er like housing or looking at apartments and stuff and the guy calls in like all these different voices with different names and stuff, like I think that's terrible like if you're black and have the same credit history as a white person what's the problem with getting an apartment they're gonna pay their bills (.) like I think something needs to be done about stuff like that 'cause just because (.) I don't know, I think it's stupid not to get an apartment 'cause of your race or (.) I don't know

I: Right. (2.0) Yeah, that is interesting, why do you think like, like people would do that?

R: I don't know. I don't understand. It's just (.) I don't know. They have a (.) I don't know, maybe they think they have a history of like not paying their bills but if they have a good credit history like that's all you need to know. And if they have a good job with a good income and they'll be fine, I don't understand why they (.) do that.

Kaitlin tries to avoid the obvious fact that whites discriminate against nonwhites in housing due to racism. She almost seems as if the "stupid commercials" won't do anything to stop racism. Despite expressing optimism towards the decline of white-on-black racism, respondents appear quite pessimistic in its elimination, and quite limited in their thoughts on how to stop it.

Not Just "White" Supremacy

Since respondents naturalize the phenomenon of racism, anyone can be a supremacist. Thus many evoked a kind of "It's not just white supremacists that's the problem" storyline. This aids them in downplaying the (sole) role of racial supremacist in U.S. society, a role unparalleled throughout our history. This is also a frame that forces whites to tread very carefully since there really is not any comparison.

Dina goes as far as to say that other supremacists pose a greater threat to whites than vice-versa:

Umm (1.0) ↑I'd say it's about (.) like, depending on where you are I guess, or what organization it is, but I feel like a lot of the time (.) the people of another race (.) um, like if an (instance) does happen, or like a Communist man or something, then people of the other race, like it's a big deal and if that were to happen to, like, my race, because they're so many of us and stuff, it would never mean to be such a big deal, but I don't really know of any white supremacist organizations °that are really ((trails off))°

In this passage, Dina actually uses her ignorance of white supremacist activities as evidence. In addition, her use of "Communist" serves as a tool to deflect the issue of race.

Respondents' atomistic view of racism (see chapter 4) allows them to downplay the significance of white supremacists and their organizations, while blaming nonwhites for racism, even if they struggle to mention examples of their supremacist activities. In the following passage, Elizabeth spoke of other supremacist groups and I probed her on that:

R: Umm, I don't agree that <u>any</u> (.) supremacy group like not necessarily just white or like, have to do with race at all has (.) any positive connotations for society like I think it's all (1.0) not good, but I don't know.

> I: Like can you think of like other (.) like race supremacist grou:ps umm, that
> might not necessarily be white supremacist groups?
> R: Well yeah, like there's like um, what is it called, I don't, I don't know the
> name of it, there's like a black power one too, like there's ones for like Hispan-
> ics and like everybody else but, I don't know, I was thinking more along the
> lines of like (.) religious supremacist groups like
> I: Mm
> R: I don't think that's very good either because then you don't give other peo-
> ple the opportunity to get to know (.) like more about it and they get really
> closed minded.

Elizabeth tries to equal the playing field in the supremacy game, in that nonwhite supremacist groups pose an equal threat to society as white supremacist groups. Although there are groups that exude antiwhite prejudice, they simply lack the resources and desire to systematically kill white Americans. If these groups are on an equal par with those like the Klan or neo-Nazis, then why can't she name any?

I asked some respondents about their response to a man's comment once that "A black man can be prejudiced, but he can't be racist."[4] Zachary retorts to this during his interview:

> I disagree. I think that this (.) that racism can happen anywhere. I think that if
> you live in a predominantly black community, and you were the only white
> person there, and you, you know, I'm sure you can experience racism at times
> because people are closed-minded, and I don't think that everyone, you know,
> receives people the same way, so I'm sure that if you live=if that was the case,
> you know if I lived in the ghetto somewhere, you know, I'm sure that peo- ya
> know, I stuck out or I was a various perception about me, just because the per-
> ception might be, you know, 'oh, that you're,' let's just say that 'you have a lot
> of money or you don't belong here because you're white,' that doesn't make it,
> you know, right and it's still considered to- at least I consider it to be racism.

Like the solid majority of respondents, Zachary lacks understanding of racism, and believes it to be a state of mind, and misrecognizes the importance of power in who can discriminate and who cannot.

Ambivalence towards White Supremacy

There is a pattern emerging in how whites enable themselves to express ambivalence towards white supremacy. First, they equate "racism" with individual prejudice, and see prejudiced black individuals as "racists." Hence, anyone is capable of racism, even if they say that nonwhites are less likely to do so. This allows them to go as far as to naturalize the phenomenon of race supremacy, to even say that everyone is prejudiced, racist, and thus supremacist. This brings the process to expressing ambivalence, in which whites conclude that racism cannot be dealt with in any meaningful way. While respondents overwhelmingly believed that the freedoms of everyone should be protected, they were not nearly as unified in their desire to see the law eliminate supremacist organizations (Table 5.1).

Table 5.1   Questionnaire Results for Attitudes towards Supremacist Groups and Protecting Liberty

Question	Mean
The law should eliminate race supremacist groups and their activities.	3.60
Society should protect the freedom and liberty of all citizens equally.	4.63

Study participants commonly respond to the issue of white supremacy with ambivalence, largely due to the result of their existence in the white bubble. Angie, for example, remarked, "I don't know. I guess that people do feel pressure from white supremacists, but I really can't bring anything up." Similar to other topics, respondents often project incoherence, such as the following excerpt from Jane:

> U::mm, I don't really know if racism is increasing? because there's so many efforts today to make racial equality (.) I mean there's always going to be people out there who are racist but I don't really know if it's increasing u::m and I don't know if it's decreasing but I don't know if it's increasing.

Responses such as these are difficult to comprehend, which I believe is no accident: whites walk on eggshells in their quest to preserve their dominance (however subconsciously) while attempting to come across as someone else. In this section, I present three ways in which respondents express their ambivalence towards white supremacy: first, by suggesting that if they do not see reports of white supremacist activities on the news, then it must not be a concern; second, they fail to recognize white supremacy in action, even when it unfolds right in front of them; and third, some respondents went as far as to accept white supremacist ideology and engage in supremacist actions.

"It's Not on the News, So..."

Sociologists have documented how the media socializes us to see the world in particular ways. The media delivers us messages of what is and what ought to be. Specifically regarding the news media, they implicitly tell us what is important to know about and, at the same time, what is less important. The influence of the media on perception is especially persuasive with the more one consumes.[5] Based on (at least perceived) lack of news coverage on white suprema-supremacist activities, some respondents do not think they pose a serious threat.

For example, I presented in chapter 2 how Irene downplayed the significance of race in U.S. society due to her own experience living in a racially diverse community. When discussing the presence of white supremacists and their organizations, she claims "it's (1.0) I don't see it on the news, I don't see it." If it isn't talked about on the news, then it must not be a problem. Meanwhile, Kaitlin makes sure to mention how much she despised what white supremacists stood for prior to dismissing them due to their absence in the news:

> Um↑ I don't think I mean I think they're very wrong? but I haven't noticed them much like they're not in the news or anything like that so I don't think they should exist I think they're terrible but (.) I mean, I don't think they're doing anything bad right now are they? I haven't really heard anything in the news like the KKK doing anything like I don't think it should exist at all I think it's terrible so I definitely think it's a problem but (1.0) it's not like at least from what I've heard it's not like they're killing people or anything right now (laughs)

I find it disturbing how she only seems to take white supremacists seriously when they are "killing people or anything." Like I mentioned previously, respondents feel a need to agree with the general notion that they indeed are a problem, but just not that much.

In the next passage, Renee recalls hearing about other hate groups being a problem, while white supremacist groups are dormant:

> I don't really know about *a bunch* of white supremacist groups in our society, I guess there's still like instances with like (.) KKK people? I don't (.) I don't know, like I never really- I hear more about like hate crimes (.) more of like homosexuality I feel like, but I'm sure that yeah I guess this is probably a problem with this. °I've never heard that much about it to think today society (?)°

Here, Renee sounds as if only having one or two white supremacist groups—not "a bunch"—is not enough reason to justify concern. I do not recall any antiwar critics who argued there were only one or two terrorist organizations out there, and thus could not justify the "war on terror." She almost seems afraid (ashamed?) to admit she has not heard of problems these groups have caused.

There were times during the interviews that I provided them instances of news stories about white supremacist activities, such as the following exchange with Harriet:

> I: Near Chicago the Klan applied for a permit to march and have a parade or something? And it was like a predominantly Jewish American suburb and it

was a really big deal, like it got a lot of attention, ultimately they were allowed to have the parade, but (.) But you don't think (.) I mean, as far as white supremacists increasing I mean in (.) as far as in popularity, you don't think that's happened?
R: I don't think so, I mean I don't watch the news nearly enough to know for sure but just from what I do, I don't think that it is an increasing problem but I hope it's not.

Despite my own reference to a particular instance of white supremacist activity, Harriet prefers to remain inside her white bubble and deny their significance. She then adds the final semantic move (often respondents utilize a kind of serial semantic moves), which serves as a face-saving mechanism.

Respondents also believe that the stigma associated with joining such an organization keeps people away from them. They seem to conveniently forget the proliferation of the Internet and ability to share information without other people knowing about it. For example, Elizabeth disagreed that white supremacists are increasing in U.S. society:

R: Um, I don't think so? I think it's (1.0) maybe not necessarily getting any better, it's just different than it used to be like, people aren't (1.0) like so widespread like, killing each other and just (.) doing like awful things to one another but there's still (.) like prevalence in society of it, but I don't feel that it's any worse than it was before, and I'm hoping, like hopefully I think it's getting a little bit better.
I: Well, like, white supremacist groups, do you think that they might be increasing?
R: I hope not, I think they're decreasing, I would guess, just because of the taboo like being in one, I can't imagine, like (.) knowing somebody that was in one, that's just insane to me, I don't know, I can't even picture it, so (.) I would say they're on the decline, but I don't know.

Similar to Irene, Elizabeth believes that based on her own relationships with nonmembers of white supremacists, there must not be any. As long as they remain under the surface of U.S. society, then they are not a problem. Meanwhile, Betty dismisses the portrayal of white supremacist gangs in the film *American History X* and only thinks they are important if she were involved in their activities:

Not that I've encountered, because I've never myself have partaken in any of these white supremacist groups, and I've never seen any of my black, Hispanic, like any different kind of racial friend discriminated against because it's you know who they are, but I've never myself ever come across an actual group of white kids that were against you know blacks or Hispanics or what not, I mean you've seen it in movies, but I mean how accurate is that? Um I think it was *American History X*, you saw the skinheads, but I've never myself encountered them, and I've never approached or ask- joined, or (.) you know, so I'm sure they are in existence, but as far as the places I've ever lived, and the people I've ever been in contact with, I haven't come across it, and in [city in the Midwest], if you're in a white supremacy group, you're not gonna last ve(h)ry long, just because you are the minority, and uh you sink or swim=I don't think it's a good idea to ever like (.) you know, outright come out and say that you're against a certain race, like that's ridiculous, at least I think so

In this passage, Betty fails to recognize the reality that most white supremacist activities are covert in today's society; e.g., known as usernames passing hate messages and literature over the Internet. In fact, the example of the story reported by CNN exposed racist video games available on the net, such as one in which you tried to shoot as many Mexicans as you could as they try to run across the border.[6] She seems to believe that because she does not think it would be "a good idea" to join a white supremacist organization, no other whites would either. She then closes with the "that's ridiculous" line; what are the repercussions of this phenomenon of saying something is serious but not all that serious?

Failure to See White Supremacy in Action

The ambivalence of my sample when it came to recognizing white supremacy was rather disturbing in that they would not call an activity "white supremacist" even when it was painfully obvious. As long as they were not actively killing people and out from the shadows, they aren't a threat, according to the respondents. They also speak of it in odd ways: for instance, when speaking of white supremacists, Irene remarks, "they're there, but I don't think there are more than there were in the past."

But what about respondents who did witness an event involving white supremacist activity? During Odella's interview, her conceptualization of "white supremacy" was ambiguous and serves an example of failing to see racism right under her nose. First, when recalling an instance of "racial tension," she speaks of an event at her high school in which white students hung a "black doll" (human-sized mannequin wrapped in black trash bags) from a tree, and lit it ablaze on campus:

R: At my high school, there was a big news story about there was a uh southern boys group at my school, and they um hung a (.) black doll from a tree at my high school, and that caused a very big news story and a huge, huge problem, and (.) the two groups, the black kids at the school, and the southern boys group had to go through this huge counseling, and they were two really big groups, but it kind of affected the whole school, and um (.) there was a petition to make the confederate flag not allowed to be worn or put on cars at our school, so there was a lot of debate over that, and it caused tension (laughs)
I: How did you like respond to all of that going on you know around you at the time?
R: Um (.) I thought that um the southern boys group handled the situation very poorly, and um (.) that it cau- like it- I couldn't believe that they like did that, and um (.) that they were so insensitive? And (.)

I: Well like, it was- like as far as some of the details, I mean I'm not familiar with the story but like you said that a black doll they- like this was on campus? Like they

R: Yeah, it was at our school.

I: Okay. Like and they um just like (.) I mean it was like just a regular-sized doll?

R: No, like a human sized

I: Oh, okay. Hmm (.) What and it was like dressed in real clothing?

R: It was just like, it was like cloth and uh a trash bag

I: Oh, okay.

R: in the shape of a person, hung from a tree, by the neck.

I: Right. God, that's interesting. And so there was just like I mean you mentioned like the principal and

R: Yeah.

I: They were all (.) mobilizing as far as to deal with it

R: Yeah, and yeah (laughs)

I: And what about parents, were there parents getting involved to with it and stuff

R: Yeah, it was like a whole, huge (laughs) huge like news story with news stations at the school, and um but it resolved itself pretty well in the end. Like everyone realized the (.) stupidity of it.

I: Yeah.

In her statements, she provides details of the incident, and the fallout. It was interesting how she mentions that there was the debate to forbid display of the Confederate flag, and includes the debate into exacerbating the racial tension. Later in the interview, I made reference to the issue and she called it "an isolated event."

Then, when discussing the issue of white supremacy posing a "major problem" in our society, she says:

R: I don't think white supremacy is a serious problem in our society, I know it exists, but um (.) maybe I just don't see it (.) like maybe in other places it's more prominent, but I (.)

I: Well, like the example from your high school, do you think that that like constitutes white supremacy?

R: Well it pro- yeah, yeah probably. But I think it was kind of a spur of the mo- I don't know, like (.) I don't know how someone justifies that, and they realized that they ma(h)de a ba(h)d decision, so (.)

I: Were the people who put it up there, were they pretty outspoken about it, and like "we did this," or

R: Yeah, they were. Um and they were like uh good ole southern boys, they wore confederate t-shirts and cowboy hats

I: Right. I'm not originally from the south, but like maybe for people who might not be familiar with like good ole southern boy like you mentioned, like you mentioned cowboy hats and confederate t-shirts

R: And that was definitely a minority at our school, like a very small group, there were more black kids then there were of them.
I: And what were the reasons they gave as far as like you know "why we did this," like what was you know this stunt supposed to prove or say or whatever
R: I'm not really (laughs) entirely sure.

Thus, she appears to define "white supremacy" as something remote and not something she has experienced, despite her own experience of the effigy incident at her high school. She refuses to agree that this was an example of white supremacy, saying that it was "isolated" and "spur of the moment," suggesting, then, that to be white supremacist one must do these things all the time, even if this particular activity fits the bill of white supremacist activity. It's really hard to eliminate white supremacy when you fail to see it happening before your very own eyes.

Similar to the others' "ridiculous" commentary, Odella delivers this final analysis of the situation at her school: "Yeah, it was like a whole, huge (laughs) huge like news story with news stations at the school, and um but it resolved itself pretty well in the end. Like everyone realized the (.) stupidity of it." So despite this experience, she comes to the ambivalent conclusion that white supremacy is not much of a problem in society.

Implicit Acceptance of White Supremacy

A few respondents go as far as to implicitly accept white supremacist activities, or at least are unwilling to do anything to stop it. In his interview, Troy recalls his experience as a bouncer and the "training" he received from his white boss:

R: I work as a bouncer in a club downtown, a:nd a lot of times like, you know, you kind of have to be racist at the door it's (.) you know, it sounds terrible but it's kind of like the line from *The Godfather*
I: Mhm.
R: "It's business, not personal," um (.) a lot of times you know your [boss?] will come out there and tell you (.) like what people that dress in a certain way
I: Oh.
R: Or look a certain way, you have to deny them at the door um 'cause basically they're looking to maximize profits um (.) and based on past experience they'll see that (.) you know the (.) black guy's coming in wearing ya know baggy jeans, Fubu clothes and all that
I: Mhm
R: They're really not gonna buy much drinks and if they do↑ then they're probably not gonna tip the bartender, um
I: Right
R: And also the majority of fights tend to be started by ah (.) you know, black guys (.) and painting that kind of description um so downtown in a lot of places um you know, they'll even hire me and some of my friends and come in and work the door, and they'll be like, like absolutely no black people whatsoever, um (.) 'cause some places like ah [name of a different establishment] uh a while back they were going through some changes and, you know it kind of

turned into a place where a lot of the black crowd was going, a:nd they started seeing a loss in profits and all so they brought in some new people and basically they told us like "you have to stop them from coming in the door" like, you know? Um, they gave us like a general outline for ah (.) you know, clothing and all ah (.) even if they do, you know, follow the clothing outline, if you can look at 'em and kind of get that general opinion like "find something with your clothing"

I: Right. So the clothing outline, was it pretty specific where they like gave you a list of stuff [like what's allowed and what's not allowed

R: [Yeah↑   You know, they basically left it up to our discretion, they're like you know you're typical stuff that you know your inner-city ghetto hip-hop whatever you wanna call it crap, kind of stuff they'd wear um

I: So I mean like (.) baggy jeans like Fubu like you mentioned=

R: =Yeah. Any kind of jerseys, um (.) you know they say [baggy?] jewelry, big chains all that um a lot of places like they go as far as saying "no Timberlands at the door" the shoes are pretty popular, and just general stuff you find uh 'cause they can't just come out and say 'all right [don't] black people come in' so they have to make a dress code and basically they find stuff that applied to you know (.) kind of black crowd and say you know 'you can't come in wearing that.' You know, I don't know how much of that is just based on racism or if they're just (.) you know, looking at it like they've got bills to pay, so you kind of have to

In Troy's statement, we see how formal rationality, coupled with the pursuit of profit, excuses discriminatory behavior. Similar to individualism trumping the value of diversity, here laissez-faire capitalism and economic "freedom" trumps the value of equality. This example serves as a great example of rationalizing racism, and it appears likely that, as an owner in the future, he will conduct business the same way (in fact, the line blurs between what his boss taught him and his own thoughts).

In a different example, when dismissing white supremacist groups as ridiculous, Wanda tells a story of a male floor mate and what she would (not) do about him if she were a resident assistant:

R: There are people that take it like they're too extreme, and (.) not a serious problem, just like goes both ways, like whatever you stand for, if you (.) there are some like ridiculous organizations (.) but just people like taking their freedom of speech...they're allowed to say what they want, I never really listened to them, but I know (.) they um they're like um (.) towards white people (.) there's someone on my floor on the boy's side, he has stuff on a board outside his door with "I smell goyim" on it, and I asked a friend and it's like (.) that's everyone who's not white, and when you feel like- I walk by his door I like (.) like a bad like (.) vibe

I: Does he have any swastikas or anything like that?

R: No, just that.

I: If you were the RA, what would you do?

R: If it was just like [a] thing on his door, if he did anything else, or like (.)
then, maybe but (.) but if even like one person I guess like said something
about it I guess then I would do something (.) I'm like offended by it, I'm
white, but I'm offended by it

In the following excerpt, Wanda takes the common approach that as long as she
personally ignores them, white supremacist groups are not a problem. She also
tries to take the attention away from white supremacists by claiming there are
antiwhite groups (though said with considerable incoherence). According to her
response, she fails to recognize how the student's form of speech was more than
mere "speech"; by putting a sign on his door, it was an action. In addition, she
offers no idea on how she would deal with this situation, defends his right to free
expression, and seems prepared to defend supremacist speech. I discuss this issue in more detail in the next section.

Protecting White Supremacist Speech

Freedom of speech is a strongly held value of Americans. However, in civics
courses we learn how not all speech is protected by the First Amendment, and
the example we commonly learn of as unprotected is the person falsely yelling
"Fire!" in a crowded theater. This form of speech is not protected because it
endangers others.[7] Following the events of September 11, 2001, Americans have
heard of the government's warrantless wiretapping of suspected terrorist organizations associated with those attacks, and surveys show many Americans support those measures. The support is likely linked to the suspicion they have of
individuals who express themselves in such a way and the actions that have
harmed others.

But the issue of whether the wiretappings are constitutional is not my concern here; rather, my concern lies with the rather incredible reversal in response
to white supremacist speech, and linked to specific organizations that for decades engaged in terrorist activities against blacks and other nonwhite Americans,
including honorary or borderline whites such as Jewish Americans. In this section, I present data from the interviews that respondents almost go out of their
way to protect white supremacists' right to speech and organization, despite the
fact that they are terrorists. Second, I offer examples in how respondents do not
give black Americans the same right to speech than what they give white supremacists.

Aiding and Abetting White Supremacy

When responding to the statement "White supremacists and their organizations are a serious problem in our society," respondents generally did three things: first, they admit their existence and often condemn them (usually as an impression management tool); second, they downplay their significance; and third, they defend their rights to engage in such activities, when in fact those rights do not exist. For example, Bill responds this way:

> R: I don't know if they're a se↑rious problem, 'cause I know they exist, but I don't [know] how (.) prevalent they are...but they definitely are somewhat of a problem because (2.0) they're (.) just not good people(h).
> I: Hmm.
> R: Ignorant people that cause pro-problems.
> I: Right.
> R: But they're allowed to organize peacefully and all.

With a past like that of the KKK, how can we assume they are capable of "peaceful" assembly? At the same time, why are we willing to give them a podium to speak their minds while our former President called for Osama Bin Laden's head ("wanted dead or alive")? Similar to previous findings, participants in the study generally failed to recognize the structural components of racism.[8] Meanwhile, respondents are overwhelmingly convinced that anyone is capable of racism in U.S. society. Despite their little knowledge of white supremacist groups, respondents are largely ambivalent when white racism occurs around them, whether on campus, in the workplace, etc., suggesting that their ambivalence comes close to outright acceptance of this behavior and thinking.

White supremacists and their organizations are terrorists. Worse, too often whites in the sample come to their defense in the name of free speech. Despite their reported repugnance for these individuals and desire to see them disappear, respondents claim there is nothing that can be done to stop their activities, due to their poor conception of "racism." Whites appear willing to defend the rights of white supremacists, even when those rights do not exist in legal reality. For example, George believed their actions are horrible but there is nothing we can do to stop them:

> Um, as far as white supremacists, it's a problem but you can't really deal with it because of like the basic freedom of speech or whatnot as long as uh (.) but as far as sociologically or towards the society, it can like (.) cause problems and sentiments in the people who've been affected by them in the past, like uh people had like (.) uh, great grandparents who'd been lynched or anything like that

In his remarks, note how George limits their significance to the past, and spoke of their impact on society in an abstract way, which highlights the insulation whites have from the horrors experienced by black Americans. He speaks of "great grandparents who'd been lynched." How would the siblings of James Byrd Jr. respond to such an uninformed statement?

This line of discourse continued throughout many of the interviews. It is interesting that probably the most essentialist of all respondents, Amy, claims that these groups, "if they're still around, they should be shot, they don't deserve to have an organization like that, it shouldn't be legal." Jane also spoke in this vein:

> Um, I think white supremacists are a serious problem because (.) um, to think you're better than someone else just because of the way you look it's (.) definitely not right um I mean there's not really anything you can- I mean, you can try and get rid of them but (.) they have freedom of speech so you can still uh (.)

Some respondents even joked about the seriousness of white supremacists. Troy, for instance, said the following:

> You gotta stick by the first amendment but (.) really, ev(h)en though they're pretty ridiculous (laughs) you know, as long as they're not really acting out on, you know hurting anybody, you know I'd just- you know, I'd let people say whatever they want (.) you know, as long as they're not breaking any laws

The ambivalence almost trivializes white supremacy, and hence the violence they commit against nonwhite Americans.

In Jane's response to my query on how to best deal with white supremacists and their organizations, she equates them to political parties in debates:

> R: Um (2.0) I don't know. You can't take away their freedom of speech but (.) like even at um like a Presidential Election like when they would in the debates between Bush and Kerry like I'm pretty sure like (.) they would allow people who didn't support Bush to still come but they had a designated area I think
> I: Mm
> R: You can't stifle like freedom of speech you can't even if it is wrong to think that I mean I don't know what you'd do to get rid of it entirely but I mean I guess if you allow them their designated time when to speak (.) only a certain amount of time or a certain place then it might like (.) they still be happy 'cause not- no one's ever gonna be happy like, both sides are not going to be happy, so (.)
> I: Right.
> R: But uh I guess going through the government and passing laws to like prohibit racial inequality and laws like not allowing permits to go through would be good way to stop that.

Although she offers methods to limit white supremacist activities, she misses the point that the Klan in Illinois was granted a demonstration permit. Due to respondents' atomistic view of racism, they view groups like the Klan and the

Nation of Islam as "supremacy" groups, though the latter has never systematically killed white people, raped white women, or destroyed white property. By using this false antithesis, they can claim everyone deserves a right to speak and should be given time at the podium, just as the representatives of the corporate political parties have in Presidential debates.

Ignore Black Freedoms

In addition to leveling the speech of white supremacists to other opinions in society, a few respondents take it a step further: they questioned the ability of black Americans to voice their opinions. I found it interesting how these respondents appear more willing to defend the rights of white supremacists than those of black Americans.

I conducted most of the interviews following the natural disaster (and human fiasco) of Hurricane Katrina. During a telethon to raise money for victims, entertainer Kanye West was visibly shaken and, apparently refusing to read the cue cards, said "George Bush doesn't care about black people." At times during the interviews this issue came up. For example, Penelope responded to West's comments this way:

I: Did you hear Kayne West's comments?
R: Yeah.
I: Like what did you think of that when he said that about George=
R: =Well, I am anti-Bu(h)sh, so(h): I guess I have bias towards that, but at the same time, I don't think he had a right to say that.

Why would she feel he had no right to state his own opinion, regardless of the validity of his statements?

Meanwhile, in Jane's response, she makes the connection between supremacist speech or supremacy and West's comments:

R: I don't know if you watch the uh hurricane relief and Kayne West said 'George Bush hates black people' which
I: Mm
R: I mean (.) that's entirely not true you know I don't know maybe there are certain other advantages for white people but the fact that you can't just go out, you can go out and say that he hates [black people] definitely not, you know
I: Right
R: In the right context. So um (.) I think anybody can be racist in American society because (.) um (.) I don't know, I think it has a lot to do with how you were raised and your experiences in life because if you're a child you're not going to know what to expect, you're only going to know what someone told you.

In the above passage, Jane weaves her response to the white supremacy statement with West's comment on Bush, thus suggesting that his comments relate to
something supremacist. This is an utterly false comparison because no black
organizations or individuals have ever been part of or affiliated with the systematic killing and raping of white people. Despite the fact that earlier in her statement she supported the need to protect the speech of white supremacists (considering they are responsible for much more than hate speech), here she appears
unwilling to protect Kanye West's own right to speech.

Cynthia also addresses the issue of West's comments and the debacle of
Katrina:

> R: I don't know, I just thought that was a general uh very general comment, I
> mean even though it was his opinion, um (.) it kind of was taken as that's what
> all black people think, but um (.) you know, that the government really doesn't
> take into consideration their needs, which I think um the government definitely
> does, but maybe not to an extent where it should, in terms of just like welfare,
> and work, the majority of (.) minorities and such um and different races other
> than whites um [are]
> I: If Katrina had hit Miami or Tampa, do you think the response would have
> been different?
> R: Um, I don't know how much of a factor, but I mean, I think race is definitely
> factored into there (.) but in terms of say if it were to hit [a predominantly white
> area] um (.) we tend to vote more in elections, and where Katrina hit, it's more
> of the poorer people and people who don't vote, and I mean so in my opinion I
> think the government wasn't as responsive? But I also do th- just because of
> that factor that it's kind of forgotten about? But I think that race is definitely a
> part in that? just because you look at the voting statistics like whites are more
> (.) vote more, you know, and blacks uh they don't, and it would be (.) you
> would've responded more quickly and effectively if say it more (unintelligible;
> laughs)

Cynthia's statement "it kind of was taken as that's what all black people think"
has a lot of discursive work going on, including the diminutive "kind of" to soften the blow of a potentially controversial statement, and use of the passive
voice "was taken" to hide the subject when making the claim that all blacks
thought the same as what West had said. Although she initially tries to distance
herself from this statement, she then provides "evidence" to back up her claim,
such as suggesting that blacks and other Americans of color make up the majority of welfare recipients, a common misconception within the white mind.

Cynthia presents a critical contradiction to understanding race and power in
U.S. society: first, she implicitly condemns West for making a "very general
comment" (despite the fact that it was directed at a specific individual). Then,
she ambiguously (through her usage of the passive voice) criticizes his comments because (white) people took them as representative of the thoughts of all
black Americans. Thus, she places the blame on West for white generalizations
of black people and their attitudes. Even worse, she rationalizes the ethnic
cleansing of New Orleans with the excuse that black Americans do not vote as

regularly as whites do. Finally, Cynthia presents another image of the racial Other (and thus of the lily white): that they are less likely to vote. She rationalizes this as justification for why blacks get less assistance from the government to address their concerns, while failing to offer reasons for voting less often (e.g., state laws that bar convicted felons from voting). I believe that an image of less voting is linked to an image of being less responsible than white Americans.

Enjoying Racist Jokes

In addition to downplaying the significance of white supremacy and protecting the speech of white supremacists, respondents also report enjoyment in listening to, and actively engaging in, racist joking. In this section, I examine the way whites in the sample respond to the social phenomenon of racist joking. First, I present the indifference many respondents report to the jokes they encounter. Second, I examine their involvement in joking, both indirect and direct involvement.

Indifference towards Joking

When responding to the statement "I can recall a conversation in which someone told a racist joke," most respondents project ambivalence towards the jokes. They did this in three important ways: first, there was passivity towards the jokes because the jokes did not personally insult them. Second, I focus on the responses primarily from Jewish respondents in their articulation of the notion that a certain line should not be crossed (a repertoire that did not exist nearly to the extent for other respondents, due to Jewish Americans' status as honorary or borderline whites). Third, I examine the ways in which respondents minimized the significance of racist jokes, even blaming blacks and other nonwhite Americans for being hypersensitive.

Passivity towards Racist Jokes

Some respondents dismiss racist jokes as silly nonsense, and no harm done. For example, Nadine says that, upon hearing a racist joke, she quirks "I think it's funny, you know (.) I don't join in, but I don't necessarily stop it." Quilla spoke of a friend of her father's racist joking and her response to them:

R: Yeah, one of my friend's dads tells a lot of racist jokes?
I: Oh, really?
R: Yeah. Uhm (.)
I: Like when, like or where like would he=

R: He'll tell them to her, and then like she'll tell us, and then whenever I went down to her house, uhm it was just me and her family and she was like 'oh, oh tell us some more of your jokes' ((mocking tone)) and (.) I don't know, like I wasn't personally offended? But I can't imagine like I was just kind of like 'why are you telling this?' you know what I mean=it's not like it was like offensive towards me, but I still didn't understand the point of it really, I don't know.

As a result of her mocking tone, it appears as if she disapproved of the racist joking, but then casts ambivalence. Furthermore, since the joke did not offend her personally, she did not see it as a problem.

Some Lines Shouldn't Be Crossed

Responses to recalling a situation in which someone told a racist joke was particularly interesting for those of the Jewish respondents in the sample. They generally argued that, similar to the other respondents, are ambivalent or even enjoy racist jokes, at least in the "right" context. What makes the Jewish participants' responses unique from the others is that they are more likely to be a target of the jokes. This gives them a better understanding of the harm racist jokes cause. For example, Penelope responds this way:

They happen all the time, you know, and they're always premised by 'okay, I'm not racist, but this is just a joke' (said in a mocking tone) and like uhm (.) you know, well you take it, like there's Jewish jokes, and I think they're funny, but uhm (.) the serious racist joke, like really [cracking light?] like somewhere where I heard them say something, and they thought it was hilarious, and I was just like 'are you disgusting?' I can't really re- (1.0) I don't really like know where- like I said, I would probably not associate myself with someone like that, so (.)"

Unfortunately for Penelope and other nonwhites (or honorary whites), sometimes you have no choice but to associate with "someone like that."

However, there were some Jewish respondents who did report an enjoyment or ambivalence of racist joking. For example, Amy replies this way:

The racist jokes? My husband tells them all the time, they're very funny. They're also very mean, but just as he can tell jokes about black people, like I'll tell jokes about Jewish people and I'm Jewish, and I can laugh at it, it's funny, like it's just a joke, it's based on history, it's based on people's reputations, and it's not saying everybody's like that, it's just how people are labeled, and that's just the way that it is.

She seems to naturalize the phenomenon when she says "that's just the way that it is." Meanwhile, Zachary takes this a step further:

R: Yes, I've heard a million racist jokes, and I've laughed at them, you know like um they don't bother me, I think a joke is a joke

I: Right. What about Jewish jokes? Like 'cause I've had some respondents talk about Jewish jokes that=
R: They don't bother me at all. I think that (.) I think a joke is a joke. And if you don't have fun in life and you're not smiling and laughing, I think you have a serious problem=if you can't joke about yourself, I think you have a real issue, and people make, you know, jokes

It is important to note that the status of Jewish Americans as honorary whites makes jokes less effective in causing harm than for nonwhites. This can be linked to other nonwhite-turned-white groups like the Irish, such as *Saturday Night Live* skits in which Senator John McCain, Conan O'Brien and others poke fun at Irish heritage and stereotypes of the Irish drunk. The images of the Irish drunk or Italian mobster are almost "cool" these days. Also note Zachary's total lack of empathy and understanding of the onslaught of "harmless jokes" towards nonwhites.

However, Zachary does add a wrinkle to the mix when he adds "I think there's a line that you can cross, to make it extreme, but I think you have to know your audience when it comes to a joke." So although he says that people are too sensitive when it comes to racist jokes, he does suggest that there is a line that should not crossed; e.g., that the joke not be too extreme. Harriet responds this way:

R: I can recall a situation when someone told a racist joke. I kno- my friends say them all the time, but they're not serious about 'em
I: Mhm.
R: It'll just be like (.) against like (.) Jewish people or whatever
I: Oh.
R: And I have friends that are Jewish that joke around about it too (1.0) so it's ea- it's not really (.) getting too serious
I: Right.
R: And like if I hear "oh, that's awful," and sometimes it's like it's funny but not funny you know?
I: No.
R: I don't kno(h)w. It's funny when it's [a] really bad joke
I: Yeah
R: I guess
I: You were saying before about like you know joke telling um (.) like if you were in a situation in which somebody told a racist joke, say at a family reunion or something, and how would you react in that situation?
R: I think just depending on the degree of the joke (.) a lot of times. Sometimes like (.) the Jewish jokes are really bad and I just don't think that they're- I'll go "that's not funny."
I: Yeah.
R: But if it's a joke that's not (.) that bad that doesn't offend like the opposite like other people (.) I know like in *Guess Who?*
I: Mm mhm

R: Like Ashton Kutcher's telling like a bunch of jokes and then he says one
joke and takes it too far.

I: Oh

R: I think in that case, 'cause like at first they were all laughing and stuff you
know at the jokes

I: Right.

R: And then he said one that was just like really bad.

I: Do you recall what it was 'cause I haven't seen that yet.

R: Oh you haven't seen it?

I: I saw the original, like the old one.

R: Right.

I: Um, I haven't seen the new one.

R: I can't remember what the jokes were, but the ones he told first you know
were just were a few words and you know everyone was laughing about it but
then I can't remember what it was but it was one that was like

I: Like Bernie Mac's family was there?

R: Yeah, Bernie Mac's family was there. And Ashton Kutcher was the only
white guy there. And they were laughing about it at first and then (.) he took it
too far.

I: Oh. And just suddenly everybody got quiet and

R: Yeah, exactly. And there was like, Bernie Mac got like really mad and

I: Oh (.) yeah.

R: I think there's like a degree to the jokes.

In this exchange, Harriet includes the ambiguous statement that sometimes jokes
are funny and not funny. She then inserts an appeal to the recipient, and I delivered a rare rejection to that appeal, in which she responded "I don't kno(h)w. It's
funny when it's [a] really bad joke." Although her latter statement is even more
ambiguous, this serves as an instance of an interviewer's role in producing discourse, in which she made a statement and then seemed to back off when I failed
to agree or understand the interlocutionary force of her utterance.[9] Like Zachary,
she argues that there is a line that should not be crossed when making these
jokes, although she is ambiguous on what that line is (e.g., it is interesting how
she recalled a specific joke from the film and then chose not to say it).

Minimizing the Impact of Racist Jokes

In addition to suggesting that jokes should not get out of hand, respondents also
minimize the impact of such joking. As presented in prior chapters, whites in
this sample have a knack for placing the onus on black Americans for racial
problems, while deflecting any responsibility for those problems. When discussing racist joking, many respondents reduce the joking to something irrational or
silly and considered complaints by blacks as being overly sensitive and unnecessary.

For instance, similar to Odella's blame of the effigy incident on "good ole
southern boys," Linda also blamed the occurrence of racist joking on growing
up in the South:

I think a big part of it is 'cause I've always lived in [state] in the south and people here they're like (1.0) I guess their parents will be kind of like racist and they just wanna be like that too=and a lot of people seem like they just want to come across to others like they're funny because they're making fun of like other races you know like (.) I don't know. It just doesn't seem like they're (.) especially like, like when I was younger like in middle school and stuff they didn't (.) it didn't even seem like they knew what they were talking about a lot of times like looking back, I don't see how (.) I don't know.

In this passage, Linda exercises one method of minimizing racism by claiming ignorance of the orator to racist beliefs that manufacture the jokes. She defends their racist joking as innocent youngsters who did not know any better.

Often whites associate racism with childlike, mentally challenged, or pathological behavior. Later in the interview, Linda provides an experience in which a black coworker was hurt by comments made by a camp resident:

R: Okay. Actually, I can think of one=like I was talking about my like coworker at camp who I sat with at meals and one of the sessions like there was a girl with Down syndrome there and she just like (1.0) she didn't know what she was saying a lot of times and like (.) but like my friend didn't really- she was really sensitive to like (.) racist comments and like (.) she said something to her about her being black I don't even remember what she said but
I: Mhm.
R: Like my friend was like (.) really like (.) torn up over it and like talking about it at dinner and just like really mad like she wasn- it, I would have dealt with it better if she had just been upset over it like sad but she's like mad about it but like (.) I wasn't gonna (.) like I didn't wanna make her believe that it was right to like be mad at the girl with Down syndrome just because she didn't really know what she was saying you know like
I: Mhm.
R: She wasn't even trying to be rac- I just didn't know how to deal with it. Was that the kind of situation you were talking about?
I: Yeah. Well like um were there other leaders there besides you and the one black woman?
R: Mm mhm. Oh, she told several people about it and like there are other counselors there like (.) when the girl had said it but (.)
I: Like how did they react to it?
R: They like (.) uh it felt like a lot of them to her face were like 'yeah it was'- I mean it was wrong of the camper to do that but she didn't know that and a lot of people would like comfort her and like try to make her feel better about it and that's pretty much what I did I mean I didn't really know how to deal with it. 'Cause like part of like your job out there is to like make sure like (.) you're not supposed to get mad at the campers you know, like (.) it's just kind of like torn between like what we're supposed to do and like (.) being a friend to her and stuff

When reading this passage, I think of Jack Nicholson's character in *As Good As It Gets*, in which a man with obsessive-compulsive disorder makes racist comments about blacks and Jews, and how the message from the film is that racism is a product of sick thinking, something pathological. Here, Linda believes her coworker overreacted to the comments made by the resident with Down syndrome. Meanwhile, she fails to recite what had been said, suggesting that the comments were insignificant. Furthermore, she implicitly blames her coworker for putting her in a difficult position: on one hand, she has a job to do, making the case for formal rationality; and on the other, she is "being a friend to her and stuff." It sounds like her "friendship" was for purely superficial purposes.

Thus, respondents place the onus on blacks for being oversensitive. Poor whites, who mean no harm when making these jokes, think they must walk on eggshells around blacks due to their hypersensitivity, while failing to reflect on the impact of the jokes on those targeted. For example, Jane speaks of living with her black resident assistant in the dorms:

> R: Um, I actually live with an R.A. and she's black, and it's my first semester but sometimes we joke around about rap music and stuff=there's never been really like tension but you kind of don't want to step on anybody's toes if you say something or if you joke around about stuff [you have to be careful
> I: [Sure. Like what kinds of things might you or your R.A. joke around about?
> R: Just like stuff on like=say we're watching something on t.v. like
> I: Yeah
> R: And my friends think it's funny and then she might just be like 'oh, well why is that funny to you?' you know, so (.)

Thus, the joking itself is not a bad thing, just the context in which you tell the joke.

Besides blaming blacks or other nonwhites for being hypersensitive, members of the sample also defend fellow whites that deliver racist jokes and "get caught" due to slippage, or the situation in which a white person tells a racist joke and fails to realize that a member of the targeted group is within earshot of the utterance.[10] In such a situation, Ursela spoke of an occurrence involving her father:

> R: Dad told a racist joke (.) involving like Hispanic people, and he didn't know that like one of the people there was like part Hispanic or something, and like I knew? So I just sort of like looked at the guy? Just to see his reaction? Like (.) you know, and he just sort of (.) laughed it off, because my dad was his boss or whatever (.) um, I don't know if I said anything to my dad after the fact, but I probably should of (.)
> I: It was a kind of wisecrack or something?
> R: It was just like a joke, like a little (.) like "a Mexican walks into a bar" or something like that (.) I don't remember the joke exactly, it's just something like that=like it wasn't really, it wasn't really, really mean? I mean, if somebody had told me a white joke in front of me, I really wouldn't care, but (.)

that's because I'm white and I feel like the experiences in my life (.) that being said like I don't know, it wouldn't bother me for that reason, just because I've always had the upper hand in society, you know, in a way.

First, Ursela neglects the important role of power in this exchange, in which the "part Hispanic or something" male was in a subordinate position to her father, and thus could not respond to the joke, although she did interpret the situation as such. She then minimizes the significance of the joke, with the use of diminutives ("It was just like a joke, like a little..."), while using the familiar tool of forgetting the content of the joke itself. It is almost funny (yet sad) in her "it wasn't really, really mean?" remark, in her minimization attempt. Finally, by saying that antiwhite jokes would not bother her, she thus blames nonwhite Americans for their hypersensitivity. Despite her ability to recognize her own privileged position in society, yet she cannot connect the dots and realize how antiwhite jokes (like objectifying male bodies) lack the consequences that antiblack or anti-Other jokes (or objectifying female bodies) have.

Involvement in Joking

In addition to downplaying the significance of racist jokes, some respondents even speak of their own involvement in joking. In this section, I first present how a few respondents spoke of the fun they have with joking, and even the pride they take in telling racist jokes. Moreover, respondents communicate how they and their friends feel it necessary to tell jokes in more covert settings. I present evidence that the "new racism" is going to blossom via the Internet. Lastly, I examine the inability of whites to speak out against the practice, despite their objections. They ultimately are involved in the joking, since silence is acceptance.

"They Are Hilarious"

A few respondents speak of the fun they had when sharing racist jokes with friends. For example, Casey goes as far as to express pride in sharing jokes with his black friend:

> R: Ye(h)ah, I can recall, I've told racist jokes before.
> I: Oh yeah?
> R: Yeah↑ My friend
> I: Oh↓
> R: We ca- we can joke about it, that's the cool thing, that we can joke about it, like, some people can't↑

Here, Casey almost seems proud that he has the privilege of telling racist jokes within earshot of a black person who does not mind (or so he thinks).

This repertoire was more prevalent among the males of the sample; for instance, Vincent tells of sharing jokes with his friends:

> Like I've a couple of black friends that have grea:t white people jokes, they are hilarious. We laugh all the time at 'em. I mean they're great, and they laugh at our black jokes and it's all in good fun, and we know that, but we try and make sure that we're not in [campus area] you know, like boasting them out, because we're probably gonna get beaten for that, like unless you're in a closed area with just our friends, we know what's going on, so yeah.

In this passage, Vincent contradicts himself when he frames the joke telling as one big multiracial event, but then adds that he and his friends cannot say such things on campus for fear of physical harm. Both Casey and Vincent seem to think that if only blacks understand that the jokes are not meant to be taken seriously, then we could get along. It seems as if they wish this kind of world could exist.

In the next statement, Cynthia places the onus of blacks as racist joke-tellers with her example of black comedians, in which "they target (.) some people take it as derogatory and offensive, and you know, it could be in all, all in fun, too, so it depends on how you take it, but (.)," and she does not bother to complete the semantic move. She also did not state who black comedians target in their jokes. This suggests the absurdity of how these respondents see antiwhite jokes on par with antiblack jokes. Despite the similar content, the form of the jokes is much different.

Covert Joking

Although there were a couple of respondents who speak of taking pride in racist joking, more common was the practice of speaking within "safe" social settings, usually in backstage domains.[11] Another instance of slippage takes place with Angie in her dormitory:

> R: I know that we like joke about it sometimes
> I: Mm
> R: Like one of the guys on my floor last week was Chinese
> I: Mm
> R: And before he got there the other three guys were just kind of [telling a joke] and they told him about it and he thought it was hilarious, so
> I: Can you recall like the specific joke?
> R: Yeah it was uh they were ta(h)lking about, 'cause he was Chinese like, making Chinese food out of him
> I: Oh↓
> R: And (.) they were saying it like all the time and he was the last person to get there and I was like 'you guys are gonna slip up and say it in front of him, and I'm not sure how he's gonna take it' but he laughed, he thought it was funny.
> I: Like they were gonna make Chinese food out of him?
> R: Yeah, like, put him in the freezer! ((laughs))
> I: Oh, okay.

R: ((laughs))
I: Huh (3.0)

Although Angie is not the initiator of this particular joke, she does begin the statement "we like joke about it sometimes," so there was no distancing between herself and the others there. She does, however, act as a kind of lookout for the group (apparently all males), providing an intruder alert.[11] Hence, she was an active participant in this racist joking, though perhaps due to gender, assumed the role of a lookout (caregiver) for the joke-tellers. She also made it sound as if the "Chinese" man thought the joke was funny, too, suggesting the complete lack of reflection on their part.

Vincent is the most candid about racist jokes when he says that he engages in them "when the race you're talking about is not around. That is the situation which I've heard many of them, and believe me, my friends and I, we've got all of them." Nowhere is it easier to avoid slippage and intruders than sharing jokes (and other supremacist materials) on the Internet. Troy provides insight into the primary vehicle for the new white supremacy movement, where whites speak openly without the restraints of impression management:

R: I hear hea(h)r them all the time (laughs).
I: Yeah?
R: (laughs) Yeah. Pretty much.
I: Where are the common situations you tend to hear them in?
R: Mostly↑ you hear in: situations were people don't know in situations where people don't know who's saying it, and that would be like on an internet discussion board
I: Oh, wow mhm.
R: You know, one of the ones I go to for uh you know, it's for like weight lifting and all that, power lifting and all (.) uh, they have a conversation lounge, where people could just go off on anything and
I: Right.
R: Basically, there's a group of people um not that they don't want to invit-you'll just say stuff to piss people off, and get a reaction out of people, so (.) you know, we hear stuff like that all the time in there, of course you know it's (.) it goes back [and] forth
I: Yeah.
R: It's pretty funny in the end, but some people get really riled up over something they read on the internet it's just (.) empty-faced writing on the screen but (.) um I'll admit to having some fun with that, you know (.) just, you know (.) randomly pissing off some people (laugh) that's just something I like to do for some reason, I don't know it's just I always found it weird because it takes a whole lot to you know get a rise out of me
I: (laughs)
R: If he said something bad about me on the Internet, you know, makes a little joke I'm just like 'alright, whatever,' but some people just go off on these rants and they're pretty funny, they just (.) keep pushin' their buttons and playing with them and (.) so, you now a lot of times you know somebody started a

thread on a- pushed a racist joke to you and there's pages and pages of 'em, for every kind of racial group, too black white Asian whatever, (laughs) I don't know (.) as long as it's used in the right context, if you're not like (.) you know, if you're just joking around like (.) you know, the- some of the places I work there are black bouncers, and we joke back and forth like, you know, with each other about black and white stuff, as long as there's no real (.) you know, malcontent based behind it, then I could see a proper time just to joke around and whatever.

In Troy's statements, he dismisses the racist comments as mere "empty-faced writing on the screen," and almost mocks people who express their disapproval of such comments. Like other examples in this chapter, he argues that jokes are all right in certain contexts, and attempts to support his claim with sharing jokes with fellow black coworkers (like Casey and Vincent).

Fear of Expressing Disapproval

Sometimes respondents do object to fellow whites who crossed the line with their jokes, as well as the joking in general, but fail to speak up in defiance of the joke telling. Sometimes they even question why they do not speak up. Nonetheless, members of the sample usually defend fellow whites, dismissing their behavior as trivial, and minimizing the significance of racist jokes.

For example, when recalling a situation involving race in which he had to make a decision, Frank speaks of the regarding the racist joke telling of her sister's boyfriend, despite his own omission of doing some joke telling himself:

R: I don't know if I can think of a (.) strong situation involving race but, try to think of a specific one (4.0) um (1.0) I mean I guess (1.0) I mean more generally just being (.) um having mostly white friends I mean I guess that that situation does come up because you know a lot of white people are very are, well not very, but are racist but (.) it's hard when you get people around you that are all, they all have the same views but at the same time like (.) I wouldn't want to you know just sit there and agree with them about (.) like racist things
I: True
R: I mean I'm sure of being things caused me to (.) you know like (.) tell a few racist jokes or like (.) do things that I shouldn't (.) say like that, but um (1.0) I can't think of a situation.
I: Um how would you respond to a parent of yours or a friend or somebody, like do you have any brothers or sisters? Like in this case like a white person or (.) it could be anybody, you know, as far as making a racist joke, like how would you respond, do you think, to that?
R: Um (1.0) like, I guess the one example would be like my sister, she lives with her boyfriend but uh I mean he's definitely a little more like (.) like racist than me and, though I wouldn't say I'm racist but he's definitely a little bit racist but uh he'll tell racist jokes sometimes and I don't really know what to say I mean, I don't know if I would say like, tell him not to say that but like I definitely don't uh (.) like egg him on or feed the situation at all 'cause I don't think, I mean I think that's pretty bad but (.) uh, I guess um (.)

Although he admits to his own joking, he apparently thinks his sister's boyfriend takes the joking too far. Does he ever imagine how other people see him when he tells his racist jokes?

As I alluded to in the previous section, gender appears to be a factor in the phenomenon of racist joke telling. Women in my sample report more feelings of conflict with the racist jokes, though they often do not act, while defending the jokers. For example, Xena recalls instances in which she knew nonwhites present felt uncomfortable:

> Um, like definitely I think the racist jokes, like (.) it's (.) people think it's a big deal, even like=I've even had friends say jokes you know around my other friends that are racial, and they like laughed at it, and I'm sure they felt uncomfortable, and you know deep down I was thinking 'that's not right,' but I didn't really voice my opinion on it, or say anything, just because like I really didn't want to start something, you know 'cause I don't know, it's just something, it's like hard to talk about when you're not the one=you know? When you're not the one it's against, but (.)

Xena rationalizes her inaction for not being the target of the joke. Yet, when blacks are the target of the joke and speak up about it, they are labeled as hypersensitive. Meanwhile, Odella recalls joke telling at her high school in which the effigy took place:

> R: Just like at school, at lunch, the guys would usually laugh and the girls would usually (.) you know, "that's so stupid"
> I: Yeah, why do you think that happens, where it seems like people will say that a lot where guys will (.) like a lot of times like the perpetrator, you know, like the person who says the joke usually in a situation is male, and like the other guys laugh, and like the girls are kind of quiet, or even if someone is a little more straight-forward and says like 'that's wrong' or whatever, li(h)ke why(h) do you think that happens where it's like that?
> R: Well, I think in this situation this person told a racist joke, but I don- he's not racist, and I think the girls kind of tell him 'no, that's wrong,' just because they feel like that's what they have to do, and the guys realize that he's not a racist, and that it was just like a joke, so they (.)
> I: Hmm. And that was at your high school?
> R: Yeah.
> I: How often do you think that would happen where guys told racist jokes?
> R: Not very often.

Despite her experiences both with the effigy and the joke telling at her high school, she does not think that white supremacy is a problem. Moreover, she initially speaks generally of this behavior of the white boys, but finishes her statements that these incidents did not happen very often. She evades my question of gender difference in racist behavior and instead defends the joke-teller and minimizes the joke's importance.

Summary

In this chapter, I examined the contradictions within the sample's discourse as they discussed white supremacists and their activities. I presented evidence in which these whites constructed ambivalence through a process involving the color-blind tenant of equating race with racism, naturalizing race supremacy, and considering anyone capable of racism. Ambivalence is a construction, not a condition. This process aids them in their ability to dismiss white supremacists while maintaining face. Respondents go out of their way to deny any existence white supremacist activities, and the need to address the issue. Furthermore, their ambivalence gives them leverage to protect white supremacist speech, that it is legally protected (even when it is not), harmless, and trivial. They appear more willing to protect the speech of neo-Nazis and Klansmen than ordinary black Americans. Similarly, they see no problem with racist jokes, unless black folks are within earshot of the jokes. Additionally, they label nonwhites as hypersensitive when they complain about them. Despite the gender differences in the role taking of racist joking, most whites in the sample either actively engaged in racist joking or refused to object to the joking. This evidence highlights the retrogression we find ourselves in today's society: a young, white population that is ambivalent towards white supremacy and a willingness to defend their rights of speech and organization.

Notes

1. In fact, there are probably at least a few Clinton haters out there who still believe that they killed Vincent Foster!

2. Explanations offered for the media attention given to the birthers vary, including the incessant drive of corporate news media outlets for ratings, sensationalist tendencies (often used to push ratings up), or a desire for Obama supporters to keep it in the news. For an example of the latter, see Alex Koppleman, "The Boy Who Cried Birther," *The New Yorker*, May 24, 2012. Available online at www.newyorker.com/online/blogs/newsdesk/2012/05/bennett.birther.html (accessed July 13, 2012).

3. This point was inspired by John Isbister's comparison between modernization and dependency theories' divergent perspectives on the concept of "development." He wrote that "To the modernization theorists, underdevelopment is a state or condition; for most of them, it is synonymous with tradition. To those in the dependency school, however, the underdevelopment is a process. Underdevelopment is not just a failure to develop, it is an active process of impoverishment." John Isbister, *Promises Not Kept: Poverty and the Betrayal of Third World Development*, 6th ed. (Bloomfield, CT: Kumarian Press, 2003), 42.

4. This man appeared on the television program *Politically Incorrect with Bill Maher* back in the 1990s; unfortunately I could not find his name.

5. This point was made by George Gerbner in the film *The Killing Screens: Media and the Culture of Violence* (Media Education Foundation, 1997).

6. The name of the video game is "Border Patrol," a browser-based game first appearing in 2002. The CNN story aired April 26, 2006, entitled "'Border Control' Game Outrages Activists," and the transcript is available online at transcript@transcripts.cnn.com/TRANSCRIPTS/0604/26/lol.03.html (accessed July 13, 2012).

7. The reference to someone yelling "Fire!" in a crowded theater when she or he knows a fire does not exist is from Justice Oliver Wendell Holmes, Jr.'s opinion in the Supreme Court case *Schenck vs. United States* (1919).

8. Bonilla-Silva, *White Supremacy*.

9. Hak, "Interviewer Laughter as an Unspecified Request for Clarification."

10. Picca and Feagin, *Two-Faced Racism*, 96-100.

11. Picca and Feagin, *Two-Faced Racism*, 178-181.

Chapter 6
Antiracism in Progress

So far in this book, I have documented how young white Americans (or at least a sample of them) seemingly contradict the notion that Americans of their type are more open-minded on matters of race and less supportive of discriminatory treatment of racial minorities. Such findings may leave readers cold, even including some sociologists. So what exactly is going on: are white Americans increasingly opposed to racial prejudice and discrimination or not? After all that has happened in our country's history to bring about greater equality for all Americans irrespective of race, how could we still appear to be so far away from our ultimate goal?

Unfortunately these are the wrong questions to ask, for at least three reasons. First, race is embedded into our social system to such an extent that meaningful social change will likely take generations to move closer to a society characterized by racial justice and harmony, not oppression and division. Second, opposing prejudice and discrimination simply is not good enough; taking the actions necessary to end them is needed to bring about a truly "post-racial" society (i.e., that race does not matter in determining one's life chances). Finally, what exactly is "our" ultimate goal, anyway? A "post-racial" society is highly problematic since whiteness is defined as normal and raceless, so a society devoid of "race" seems to suggest doing away with racialized beings—namely, racial minorities.

Of course, with the exception of some overt white supremacists, no one is calling for the extermination of persons of color. However, as presented in previous chapters, white Americans generally wish to hear less from racial minorities and allow whites to maintain their privileged positions in society. But they often express these sentiments in a way that maintains face ("racism with a smile," so to speak). But it would be an incomplete analysis without the instances (albeit rare) in which study participants expressed antiracist views on various subjects we discussed during their interviews.

White Americans like John Brown, Harriet Beecher Stowe, Gloria Steinem, Tim Wise and others have played an important role in the movement for greater racial justice and equality in this country for generations. Their presence continues to be of great significance in that they provide credence for Americans of color by voicing their opposition to racial prejudice and discrimination. Unfortunately, however, antiracist whites have been, and continue to be, greatly outnumbered by whites who either actively defend white privilege and the social structures that create it, or who, regardless of intentions, fail to challenge that system that they benefit from. While there might not be any antiracists in this sample (yet), I argue that, given some time, patience, and hard work, there could be at least a few.

In this chapter, I present these rare gems in which agency overcomes structure (i.e., WRD), often based upon unique personal experiences that few white Americans have. I posit that these whites possess the potential for becoming active antiracists, something needed to continue the struggle for greater racial equality in U.S. society.

Moments of Antiracism

In this section, I present moments in which respondents break the mold of typical color-blind responses and break the "rules" of WRD. First, I provide instances in which a few study participants offer confessions or epiphanies surrounding some racial issue that could bring them on a road to antiracism. Then I offer several examples in which respondents cite experiences at work or at school that gave then valuable insights into the reality and consequences of racial domination and oppression. Finally, I show how several members of the sample were in a unique position to question white privilege and supremacy, whether due to ethnicity, sexual orientation, or residence, along with the unique experience of witnessing an act of discrimination.

Confessionals and Epiphanies

One rarity is when white Americans offer a *confession*, or admit to believing or doing something other (white) people would presumably disapprove of; namely, practice antiracism. Confessions are probably quite unlikely in frontstage performances than in more backstage settings (such as writing autobiographical accounts[1]), given the possible fear of being criticized for their candor. In this study, I did not know the participants prior to the interviews, so there was no established rapport with respondents. In fact, the following passage from Casey is the *only* explicit example I could find of a confession among the respondents. After expressing anger towards those who disapprove of interracial marriages, I then shifted the discussion to the ABZ Hybrid question:

I: Do you think that still goes on with a, you know, as far as like, you know, employers like, like

R: Oh, ↑heck yeah. ↑Heck ya. Yeah.

I: Well, I mean like the idea that you know it- you have like one candidate you know and another candidate an-

R: It's gonna continue to go on.

I: Yeah.

R: (2.0) I mean heck, I mean, it would probably apply to me too I'd probably (.) I mean I can't [lie.   So

I: [Yeah.   How do you think we can deal with it? I mean, do you think (.) we're (.) dealing with it, like in a good way now already, or

R: ↑Umm

I: Is there more to do, less to do, like

R: I don't thin- I don't know that's the type of question, I don't know the solution, like luckily I can see past- like if, honestly, if someone came into an interview, like it probably would be a problem actually but I could past it and like, I wouldn't have a problem hiring a black person over a white person, that would not like phase me one second. Like () but (1.0) I'm just like lucki- like, blessed, I guess, too, like I don't know (1.0) some people say I'm an idiot probably for saying that, but I mean (1.0) I- u↑mm↓, I don't know how long it's gonna take to have a solution (or?) if there'll ever be one (1.0) it's gonna take some ((unintelligible)) to deal with th(h)at.

At the beginning of this exchange, it is a bit unclear at first exactly what Casey is referring to when he says "I mean...it would probably apply to me to I'd probably (.) I mean I can't lie," an instance in which perhaps the bridge from one subject matter to the next was too abrupt. Nonetheless, later on he makes perfectly clear that, unlike most respondents in the sample, he would have little trouble hiring a black candidate over a white one, and that doing so "would not like phase me one second." Furthermore, although he struggles to say so, he feels "lucky" and even "blessed" to be in such a position, while acknowledging that "some people" (I assume he refers to whites in particular here) would disapprove of saying such a thing. Also note his semantic move "some people say I'm an idiot probably for saying that, but I mean (1.0)," and he fails to complete the thought. This suggests how whites are defended (e.g., he does not actually specify that he is talking about white people) in WRD, even when a speaker is conveying an antiracist message.

In the next passage, Kaitlin also responds to the "angry" statement. Not as obvious of a confession as Casey's response (though perhaps a kind of semi-confession), she laments the ways some white Americans complain about immigrant laborers who try to make a living like anyone else:

R: Umm it makes me- this isn't really about like the other races=it's kind of about our race but

I: Mhm.

R: When people get angry about like (.) people of other races taking our jobs
and stuff like that
I: Mhm
R: Like if they live here it's (.) just as much their opportunity as it is ours (1.0)
and that bothers me 'cause like (.) they want the jo- they want them to have like
'cause they come and you know they like (.) do lawn work like (.) you know,
like they're not supposed to work here=I mean there's definitely illegal immigrants like workings in factories and stuff like that and (.) on farms and stuff
and as soon as like (.) economically like our like our government falls or something like that they get all pissed off and they're like "oh, they're taking our
jobs" but they would have never done it like even thought of doing those jobs
before (.) like that bothers me (.) when people do that.

In chapter 2, I presented the opening of this exchange in which Kaitlin appeared
to associate "race" with nonwhites. Without any prompting or prodding, she
chose to address this particular issue of "people" (i.e., whites) getting mad about
"people of other races" competing for jobs (certainly it is safe to assume she was
referring to white Americans because of her use of the possessive pronoun
"our"). As she rightly points out, the notion that these workers are taking away
job opportunities for white Americans is largely not the case.[2] Kaitlin argues that
all people in society should have the opportunity to earn a living, and that those
who complain about it are irrational for doing so.

Another interesting feature of this excerpt is that Kaitlin appears to explain
white opposition to "illegals" seeking work in the United States by utilizing the
frustration-aggression hypothesis, in that dominant group members scapegoat
racial minorities and/or immigrants for economic downturns or political problems ("our government falls or something like that").[3] Despite her lack of quality contacts with persons of color (as presented in chapters 1 and 2) and ignorance of white supremacist groups (appearing in chapter 5, with the "it's a
problem but it's not" semantic move), Kaitlin here appears to have developed a
rather sophisticated method of analysis of social phenomena, likely acquired
from her education. I cannot say that this appears totally out of the blue: in chapter 5, she perceived housing discrimination as totally irrational, saying "if they
have a good credit history like that's all you need to know." Unfortunately, she
(like so many others) perceives racism to be a product of irrational, even pathological, thinking.

Another rare occurrence in the discourse was that of the *epiphany*, or when
a respondent comes to the realization that things are not as they seem; or, specifically for this study, whites are *not* under attack from racial minorities (e.g., they
do not steal "our" jobs due to a quota) and the reality is oftentimes the opposite.
Sometimes when respondents had difficulties thinking of a situation involving
race, I talked about an incident I experienced while in high school that caused
me to reflect on my own subconscious fears of black men, an epiphany of my
own. One epiphany I came across in the responses came from Vincent when
discussing whether or not racism was increasing in U.S. society, with a particular focus on hiring discrimination:

I think so. I think it is on the decline because uh actually, um an experience is that my dad hires a lot of people (.) and I was curious one day when I was back home, I just went through his files and there was a lot of- I mean, there's a different variety of people in there, and actually the minority of the group were white people that he hired, and because what I found is that (.) 'cause my dad went to [university in the Midwest] so I mean yeah it's a Catholic white you know whatever, but that's not what he does, um there were two applicants in there, one was Mexican and the other one was a Cuban I think, and he was an illegal, but he has paperwork now on this stuff, so when I looked at their files and read their applications=my dad didn't see this, so, not supposed to be in there, but I was very impressed by him, I mean I went ahead and you know put my hand over what they were, and then read it off and I was like 'wow, that's pretty impressive (.) pretty interesting people,' and then I went to the two white people, and I was like (.) 'okay, I mean, they got the minimum, but'

Vincent reports that he did some "undercover" work by going through his father's notes without his permission, and compared various job applicants of different racial groups. Although he does not complete his semantic move to close this passage ("they got the minimum, but"), he makes clear that, as a result of his "research," minority job candidates for his father's business were *at least as qualified* as the white candidates, if not more (it is interesting that he did not quite bring himself to say it, however). Vincent provides evidence for why he was the only respondent of the sample to answer the ABZ Hybrid question that he would hire the black candidate (as presented in chapter 4).

Benefits of Quality Contacts

As Gordon Allport stipulated long ago, "quality" contacts are likely to decrease antiblack prejudice among white Americans. As others have pointed out, younger white Americans will have more contacts with people of color than their parents or grandparents did due to the changing racial landscape in U.S. society.[4] However, with Allport's original hypothesis in mind, the more pertinent question to ask concerning young whites today is the following: are their contacts merely superficial and fleeting, or are they informal, thoughtful, and lasting? As I presented in chapter 3, the majority of respondents reported few quality contacts with nonwhite Americans, experiencing mostly superficial interactions that would be unlikely to decrease antiblack or anti-Other prejudice, while perhaps even increasing contempt and hostility towards nonwhite Americans. However, there are a few exceptions. In this section, I present in detail how having such contact with people of color does at least have the potential to affect white attitudes towards nonwhite Americans. As we will see, however, this change may not happen right away; in fact, I should point out that compared to Frankenberg's sample of white women, most of whom were in there 30s or older,[5] perhaps at least a few of these whites could become increasingly antiracist as they get older.

The first example I present here is from Betty who, as I pointed out in chapter 3, was the only respondent to have had an ongoing intimate relationship with an African American. After living in a white bubble until she was 12 years old, she and her family moved to a large city in the Midwest, and attended a school she characterizes as "majority black." In the following excerpt, Betty discusses her time in the new school and the issue of interracial dating:

> I have never really thought about dating a black person before, it just never like crossed my mind, and uh for a while a lot of people thought I was a lesbian because a lot of like black men would show interest, but I- well, at that age you're not even interested in boys, or at least I wasn't, but um (.) like once you're-those are your friends and like (.) you don't even see color after a while, although yes, I did when I first got there, I was like 'it kinda sucks to be the minority,' but um it's not a problem, because they're not gonna treat you any differently, or at least that's what I've discovered, it's all based on how you carry yourself and how you treat other people

Betty recalls how she initially acknowledged race but over time got used to being around people of color. She argues that her age kept her from dating guys at the time, and insists that race was not a factor (while contradicting herself). In fact, note how she fails to complete the semantic move ("a lot of like black men would show interest, but"), perhaps a bit of face maintenance at the moment. Additionally, she asserts that she "discovered" that she could get along with her (predominantly black) peers, although at first she was skeptical. That skepticism could have come in part from her parents, whose mother upon learning about her first relationship with a black guy was "in shock, and then angry and mad," though interestingly Betty blamed her opposition to it on her drinking and opinions that had since changed. Meanwhile, recall in chapter 3 how her father persuaded her to take down pictures of her boyfriend so as not to upset her grandfather.

This transition to a predominantly nonwhite social setting did not come without some difficulties, though. In the next segment Betty talks about an experience while trying out for the cheerleading squad:

> R: The majority of everybody was black and the minority would be white and the middle in-between would be Hispanic or Mexican, majorly, and I was the only white girl, and the dancing was different, and it wasn't anything I had ever been exposed to necessicar- I mean, I'd seen it before, but I've never done it myself, and uh a lot of the moves were a little more sexier, racier, and um but it was really funny because I was wearing a cheerleading uniform on the day of the game-day, and I was um at my locker or something and a girl made a comment, I had a friend with me, and another girl made a comment about how it looked really wrong that I was wearing that uniform, and I said 'well, what do you mean by that?' and she's like 'well, white girls aren't meant to wear that uniform,' and I assumed she meant or at least not at this school, you know, and

my friend was instigating 'well, you should like say something back to her' or bitch her out or start a fight or something, but um like I said I'm not a big conflict person, and I thought it was really rude, and I got upset about it, and it hurt my feelings that anybody would say that because I- you know, if it's so wrong for me to have this spot on the team and me wearing this uniform, why didn't you go out for the spot? Like why weren't you here? Because we're all here because we show up to practices and whether we're good or not, we make the effort to do this, and like I don't see you here, and uh that really upset me, but as far as (.) I don't know, like she did say it because I was white, and uh it's definitely a difference when you're the minority, and you have black people discriminating against you, and it's like 'wow' you know, it's really weird to think that if a black person were to hang out with a group of black people, like white people would be not necessarily accepting, but they'd be a little more polite about it, and they would, they would you know try and include somebody, but if you were a white person going into a group of black people, you have to prove yourself apparently, and uh both groups neither one are more accepting than the other, but I guess at least in my situation, my opinions, like you have to prove yourself to them, you have to prove that you're cool, like that you can do what they can do just as well, but uh and it sucks! Because like if I brought you around my group of white friends they would never put you through like the kind of like not torture but the kind of like questioning and all the stuff that I would have to go through to hang out with their friends, and but it's so different in family situations though, because if it's a family and I'm going to my black friend's family's house and I'm meeting all of them, they're like the most warm and loving people, but if it's like a group of your peers, and you're in the minority, they want you to prove something, and whether they come right out and say it or not, they're always looking for you to prove yourself and for them to accept you ugh

I: Like what things would they want you to do to prove yourself?

R: Well, it's not so much specific things that you have to do like joining a fraternity or sorority, it's um more just like being there, like being there constantly, like you're not just there for like that one instance and then you're all of a sudden scared of everybody, it's more like sticking it out and like being willing to put up with a little bit of criticism and then after a while like you're accepted and you're asked to go out and hang out and go to the mall and ditch school, that would be the only thing that I could think of like that would make you- not necessarily cooler, but like you were more one of them, like it would be like you know skipping school and going out to lunch, and...then they don't even see color at that point, and hopefully they're a little more open-minded so the next white person that comes along

In this exchange, Betty felt hurt by another girl who had questioned her right to tryout for the squad, feeling as if she had been discriminated against. She then insists that a black person would never be put through the "torture" that she had been through as a white minority trying to fit in with blacks. Like the earlier excerpt, Betty emphasizes the significance of being in the minority, and unfortunately here fails to understand the pain and suffering experienced by nonwhites while attempting to get along in majority-white settings. Nonetheless, after time she "stuck it out" and found that her peers were willing to accept her. She then adds that hopefully others would not have to share the same painful experiences that she did.

This exchange perhaps shows where many young whites are in this society, and offers up a reason why there may be some guarded optimism for future race relations. Although there is a total absence of reflection on her part and lack of understanding why her black peers would be distrustful of her, she nonetheless appears to have learned a valuable lesson about the significance of integration and more specifically, beneficial contact. Growing pains hurt, and Betty discovered that at this school she attended. Sadly, too few whites "stick it out" and get past that barrier. What whites like Betty need to understand are the reasons for the initial distrust and even hostility directed at them by persons of color, including the numerous occasions of which white people came to neighborhoods of color offering "help" and instead gave them even greater misery and (at least in some cases) even death.[6]

As I mentioned earlier in the book, authority approval is a necessary prerequisite for beneficial interracial contact to occur. Perhaps the bar has been set too high by Allport; antiracist whites must do all they can to increase racial harmony and equality. In the next passage, Jane talks about overcoming parental disapproval of interracial friendships:

> In middle school, um a black girl [name] I used to hang out with her and there was never an issue with [my] being friends with (.) um a person of color because you know my parents, they're not racist, they just don't agree with certain things about dating and stuff. But they were fine about being friends with them, and there was never like (.) it was kind of concentrated [with] my dad because I didn't know what he would think, but you know part of me didn't really care so like 'this is my friend' and you know 'you don't have to like it.'

Although she initially defends her parents ("they're not racist"), she does (eventually) come around to saying that her father was opposed to her relationship with her black friend (though said with some uncertainty).

Later in the interview, I ask Jane about how her parents would react to her dating interracially:

> I: Like if you happened to (.) maybe you know bring home maybe (.) well, whether a black man or a Latino man you know and like 'yeah, this is my boyfriend,' like (.) how would your parents react to that?
> R: I think my mom would be more open than my dad would but I think at first (.) my dad would probably be like 'no way' you know, I mean but (.) a man like- they can't tell me who to date, and they (.) I think that even if they disagreed with it, they'd eventually accept it, whether they liked it or not (.) so I mean they'd have to get over that but I think a lot of the reason my dad is the way he is because of his dad, like his dad's like 'this is what's right, this is what's wrong,' so my dad is not as much like that but he's still like that

In this excerpt, she is much clearer in her father's disapproval of interracial relationships. As in the previous instance, she claims she would be undeterred by any parental disapproval about the hypothetical relationship. Despite the possibility that saying is one thing and actually doing is another, it does seem possible that ones thing can lead to another; in this case, that real friendships with blacks or other persons of color can lead to greater acceptance of such relationships, which in turn could lead to dating or even marriage.

Eye-Opening Experiences

Living in a hypersegregated society limits opportunities for white Americans to develop empathy for oppressed minorities. Sometimes whites can experience (however brief) moments that challenge preexisting notions about the racialized social system; namely, that we live in a land of opportunity for all people, regardless of race. Unfortunately, these experiences are unlikely to adequately modify white attitudes and alter their actions. Sometimes the eye-opening experience occurred while at work. In the excerpt below, Zachary recalls his experience as an intern for a public defender's office:

> R: I had the opportunity to go into the county jail and do pretrial interviews, and (.) I've been to [a different county jail in the state], and what I've noticed here from the interviews, the inmates were predominantly African American males from 20 to 30, and they all you know basically complained about that they didn't know, I just think that it was a really clear way of understanding that there was a big gap in understanding and in what they had learned, and just educational on a whole.
> I: So how do you put that into that frame, like racial identity?
> R: I think that it just shows that maybe locally or on a national scale that African American males are predominantly at a disadvantage as far as education is concerned.

A clear deviation from the typical duck-and-dodge strategy associated with WRD, Zachary is straightforward about the racial inequality in the U.S. education system. Unfortunately, later in the interview Zachary shows that this experience alone was not enough to affect his views on a host of issues, including his opposition to government involvement in increasing racial equality (presented in chapter 4). Still, experiences such as these can plant the seeds needed for whites to recognize that race indeed matters in U.S. society.

In addition to workplaces, schools also have the potential to offer young white Americans experiences that challenge sincere fictions of whiteness. Though most whites in the sample attended monoracial educational environments prior to college, at least a couple had attended multiracial schools, as did

Harriet, who went to what she characterized as "an inner city high school" that was where the "International Baccalaureate" program was located. In the following excerpt she discusses how the experience was an eye-opener for her:

R: [At the school] whites were like a minority (.) s:o in that sense (.) I guess it made you like (.) it was a really neat experience for me because I saw that like it was (.) when I first went there, it was kind of like a culture shock I guess
I: Mhm↑
R: 'Cause (1.0) my whole life I had gone t:o like a really small elementary school that (.) was predominantly white
I: Mhm↓
R: And so was my middle school. And then I went to (.) my high school that was (.) very di<u>verse</u> u::m (.)
I: You went there for like all four years?
R: Yeah, all four years. Um (1.0) it actually made me like start seeing things in a different way.
I: Mhm
R: I guess, and it (.) made me (feel?) [the] diversity in our culture
I: Sure
R: It was like a good (.) experience, um (.) I don't know, I had a lot of fun in my high school
I: Oh, yea↓h
R: Because (.) just like football games and stuff, you know, they're more (.) spirited I guess
I: Mhm
R: (.) and stuff like that.
I: Yeah
R: Um I rea(h)lly don't know how to explai(h)n it.
I: No↑, no. (2.0) Like as far as like seeing things differently um (2.0) I mean you mentioned like football games or (.) u:m (.) as far as=
R: =It's a complete ghetto I mean (.) we didn't have nice facilities or anything like that.
I: ↑Oh
R: 'Cause the place (.)
I: Yeah, like um what did you think about that, as far as not having (.) like, what kinds of facilities?
R: Um, well (1.0) I was on the varsity soccer team all four years and we didn't have like a designated practice field
I: Oh
R: For soccer and they (.) tended t:o (.) I guess football and basketball were favored than like other sports so
I: Sure
R: We didn't have
I: Like you had to use the football field?
R: That's where like (.) the stadium was where we had our soccer games and then (.) um (.) yeah, like we had- if the football and soccer seasons overlapped, we would get er have to practice on like a softball field or something because we couldn't [use (.) yeah.
I: [Oh↓   Right, yeah, that wouldn't be good (laughs).

In our exchange, Harriet provides considerable detail in the discrepancies between the facilities of her high school and (perceivably) the "predominantly white" schools she had attended prior. It is interesting since she initially begins with a discussion of her feelings of "culture shock" while attending the school, and after I encouraged her to continue with further examples, she then shifted from behavioral ("they're more (.) spirited I guess") to material observations, focusing on her personal experience with the soccer team. In addition to race, Harriet also made the link to class and poverty, pointing out that the school was in one of the poorest counties in the entire country. Similar to earlier examples in this chapter, she has yet to make the connection between racial inequities in school and supporting race-sensitive admissions policies of prestigious colleges and universities. Nevertheless, attending more diverse schools (in terms of both race and class) can provide eye-opening experiences for white Americans that may give them pause and cause them to reflect upon their own lives and the country they live in.

Influential Films in Academic Settings

Films can be educational tools. For years I have shown students in my race courses *Ethnic Notions*, a documentary showing the impact and influence of the minstrel shows on American cinema and television. On one of the slips of paper I handed students, one statement read, "I recently watched a movie that made me think long and hard about race in America." Examples brought up by students included Hollywood films such as *Glory*, *Training Day*, and *Coach Carter*. In this section I present two examples of films watched in classes they took, one while attending university, and the other while still in high school. The first is from Quilla, who watched a movie in a "stress and anxiety management class," and how it made her think about race in U.S. society:

R: We had to watch this movie where um there were five people gathered in a room with like uh you know a mediator and they were all different races, and
I: Right.
R: They were just talking about like racial prejudice and everything in like our society? And just (.) people got so upset about this movie, like I walked out like=and he said it was gonna be heavy, like it's a movie, you know I can't imagine it being that bad, but just like the guys, the white guy in the movie was very uhm (.) he was very like acting like everything's okay, he's like "oh, you're all my brothers, you're my brothers," and then everyone else is getting all upset about that, they're like 'no, like you don't act like that outside of here,' and then like there was a person who made a comment who made a comment about how uhm (.) how he's like 'oh, I have plenty of Mexican friends, like they- I have plenty of Mexicans working for me, and I go down and I say hello,' and like everyone's just like 'oh my god!' like you can't hear what he's saying.

I: Right.

R: And that, that made me think differently 'cause sometimes I think like maybe I'm like "oh, I don't think like"- I think white people maybe are judged more harshly like (.) their thoughts would be more prejudiced than they are, but like maybe (.) apparently not, 'cause that was pretty bad, like it's different when you see it on screen, I think.

I: Right. Do you think it had like those kinds of like well was it in a class of yours?

R: Mm mhm.

I: Okay. Do you think that like educational films like that can be pretty useful? for people

R: I think it was definitely useful, because I think uhm I mean obviously I think this school is very you know like um it's very diverse, and that class even was, and uhm it got people really upset and like interested in it, and it kind of for me it uhm (.) it like made me think more about it uhm in a different light?

In the above excerpt, Quilla seems to have been affected by this video, as well as others in the class. Note her semantic move ("I can't imagine it being that bad, but") as it followed her rather ambiguous line that she "walked out." *Ethnic Notions* and educational films such as these are designed to get people thinking, and clearly that was the case for Quilla in this instance.

In the next example, Frank watched *Beloved*, the film based on the Toni Morrison novel, in an English class in high school. He presents a synopsis of the movie and offers his reaction to it:

R: It's mainly a story in past tense about the narrator as the slave and how she escaped from the plantation and saved her daughter and family and how the past constantly haunts her throughout her entire life and that obviously made me uh (1.0)

I: Yeah like, did it have a kind of impact on you?

R: It kind of made me realize that uh, I never really thought about how, I mean I knew about what went on in the past but I never thought about how long- I mean even today like I wondered if black people like ever like get that on their mind and if they still felt that hatred (.) even today you know even though they personally didn't go through it, it happened to their ancestors so, it made me wonder

I: If they still (.) felt that way?

R: If they still felt like haunted by what happened in the past

I: Right.

R: If they still felt hated by (.) white people.

I: Oh.

After watching the film, Frank better recognizes the tremendous *generational* effects of slavery on African Americans. Perhaps whites such as Frank could then make the connection between the generational experiences of black Americans with slavery, Jim Crow, and covert forms of discrimination and their distrust or even hostility sometimes directed at whites.

Insights due to Unique Situations

As I have shown in this chapter, one of the best ways to turn false empathy into authentic empathy is for white Americans to be taken out of their comfort zone (i.e., the white bubble) and transplanted into a situation that is racially diverse. In this section, I present several instances in which members of the sample possessed a unique trait or circumstance that gave them an opportunity to see things from a minority perspective. In the first two examples, Jewish respondents agreed that white supremacists and their organizations are a serious problem in U.S. society, both connecting to their or their family's identities as Jewish as a connection to the problem. In the first instance, Penelope recalls an experience in which she attended a summer camp that previously had had some altercations with the Ku Klux Klan:

> I went to uh summer camp in [large city in the Southeast], a Jewish one, when I was like six through 10, and apparently it was suburb, a small town, and apparently there was a white supremacist like towns that kind of like not immediately surrounded it and I heard stories like back in the '70s the KKK actually came on horses into the camp during the summer, and was a big problem, and stuff like that, and I mean (.) it's like stories like kind of scared me, like if I saw movies about it and whatever, and I never really realized that there were still groups like that until maybe like I was more of a teenager, 'cause like when I saw movies I was like "oh, that's in the past, like the '60s and the '50s," and then like when I started to realize that there really are still people like that, that scares me like a lot, like (.) I don't get it, I don't understand how these people- they have their justifications for believing you know white supremacy and what not and uhm (.) I do think it's a serious problem, and I wish that someone would take a stand and completely eliminate them, and maybe like make a law that you'd be arrested if you were caught, which necessarily wouldn't change anything, 'cause they still meet in secret, and they still do their secret things and (.) it really sucks

Although Penelope had never experienced the clashes of the Klan with her camp, she still felt afraid after hearing stories. In this statement, Penelope appears to understand the generational effects of prejudice and discrimination because as an American Jew she has experienced it herself.

In the next excerpt, Mandy asserts that white supremacists and their organizations are "definitely a problem," bringing up the Columbine high school shootings as an example:

> R: We definitely have ↑other problems but (1.0) but it is kind of scary I know after Columbine in my high school there were threats made (.) against different teachers, there were threats made against Jews and (.) they had police there a:nd you know my mom definitely told me not to go to school one day because kids were making threats.

I: On that thought, do you think racism is increasing or decreasing or pretty much the same (2.0) everything from violence or threats (.)
R: Well I guess it's decreasing if you consider like the Civil Rights Movement I think we're more aware of it, so there might be less people? Who are more racist? But like the people that are racist? Are definitely strong in their values and would do more you know versus how before a lot of people who were kind of racist but don't really care (.) and then you have the small group who really cares so they're a stronger force just because they (.) believe their values to be stronger, so it's hard to say like there's less people, but I think they're still (2.0) influential um (.) in certain areas, like I remember coming across it, I knew there was like the KKK, it was outside the community center one year (1.0) we knew that they were there but (.) um I don't really hear much about them but I guess that's fine having ignorance (.) that they're not really do(h)ing anything.

Although she contradicts herself slightly with her closing statement ("they're not really do(h)ing anything") given her previous line that the Klan had been active (though "one year" is ambiguous), Mandy still recognizes the threat these terrorists pose in society, even if their numbers have declined.

The next example is the only instance within the sample of someone openly gay or lesbian (or at least the only one in which sexual orientation came up during the interviews). In the following passage, Yannie discusses his intimate relationships with two different black men and the resistance from people due to race as well as sexual orientation:

Well, like for him, it was the exact opposite of like high school experience for him was the exact opposite of me, he went into an almost entirely white school? And being a black salutatorian probably was a big deal for him, but they're- I remember seeing on his face like once one of his high school friends had done something when he was sitting in anthropology class, and some student said "it's so much easier to be a minority, you get so many more perks," and he's written down like "and then I thought of you, and how awful these kids were to you in high school, and I just wanna strangle this girl to death right now" ((laughs)), so I'm sure like he's experienced um (.) put-downs and what not, and then the other guy I dated um goes to ((different university in the state)), and I'm sure (.) there's a problem there=and, within the homosexual community, there's definitely a (.) sort of antiblack mentality? Um (.) when they had the uh pride student union conference up here, there actually was out of like the seven lectures offered, one of them was 'gay and black: how (.) gay interaction between the two?' because there's definitely like (.) sort of uh it just doesn't connect for a lot of people, and like I don't know why I didn't remember this immediately, but the guy that goes here, he's actually like (.) when talking to someone, he's like 'so would you ever date a black guy?' and oftentimes their response is like 'I would never reduce myself to that' they've actually said that, but those people are also kind of complete jackasses, so (laughs) it's not just a racism thing, it's more of a 'I wanna be better than you at all times' kind of thing ((laughs))

He talks about the racism in the gay (white) community and the hostility his boyfriends have had to deal with. Like most of the rest of the sample, as a young white man Yannie's ability to laugh it off may change with time, but for time being is emblematic of his white privilege.

Another way to see U.S. society critically is to spend time abroad in another country. Davis spent a considerable number of years living in France (recall from chapter 1 that Davis reported his racial identity to be "Franco-Italian"), and his experience there gave him a unique perspective compared to the sample when it came to viewing freedom of speech.

> Yeah, it's kind of funny, this whole like free speech thing, how like I can say whatever I want because I can, because it's an amendment, but you know you really think about it, it's (.) it shouldn't be fair, because you know how (.) like I know in Germany like (.) you're not allowed to have like Nazi organizations, it's like outlawed, because well, you know, Nazi Germany ((unintelligible)), but think about (.) we fought against them, too, you know, we were (.) so I think it's kind of stupid to have you know white supremacist organizations and meanwhile we're saying how we're gonna be equal, and just this awkward paradox, and you know (.)

Unlike nearly everyone else in the sample, Davis understands the limits to free speech. Later on, Davis spends more time struggling with this issue:

> I: Yeah, it's kinda like, like where do you think the line [should be drawn when it comes to free speech?
> R: [Because it's part of the fact that people find that their other rights would be more assaulted, like you know 'oh, if they take away our first amendment rights to choose to like, you know, praise white people or black peo'- you know, it works either way, uhm that obviously they're gonna take away some right pertaining to some other form of our free speech, you know, and that's the problem, you have this whole waterfall effect of which (.) snowball, you know, one little thing happens and 'oh, of course, they're gonna keep going,' and you know, next thing "you're a Communist!" and oh my gosh!
> I: ((laughs))

Although he understands how hate speech is potentially destructive and seems to agree that it should be curbed (although he never quite comes out in favor of Germany's speech limits, at least not unequivocally), he does understand the slippery slope argument that government could find further restrictions on speech as well. Despite this contradictory follow-up, Davis was uniquely positioned from his time abroad in Europe to understand why some speech should not be permissible.

In the final example of this section, Harriet worked at a public swimming pool near her high school. One day she witnessed an act of state-sponsored violence against a group of black teens:

R: I worked this past summer at the pool near my high school
I: Mm
R: As a lifeguard so, it was an inner-city pool so (.) I'd say probably 85 percent of the people who came to the pool were predominantly like African American or whatever um (2.0) so, I mean that's just a place I worked, I don't know if it made me think differently about the race or not. It was actually kind of fun I mean I'd joke around with (people?)
I: Were there like a lot of families as far as like parents goin' with small kids or a lot of teens or
R: A lot of teens, like, I'd probably from like 9 to about 17 or 18
I: Oh.
R: Parents rarely came because (.) it was almost like a (.) there were these two white boys that came everyday and their mother was never with them and if you're under the age of twelve you're supposed to have a parent with you, but their parents never came.
I: Right.
R: It was like a day care center (laughs)
I: O(h)h
R: I mean you get to know the kids like their names and stuff because you're there everyday. Um (1.0) so yeah most kids come to the pool on their own. (2.0) And we tried to like call the cops on some kids who got arrested and stuff
I: Oh
R: We have to kick people out like all the time just for (.) breaking the rules and stuff (laughs)
I: Oh.
R: But I noticed like (.) when the cops came (.) to settle the situation, they were really like rough with the African American kids, 'cause there was lightning but they wouldn't get out so we had to call the cops to get them out
I: Mhm.
R: And when the cops came, they were very forceful
I: Right.
R: The things they should- they didn't need to do, they could have just talked to them or been like "look, you need to leave."
I: Like, what kinds of force like do you recall?
R: I know they put the kids' hands behind their back[s] and (.) I don't wanna say like shove but like forcefully push them up to a wall or whatever and were holding down kids and stuff like that.

Similar to the responses of so many white Americans following the Rodney King incident, Harriet could hardly believe how the police officers treated those black kids at the swimming pool. What is most impressive about this account is how she does *not* fall into the all-too-common trap of blaming the victim for how they were treated (as was the response of far too many following the King incident); in fact, she was the one who called the police to get them out from the pool in the first place. Regardless of their wrongdoing, Harriet thought that the police officers had no reason to treat the black youngsters the way they did.

Summary

In this chapter, I presented a number of instances in which respondents display potential for antiracism. Despite reasons to be wary of future race relations based on the accounts on a variety of issues presented in earlier chapters, there are some contradictory messages being sent by this sample of young white Americans that could provide us a glimmer of hope for the future (perhaps given their youth and little time for attitudes to crystallize). Study participants most likely to show potential for antiracism included: (1) the offering of confessions or epiphanies, (2) experiences at work or school that opened their eyes to racial oppression, and (3) personal experiences that give them a unique insight into race matters. The next chapter provides a summary of WRD and offers suggestions for future research.

Notes

1. Picca and Feagin provide a great example of a confession to begin their text, *Two-Faced Racism*.

2. It is not just liberal sources who make this argument; in fact, libertarian Cato Institute has also made this point as well. Daniel Griswold, "Will Americans Line Up to Fill Jobs Now Held by Illegal Workers?" *Cato@Liberty*, March 2, 2011. http://www.cato-at-liberty.org/will-americans-line-up-to-fill-jobs-now-held-by-illegal-workers (accessed July 26, 2012).

3. Diana Kendall, *Sociology in Our Times*, 9th ed. (Belmont, CA: Wadsworth, 2013), 284.

4. Kinney and Feagin, "Diverse Perspectives on Doing Antiracism," 235.

5. Frankenberg, *White Women: Race Matters*, 245-246.

6. O'Brien, "The Political Is Personal," 256-259.

Chapter 7
Conclusion: Toward a New Race Discourse

How do young white people talk about race, and what insight does this give us in the ways in which the racial inequities that exist in U.S. society continue? Additionally, is this kind of racetalk merely a blip on the radar screen (and thus will soon be replaced by something else) or is it here to stay? Throughout this book, I explore the myriad contradictions within the race discourse of young white college students, and argue that this discourse, with momentary exceptions, casts an image of these Americans as optimistic robots. More specifically, this project answers the question of why these contradictions exist and what purpose they serve the respondents who use them. I present evidence that the contradictions assist white Americans in their attempt to maintain face while rationalizing a separate and unequal social system that privileges whites at the expense of nonwhite Americans. In this final chapter, I offer some theoretical implications that can inform future research endeavors on the topic of how racism continues in U.S. society. Additionally, I present the "rules" of engaging in racetalk for this sample of Americans, and discuss the potential for a different form of race discourse, one that resists and challenges white privilege and supremacy rather than upholds and defends them. Finally, I offer some suggestions for future research in this field of inquiry. But first let us review the findings presented in this book and the underlying themes generated from the study.

The Contradictory Nature of White Race Discourse

In this book I document the ways in which whites attempt to present a nonracist image when discussing race matters, ranging from issues of race-sensitive admissions policies of colleges and universities to understanding their own racial identity as white Americans. I argue that they speak in certain ways not due to coincidence but a deliberate (though perhaps not always conscious) impression management campaign. Simultaneously, they present our society as having race

173

problems but not anything we have not dealt with or our government should be involved in dealing with. Thus, they initially come across as optimistic towards the state of race relations in U.S. society, yet upon further examination—i.e., following the statement that would typically satisfy the requirement of answering a survey question—their optimism dissipates and even disappears.

I also present evidence that this nonracism and optimism is only skin-deep. In reality, they are optimistic robots in that they go out of their way to disbelieve the prevalence of systemic racism. I argue that they do this because they refuse to take any responsibility for contemporary race problems. Based on my findings, I can only conclude that this sample of whites is at best ambivalent of, and at worst supportive of, systemic racism. First, they define themselves as raceless beings, and "race" is defined as bad in and of itself. Second, they implicitly rationalize the prevalence of segregated social spaces in U.S. society. Third, respondents come to see themselves as the victims of racism, not people of color. Finally, they appear more willing to defend the rights of white supremacists than those of ordinary black Americans. Yet, they wish to say these things without coming across as "white supremacist." How can they succeed in such an endeavor?

In order to pull off such a conundrum, they employ a sophisticated discursive strategy that defends white supremacy while simultaneously attempting to come across as not defending it. The patterns exposed in this project provide evidence that this is not mere coincidence. In fact, these young whites have developed a kind of bureaucratized model of discourse that provides them various discursive tools at their disposal. For example, respondents often speak in general terms about black Americans (thereby stripping them of agency) while rarely doing so when speaking of white Americans. They also used diminutives as a strategy to downplay the significance of racism in U.S. society, such as the damage caused by telling a racist joke. Furthermore, members of the sample routinely used semantic moves to present a favorable image of themselves while making a potentially face-threatening statement.

After conducting this study, I found several underlying themes that emerge as the respondents of this study deliver various contradictions when discussing race in U.S. society. I focus on two primary themes: first, the bureaucratization of their race discourse and the implications. Second, I examine the underlying theme of blaming blacks and other nonwhite Americans for our racial problems, while engaging in self-victimization.

Bureaucratizing Race Discourse

The common perception held by white Americans is that less racism exists in contemporary society than in the past, and that despite difficulties that exist today, things are better now. In fact, as I have presented, whites think that efforts to combat systemic racism have run their course and need to be scaled back or even eliminated. Survey questionnaires of whites' racial attitudes have often confirmed this perception, suggesting that white Americans no longer harbor antiblack attitudes.

However, I presented in chapter 2 that the race discourse of these white college students represented a highly organized, sophisticated system of various discursive methods when discussing race matters. This form of discourse, or WRD, enables white Americans to talk about race when actually not talking about it. For instance, they often use evasive techniques to avoid expressing their "true" feelings, such as using impersonal pronouns to omit association to an action or utterance. The reason for this evasion is obvious: when actually addressing these issues in any meaningful way, respondents often spoke in ways that threatened their self-image as nonracist. Thus, the bureaucratization of WRD serves as a cloaking device for defenders of white racism.

Furthermore, I applied Ritzer's concept of McDonaldization to WRD, and how it includes the components of efficiency, calculability, predictability, and nonhuman technology (or at least a resemblance of nonhuman technology in that their discourse often is unreflective and even robotic). I described WRD as a kind of machine that delivers specific messages that portray the speakers as ambivalent, innocent, and above all nonracist. Regardless of their intentions, white Americans who utilize WRD reinforce the racial status quo.

Having said this, I do not mean to suggest that these white college students are mere cogs in a machine that cannot dismiss the tenants of WRD and choose different repertoires, whether antiracist, essentialist, or something else. In fact, a few times during the interviews respondents appeared to scrutinize WRD. For example, Mandy and I shared the following exchange over the issue of covering crime by news media:

R: But I guess also like when the media (.) like the news reports stuff, they're reporting mainly to white people? So (.) they don't emphasize white as much because they're on that one-track mind that like 'okay, it a white person,' but then when it's someone who's black, they mention it because (.) they want you to think that way 'cause you just (.) I mean when you think of a person, you think of someone who's like you, you know like you think of a white person, and then someone's black they think of a black person, like we say they all look the same and they say we all look the same, so I think it's a way of the media to differentiate like (.) tell you who it is and I don't think they realize that they (.) present an emphasis on it and then society does.
I: 'Cause it seems like you know like I mean if (.) like to say that whites watch the news and they see a story about a white serial killer or something like (.) the idea that we whites, we don't end up thinking "oh, well like all white men are like that" (.)
R: Yeah, 'cause we know we're different from that.
I: Right. But but (.) for whatever reason that happens like at least there's a tendency for that to happen with blacks, where it's like (.) we see a black <u>male</u> who's a murderer and

R: We generalize
I: Yeah, we generalize.
R: And there's something else though=what is it in psychology that's like when we see a white male doing something we assume 'oh, it's just him that's like outside of it' but if it's a black male we assume 'oh that's within him, that's like his traits' or like (.) and kind of just assume that like they're all like that, but we know that not all white people are like that because we're white and we know we're not like that.
I: Right.
R: So we like attribute it to different (.) things like internal and external I guess.
I: Right

An important point concerning this exchange is that my comments might have steered (or at least nudged) Mandy into a particular direction. At the beginning of the excerpt, she essentializes the way people of different racial groups see themselves vis-à-vis others ("like we say they all look the same and they say we all look the same"), but later concludes this passage by evoking the particularistic/universalistic dichotomy I discussed in chapter 2; i.e., whites are treated as individuals while blacks are viewed as acting uniformally, at least when the actions are perceived as negative or posing a threat to the social order. Note Mandy's use of pronouns in this exchange: initially she refers to media as "they" but in the later portion she uses "we" in reference to the way whites generalize all black men's actions as the result of "traits."

However, most respondents most of the time utilized this form of discourse. This does bring to mind an interesting question: do the respondents create WRD or does WRD create the responses? I argue that the answer is not one or the other, but rather a process in which whites have WRD instilled within them and upon using it they modify (or even dispose of) it as they use it as situations call for its usage. As I presented in chapter 6, study participants occasionally showed the ability to deviate from the rules of WRD in their responses; still, structure tends to constrain agency more than the reverse.

The bureaucratized race discourse and painting themselves as innocent victims (vis-à-vis blacks as guilty perpetrators of racial problems) puts them in a position, however willingly or knowingly, to rationalize the white-dominated racial order. As I presented in chapter 3, respondents labeling blacks as unreasonable and hypersensitive was used to rationalize segregation, and never reflecting on reasons why blacks get upset at whites for their conduct. Additionally, this discursive method allows whites to validate the white racial frame, and thus reproduce the vicious cycle of systemic racism.

Blame Blacks, Victimize Whites

Another theme occurring throughout this project is the continuous process of blaming blacks for racial problems, while victimizing whites in the post-Civil Rights Era. As I presented in chapter 4, respondents commonly portrayed whites as victims of reverse racism via race-sensitive admissions policies of colleges and universities. Despite their acknowledgement of past discrimination and the intention of such policies, they delude themselves into believing that the "most qualified" applicants do not receive the jobs. This is rooted in the racist assumption that a black candidate cannot possibly be equal to a white applicant. Thus, blacks are blamed for their alleged inferiority while whites are painted as the victims of social engineering run amuck.

In chapter 2, I presented the split identity of white Americans, in which they initially come across as innocent and ambivalent but have another side that defends whiteness through the devaluation of blackness (or Otherness). Respondents argued that whites are under attack due to the alleged stigmatization of whiteness. Furthermore, the sample believed that whites are under attack by unreasonable and hypersensitive blacks who cry racism for every "little" racist joke they get caught telling. Meanwhile, I presented in chapter 3 that respondents blame blacks for the continued segregation of society, and whites are innocent of any wrongdoing. Blacks have too much "black pride," they argue, which creates the desire to self-segregate.

What are the implications for such a stance towards black Americans and themselves? It is a process of deflecting accountability for one's social position as a white American and the privileges one receives from that particular social location. Despite the hard-fought achievements of the Civil Rights Movement, customs have largely remained intact, along with the white racial frame that reproduces negative images of black Americans. The practice of blaming blacks for racial problems and painting whites as victims undermines those accomplishments and reinforces the white racial frame.

Theoretical Implications

In addition to common themes, there are two primary theoretical implications that should be recognized. First, I discuss the implications of this project's findings as they relate to respondents' ambivalence. I presented evidence in this project that as whites discuss racial matters, they project feelings of ambivalence. An example of this projection is the frequent usage of the statement "I don't know" when discussing these topics. Moreover, they regularly deliver an appeal to the recipient (e.g., rising intonation following a declarative statement) to obtain an approval of their statement. To an average listener, s/he would likely conclude that this discursive behavior represents an uncertainty of what some-one is talking about.

When discussing race matters, it is common that whites lack an understand-ing or even awareness of these issues (since they do not have to concern them-selves with such matters). However, despite previous studies that described the racial attitudes of white Americans as ambivalent, there is an important wrinkle to this point. In reality, white ambivalence is created, not felt, and becomes a tool for rationalizing the racist social structure. I argue that this ambivalence is a deliberate, purposive *action* that is rationally used by the respondents. Projec-tions of ambivalence allow respondents to present an image of innocence. Alt-hough not all members of the sample who project ambivalence are aware of this action, the process nonetheless achieves its goal: to protect white privilege and supremacy. Thus, whether aware of the consequences or not, their race discourse reproduces the racist social structure.

As I presented in chapter 4, this ambivalence provided them an ability to display delusions of grandeur regarding the losses of blacks due to racial injus-tices and of white disadvantage in education opportunities. I find it troubling how the issue of race-sensitive admissions policies for colleges and universities was so thoroughly denounced by the respondents. It seems as if the program is not considered to affect their own lives in any way, than it is acceptable; howev-er, once they perceive that the issue might affect them in some way, they oppose the policy. The whites of this sample seem willing to do anything to defend their sincere fictions of race in U.S. society, and when confronted with evidence that contradicts those beliefs, they either ignore the contradiction or interpret the situation to support their preexisting stereotypes.[1]

The second theoretical implication I must point out is the issue of contact in its impact on white attitudes towards nonwhite Americans. Does contact really matter in the prevalence of antiblack attitudes? To a certain extent an increase in interracial (beneficial) contact could help lessen antiblack and anti-Other preju-dice, but it may not even be possible at the current time, with blacks a minority and white America as racially segregated now than it ever was from people of color. White Americans need to realize how destructive their color-blind reper-toires really are in that they make people of color invisible.

Since the general level of contact for this sample was low overall, the as-sumed difficulty to adequately measure beneficiality was not a problem. This sample does appear to have more opportunities to engage in beneficial contact, but for whatever reasons are unwilling to take advantage. Most respondents re-ported at least one "racist" family member. Apparently something is holding these young whites back, and that is the racist thinking privileging whiteness over blackness and otherness that seeps into our schools, our workplaces, and our families.

This system of oppression ultimately represses its own members by acutely obstructing interracial harmony and ostracizing those who choose to deviate. When discussing the waste of white racism, Feagin et al. asserted that "viewed in broad terms, white racist practices represent socially sanctioned ways of dissipating much human talent and energy."[2] The racism embedded in our institutions of thinking and learning create multiple tools designed to discourage and disapprove of interracial contact and to defend white supremacy.

The Rules of WRD

Based upon the analysis of WRD presented in this book, in this section I present the rules of engagement when discussing race matters. These "rules" are really strategies of resistance: resisting the mere acknowledgement of racial oppression, and thereby providing a rationale to do nothing to stop it. I stress that the speakers do not necessarily consciously use these strategies of resisting discussions of race; instead, they are rather deeply embedded within the white consciousness through extensive teachings about how to discuss race matters. The rules of WRD include (1) avoidance; (2) conversation terminators; (3) semantic moves; and (4) bailouts. Along the way I provide examples in which these strategies were used simultaneously with one another (which was quite common). I conclude this section by entertaining the possibility of the ascendancy of a new race discourse to replace WRD.

Avoidance

The first rule is to avoid such discussions (at least in frontstage settings) in the first place. Examples of this strategy are hard to come by in my findings, since the best way to avoid racetalk in this context was to not sign up for the interview. Potential respondents were told that the subject matter for the interviews would be race-related (although other particular details were left out, such as a focus on white privilege or white supremacist organizations). Still, the fact that instructors were offering extra credit for their participation may have brought some in who would have rather avoided discussing such matters, particularly with someone they had never met.

Perhaps Irene would be the best example of a respondent who utilized this strategy. As I pointed out in chapter 2, her evasiveness was quite prevalent. In fact, when she arrived for the interview, she said that she could not stay for more than one-half hour, but then following the short questionnaire said she only had 20 minutes (though filling out the survey took about three or four minutes; see Appendix for the questionnaire). In defining "society" as the "diverse" place in which she came from, she declares racism to be nonexistent or at least generally a non-issue. The following is our exchange at the beginning of her interview:

> I: Well, like the fir—the, the first one, what do you think about, um (2.0) the
> example of, like, racial privilege, do you think some people, like, uh, benefit

from racial privilege in our society, or (.)
R: No. I mean (2.0) not where I'm from, no.
I: Okay.(2.0) Okay, and how about whiteness, like, what (.) role, if any, has whiteness played in your life?
R: I mean, seriously, I come from such a place that's so culturally diverse that, if, I- I'm the minority, [so
I: [Mhm
R: It's not really, I mean, I am considered a minority from where I live so it's, I mean if anything it's kind of a disadvantage (1.0) because like, colleges, peo-ple, a lot of [my] friends are all Hispanic and they got into college because they needed (2.0) minorities, so (.)
I: Okay. I mean, would you say—I mean, outside of like, where you're from, like,nationally would you say that people benefit from racial privilege?
R: Certain things. Politics, [yes.
I: [Politics (2.0) okay (1.0)
R: Oh, um, I wouldn't say in jobs or education (4.0) I don't know.

There is a lot going on here, some of which I will return to as I discuss the other rules of racetalk. A way to summarize her discourse is she believed that, due to living in a racially diverse social setting, racism was no longer a problem in our society. In fact, if anything the tables have turned and now it is white Americans who are treated unfairly. The statement at the end of this excerpt ("Oh, um, I wouldn't say in jobs or education") is an instance of an ignorance claim, which "are as interactionally potent as knowledge claims."[3] Throughout the interview she insists that racism is not an issue (and should not be talked about) because she happens to have "come from such a place that's so culturally diverse," sug-gesting her complete lack of a sociological imagination.

Conversation Terminators

The second rule is to use declarative statements such as "I was taught not to see race" or "I don't care whether he's black, white, or purple" in order to make difficult any attempt to further an in-depth conversation of race matters, such as the link between race and power or privilege. Continuing with Irene, the follow-ing excerpt came later in the interview, when she spoke about government in-volvement in reducing racial discrimination:

R: I mean, the second one (("The government should address the losses of cer-tain racial groups who have struggled due to racial discrimination")), I don't (2.0) I think that, nowadays they like stress, racial equality so, I mean, the past is the past [and, hopefully it's (.)
I: [Mm mhm (.)

Here Irene uses the common phrase "the past is the past" which is used by whites to dismiss any contemporary discrimination while discounting any lin-gering effects of the past discrimination.

Other respondents used "the past is the past" phrase besides Irene; in fact, in the following excerpt from Penelope, she utilizes this conversation terminator while stating her unsympathetic and emotionally charged opposition to the same statement addressed by Irene above:

I: How about the second one about uhm like addressing the losses?
R: No, no. And this is something that very much uhm pisses me off, is that there's a wide variety of African Americans who uhm (.) I lost the really stupid word, but um oh are so suppressed by their past, that they think they have a right to, you know, act out, and I think that's ridiculous, the past is the past

In Penelope's response, she also uses "the past is the past" terminator as a way to rationalize her outright disgust towards African Americans who dare to talk about the continuing effects of systemic racism.

Semantic Moves

The third rule is as follows: if in a situation in which the discussion of race matters continues (which apparently for many of them it normally does not), statements employing semantic moves such as "I'm not a racist, but..." or trailing off and being inaudible and/or incomprehensible are used to avoid the label "racist," since seeing race in and of itself is racist in their eyes.

Let us return to the Penelope's denunciation of government involvement in addressing the losses of groups who have experienced discrimination from the previous section. Immediately following her conversation terminator, she continues in the following vein, while adding an additional wrinkle:

The past might have been wrong, completely, but uhm I think that they take it too far, and I think again they take advantage of their past and their situations, and I think that anybody can do anything that they want to make themselves go farther in life, there's no reason why you need to be this suppressed sad black person just because you're so-far removed ancestors maybe were slaves in America. But, I (.) that's something that pisses me off, I don't think that mhm I don't think that really there's much racial discrimination, but then again I have not lived in a bible belt of southern America where I'm sure and almost positive they're still KKK groups and what not, which is completely wrong, but uhm- and disgusting, and I think gov't should take action against eliminating them, but um I don't think there's really discrimination anymore unless people create it, and as a matter of fact I think there's a lot more discrimination on an African American's part towards white people, a:nd I'm kind of comparing that to media, and you know like rap music, and stuff like that where (.) I mean we're getting ripped apart for not giving equal rights, and there should be equal rights, and you know as far as Bush goes I could go into a whole tangent about how he could be doing better to provide equal rights for African American society? Um but (.) I don't really think there's necessarily this huge outcry like outrage over white people discriminating [against] black people, I think that's far in our past, I don't think that's something that needs to be brought up any-more, we live in an equal society and (.) like I said I think the only measures that should be taken is if there are any groups out there that are discriminatory, they should be eliminated.

This excerpt from Penelope sums up well what WRD is all about: although early on she fails to complete the semantic move ("But, I (.)"), Penelope not only acknowledges great injustices were committed in the past against African Amer-icans, but that groups "that are discriminatory...should be eliminated." Nonethe-less, this passage is dominated by her intense disgust for African Americans who have the audacity to talk about suffering such oppression. Thus, her claim that these "groups" should be dealt with should be taken with a grain of salt.

Bailouts

The fourth rule is when "slippage" occurs—often when recalling life experienc-es—and statements are made without the semantic move, at least not immediate-ly so. To overcome this "dilemma," they add a qualifier following the statement, or they might expose their ignorance on race matters, showing how little they have considered these issues previously, such as the case of Irene presented ear-lier. Her use of "I don't know" to close the exchange suggests her ambivalence towards the issue of equal opportunity in society.

Sometimes a bailout is inserted just in case there was the potential for slip-page; thus, bailouts may actually follow a semantic move. For instance, let us revisit an excerpt from chapter 3 in which Angie discusses interracial dating:

Yeah, I had friends from high school, they would date like black and Hispanic (.) people and, they were nice guys, I like them, it's a little weird, but we all make mistakes (laughs) it doesn't matter what race you are.

In this statement, Angie delivers the semantic move "it's a little weird, but we all make mistakes," and apparently believes it failed to pass muster as devoid of prejudice or as "nonracist." In effect, she believes her semantic move failed as a face-saving mechanism (specifically, that she comes across as opposed to inter-racial dating). Consequently, she immediately follows the semantic move with the bailout "it doesn't matter what race you are" in an attempt to "stop the bleed-ing."

It is important to note that the statement "it doesn't matter what race you are" is another example of a conversation terminator; in fact, bailouts tend to be conversation terminators: Not only does the bailout try to "soften the blow" from an earlier utterance but it also often delivers an end to the immediate sub-ject of discussion. A bailout could lose its power depending on the exchange with the listener (in this particular context, if the interviewer would continue to stick to the topic with an additional follow-up). However, as I have shown in this book, WRD is successful in large part due to the general unwillingness of (white) people to challenge fellow whites, at least when discussing race matters, out of "respect" for the other person. As I have presented elsewhere, at times I failed to insert follow-ups during moments like these, and in this case, I remained quiet as Angie moved onto the next topic for discussion. As a result, this bailout served her well, as it does for other whites in their normally monoracial conversations.

A New Race Discourse?

Is there an alternative to WRD out there that not only is cognizant of racial difference but also displays an awareness of the racial oppression in U.S. society that creates unfair advantages for whites, as the late Ruth Frankenberg had suggested? Penelope's example from earlier in this chapter basically sums up the situation regarding white race discourse in contemporary U.S. society: that whites are virtually incomprehensible when discussing race matters, and when intelligible they are often supportive of the racial status quo, or at least utterly confused as how to proceed. As I addressed in chapter 2, this group of white Americans seems either unable or unwilling to reject the very thing (i.e., white supremacy[4]) that delivers them myriad advantages in the everyday lives, even if they are not fully aware of all those privileges. Additionally, this defense of the white racial order, whether intended or not, is carried out by virtually all the study participants, not just the seemingly politically conservative ones.[5] Unfortunately, an inability to act allows current social structures to continue, structures that reproduce white supremacist thinking and actions. While there may be outlets for antiracist voices to make the case for resisting the current racialized social system, and furthermore, creating more antiracist whites than have existed prior, media and society have become so compartmentalized that many whites remain unaware or even hostile to such discourses. The odds are high that WRD will remain with us for some time, though it simply cannot last forever, given the inability to turn the tide against the more globalized and racially diverse society in which we live.

Suggestions for Future Research

After doing such a project, many new questions arise as others are answered. I offer several courses of inquiry for future research, including (1) where and how whites learn to speak in the way they do about race, (2) how whites respond when interviewed by black researchers, (3) gender differences among whites when talking about race matters, and (4) a closer examination of the Internet, or the primary vehicle for the "new" racism.

Where do white Americans learn this sophisticated form of racetalk? I stipulate that white Americans learn to speak about race from various institutions in society, such as within their families, peer groups, schools, workplaces, churches, media, and neighborhoods. Are there some institutions that have more an impact on the development of this racetalk than others? For example, what impact (if any) do schools have in the way whites talk about race? It is important to note that this discourse, though powerful, is (at least initially) dependent on, and a vehicle for, the white racial frame. Thus, scientists must examine how institutions reproduce this framing of the social world and, in turn, how whites learn to preserve and reproduce this worldview via WRD. Furthermore, researchers also need to examine the ways nonwhites reinforce the white racial frame (i.e., engage in symbolic violence), as well as ways they (and antiracist whites) develop strategies to challenge it.

In today's atmosphere of "political correctness" regarding race matters (which, for most whites, means not talking about race at all), defending white supremacy and racism can cause problems for individual whites in conversations on race. In this project, I presented evidence how whites navigate through "racetalk" very carefully to maintain a face that comes across as open-minded and egalitarian, while doing just enough to justify the status quo pertaining to race. I should mention that the structure has aided individual whites in their "predicament" in that whites can justify racism without mentioning race; e.g. they can talk about fearing "criminals" rather than black men.

But what about racial differences in race discourse? According to Bonilla-Silva, blacks speak in ways similar to whites[6]; for example, blacks also accept the abstract liberalism frame, which stipulates that people should be able to pull themselves up from their own bootstraps. However, there are also some key differences, such as being less likely to minimize the significance of racism in U.S. society. Furthermore, while studies like this project have shown that WRD is full of semantic moves and evasive tactics, BRD (black race discourse) is more straightforward.[7]

What about the race of interviewer as a factor, such as blacks interviewed by a white and whites interviewed by a black? For instance, how does white race discourse (WRD) differ—if at all—when speaking with a black interviewer instead of a white interviewer? I suspect that whites will be even less forthcoming in their repertoires than black respondents in the same situation. At the same time, it would also be intriguing to see the white interviewer's difference in probing techniques with black respondents, and vice-versa.

Besides racetalk in an interracial setting, few studies have explored in great detail the different ways (if any) in which white women and men express themselves when discussing race—a difference that has received little attention in previous studies. Choosing the "correct" speech depends highly on the contextualization expectations of the interlocutor(s) present,[8] and the issue of gender differences are crucial.[9] Van Dijk found that white men tend to have slightly higher prejudicial levels, due to women's higher likelihood of contact, including more friendships and partnerships.[10] However, previous studies including that of

Van Dijk do not examine the differences how white women and men express themselves when discussing race—other than the report that women are likely to tell more stories and report higher levels of beneficial contact (e.g., friendships) with people of color than men. Van Dijk helped lay the framework for analyzing white racial discourse in a critical discursive manner, but looking at gender differences has yet to be examined.

Meanwhile, as I presented in chapter 5, Troy provides great insight into the spread of white supremacist ideology on the Internet. It seems like the white supremacist's dream has come true: the ability to unmask oneself and communicate with people about their prejudice towards people of color and, more importantly, devise strategies to enforce their supremacist ideals, all the while done so anonymously (if needed or desired).[11] Although I argue that overtly white supremacist organizations are largely unnecessary in the reproduction of contemporary systemic racism, I should be reflective and realize that, due to my own status as a white American born in the post-Civil Rights era, I lose sight of the achievements made in the mid-twentieth century. These achievements have provided more black Americans opportunity and security than in past generations.

Still, the small number of white supremacists appears to be growing, and the Internet appears to be the primary vehicle for their organizations' recruitment strategies and sharing of information.[12] The size of their groups is not so important: rather, the resources they have available and willingness to commit violence against people of color. We need more research on this movement taking place on the web, and the response to this by antiracists.

Notes

1. Jay J. Cloakley. *Sport in Society: Issues and Controversies*, 6th ed. (Boston: MacGraw-Hill, 1998).

2. Joe R. Feagin, Hernán Vera, and Pinar Batur. *White Racism*, 18.

3. Derek Edwards, "Analyzing Racial Discourse: The Discursive Psychology of Mind-World Relationships," in *Analyzing Race Talk*, 45.

4. Note here that I equate "whiteness" with "white supremacy," and that "whiteness" is *not* merely a reference to one's skin tone or group affiliation.

5. As I have shown throughout this book, one certainly should not associate WRD with the racetalk of conservative whites only. For a great study on the ways progressive whites struggle to avoid color-blind racism and ambivalence, see Meghan A. Burke, *Racial Ambivalence in Diverse Communities: Whiteness and the Power of Color-Blind Ideologies* (New York: Lexington), 2012.

6. Bonilla-Silva, *Racism Without Racists*.

7. Bonilla-Silva, *Racism Without Racists*, 164.

8. John J. Gumperz. "Sociocultural Knowledge in Conversational Inference," in *The Discourse Reader*, ed. by Adam Jaworski and Nikolas Coupland (New York: Routledge, 2001), 98-106.

9. Jennifer Coates. *Women, Men, and Language: A Sociolinguistic Account of Gender Differences in Speech*, 2nd ed. (Harlow, Essex: Pearson Longman, 1993).

10. Van Dijk, *Communicating Racism*.

11. Important pioneering volumes on this issue include Jessie Daniels, *Cyber Racism: White Supremacy Online and the New Attack on Civil Rights* (Lanham, MD: Rowman and Littlefield, 2009), and Matthew W. Hughey, *White Bound: Nationalists, Antiracists, and the Shared Meanings of Race* (Stanford, CA: Stanford University Press, 2012).

12. Colleen Curry, "Hate Groups Grow as Racial Tipping Point Changes Demographics." *ABC News*, May 18, 2012. abcnewsgo.com/US/militias-hate-groups-grow-response-minority-population-boom/story?id=16370136.

Appendix

Below is the survey instrument used for the study. Participants were asked to fill out the survey on "American values" prior to the interview. Following the survey, respondents were handed slips of paper with a set of statements listed.

American values: Please use the following scale to show how important you think the following values are to you.

0 = Not important at all; 1 = Not very important; 2 = Somewhat important; 3 = Important; 4 = Very important; 5 = Essential

___ If people do not have equal access to resources, the government should take measures to equalize opportunity.

___ Society should maintain racial purity.

___ Parents should encourage their children to marry someone of a different race if they choose.

___ We should all judge people not by the color of their skin but by the content of their character.

___ Schoolteachers should encourage people to be competitive.

___ A good society should be racially integrated.

___ Society should grant reparations to those who have been wronged in the past, such as slaves.

___ Society should protect the freedom and liberty of all citizens equally.

___ People should be able to attend racially segregated schools or live in racially segregated neighborhoods if they wish.

___ The law and government policies should be color-blind.

___ College administration officials should stress racial diversity for a quality education.

___ Employers should be able to hire whomever they want for a job, regardless of race.

___ Society should provide a safety net for people who struggle against racism.

___ The law should eliminate race supremacist groups and their activities.

___ Community leaders should encourage people to practice political correctness.

___ People should be able to make as much money or own as much property as they wish.

___ Citizens should support the decisions of their elected public officials, for better or for worse.

___ People should protest social injustices.

Each of the following "sections" appeared on individual slips of paper. I handed respondents the slips of paper one at a time.

Section 1:
—Some people have certain advantages, based on their racial identity that others don't have in this society.
—I can recall a situation or interaction that later made me think about my whiteness.

Section 2:
—I recall an experience involving some racial tension in my dormitory or apartment building.
—The government should address the losses of certain racial groups who have struggled due to racial discrimination.
—I can recall a recent interaction with a black student on campus.

Section 3:
—I have been interested in a person of color romantically before (whether past or present).
—I recall someone who once expressed disapproval towards interracial sex and/or marriage.
—I can recall an experience in which someone I know went on an interracial date.

Section 4:
—White supremacists and their organizations are a serious problem in our society.
—Anyone is capable of being a racist in U.S. society.
—I can recall a conversation in which someone told a racist joke.
—I believe that racism is increasing in our society.

Section 5:
—I recall a time when I introduced a person of color to my parents or friends.
—I recently watched a movie that made me think long and hard about race in America.

—I remember a moment when I felt embarrassed to be a white person in America.

—There was an event that took place where I work(ed) that made me think about race.

—I remember one instance in which I felt angry about race in America.

Section 6:
—Everyone has had an experience of being in situations where they had to make a decision but weren't sure what was the right thing to do. I can describe a situation involving race where I wasn't sure what to do but had to make a decision.

Selected Bibliography

Alexander, Michelle. *The New Jim Crow: Mass Incarceration in the Age of Colorblindness*. New York: The New Press, 2010.

Allport, Gordon W. *The Nature of Prejudice*. Reading, MA: Addison-Wesley, 1954.

Andersen, Margaret. "Whitewashing Race: A Critical Perspective on Whiteness." In *White Out: The Continuing Significance of Race*, edited by Ashley W. Doane and Eduardo Bonilla-Silva, 21-34. New York: Routledge, 2003.

———. *Thinking About Women*, 8th edition. Boston: Pearson, 2009.

Antaki, Charles. "Uses of Absurdity." In *Analyzing Race Talk: Multidisciplinary Approaches to the Interview*, edited by Harry Van Den Berg, Margaret Wetherell, and Hanneke Houtkoop-Steenstra, 85-102. Cambridge, U.K.: Cambridge University Press, 2003.

Bailey, Alison. "Locating Traitorous Identities: Toward a View of Privilege-Cognizant White Character." *Hypatia* 13, no. 3 (August 1998), 27-43.

Banton, Michael. *Race Relations*. London: Tavistock, 1967.

Bauman, Zygmunt. *Modernity and the Holocaust*. Cambridge, MA: Polity/Blackwell, 1990.

Berg, Bruce L. *Qualitative Research Methods for the Social Science*. Boston: Allyn and Bacon, 2001.

Berger, Peter. *Invitation to Sociology: A Humanist Perspective*. Garden City, NY: Doubleday, 1963.

Bertrand, Marianne, and Sendhil Mullainathan. "Are Emily and Greg More Employable Than Lakisha and Jamal? A Field Experiment on Labor Market Discrimination," *American Economic Review* 94, no. 4 (September 2004), 991-1013.

Billig, Michael, Susan Condor, Derek Edwards, Mike Gane, Dav Middleton, and Alan Radley. *Ideological Dilemmas: A Social Psychology of Everyday Thinking*. London: Sage, 1988.

Bonilla-Silva, Eduardo. *White Supremacy and Racism in the Post-Civil Rights Era*. Boulder, CO: Lynne Rienner, 2001.

Bonilla-Silva, Eduardo. "'New Racism,' Color-Blind Racism, and the Future of Whiteness in America." In *White Out: The Continuing Significance of Race*, edited by Ashley W. Doane and Eduardo Bonilla-Silva, 271-284. New York: Routledge, 2003.

———. *Racism Without Racists: Color-Blind Racism and the Persistence of Racial Inequality in the United States*, 3rd ed. Lanham, MD: Roman and Littlefield, 2010.

———. "'New Racism,' Color-Blind Racism, and the Future of Whiteness in America." In *White Out: The Continuing Significance of Race*, edited by Ashley W. Doane and Eduardo Bonilla-Silva, 271-284. New York: Routledge, 2012.

———. "The Invisible Weight of Whiteness: The Racial Grammar of Everyday Life in Contemporary America." *Ethnic and Racial Studies*, 35, no. 2 (February 2012), 173-194.

Bonilla-Silva, Eduardo and Tyrone Forman, "I Am Not A Racist But...": Mapping White College Students' Racial Ideology in the USA." *Discourse & Society* 11, no. 1 (January 2000), 50-85.

Bonilla-Silva, Eduardo, Carla Goar, and David G. Embrick. "When Whites Flock Together: The Social Psychology of White Habitus." *Critical Sociology*, 32, vol. 2-3 (March 2006): 229-253.

Bonnett, Alastair. "Antiracism and the Critique of 'White' Identities." *New Communities* 22, no. 1 (January 1996): 97-110.

Bourdieu, Pierre. *Outline of a Theory of Practice*. Cambridge, U.K.: Cambridge University Press, 1977.

Bowen, William G., and Derek Bok. *The Shape of the River: Long-Term Consequences of Considering Race in College and University Admissions*. Princeton, NJ: Princeton University Press, 1998.

Buchanan, Patrick J. *The Death of the West: How Dying Populations and Immigrant Invasions Imperil Our Country and Civilization*. New York: Thomas Dunne, 2002.

Burke, Meghan A. *Racial Ambivalence in Diverse Communities: Whiteness and the Power of Color-Blind Ideologies*. New York: Lexington, 2012.

Bush, Melanie E.L. *Breaking the Code of Good Intentions: Everyday Forms of Whiteness*. Lanham, MD: Roman and Littlefield, 2004.

Buttny, Richard. "Multiple Voices in Talking Race: Pakeha Reported Speech in the Discursive Construction of the Racial Other." In *Analyzing Race Talk: Multidisciplinary Approaches to the Interview*, edited by Harry Van Den Berg, Margaret Wetherell, and Hanneke Houtkoop-Steenstra, 103-118. Cambridge, U.K.: Cambridge University Press, 2003.

Carr, Leslie. *"Color-Blind" Racism*. Thousand Oaks, CA: Sage, 1997.

Case, Charles E., and Andrew M. Greeley, "Attitudes Toward Racial Equality," *Humboldt Journal of Social Relations* 16, no. 1 (Fall 1990), 67-94.

Classen, Steve. "Reporters Gone Wild: Reporters and Their Critics on Hurricane Katrina, Gender, Race, and Place," *E-Media Studies* 2, no. 1 (January

2009): 1-11. Available at journals.dartmouth.edu/cgi-bin /WebObjects/ Journals.woa/2/ xmlpage/4/article/336 (accessed August 4, 2011).

Coates, Jennifer. *Women, Men, and Language: A Sociolinguistic Account of Gender Differences in Speech*, 2nd ed. Harlow, Essex: Pearson Longman, 1993.

Curry, Colleen. "Hate Groups Grow as Racial Tipping Point Changes Demographics." *ABC News*, May 18, 2012. Available online at abcnewsgo.com/US/militias-hate-groups-grow-response-minority-population-boom/story?id=16370136.

Daniels, Jessie. *Cyber Racism: White Supremacy Online and the New Attack on Civil Rights*. Lanham, MD: Rowman and Littlefield, 2009.

Delgado, Richard, and Jean Stefancic, *Critical Race Theory: An Introduction*. New York: New York University Press, 2001.

DeNavas-Walt, Carmen, Bernadette D. Proctor, and Jessica C. Smith, "Income, Poverty, and Health Insurance Coverage in the United States: 2007." *Current Population Reports*. Washington, D.C.: U.S. Government Printing Office, 2008. Available online at www.census.gov/prod/2008pubs/p60-235.pdf.

Derrida, Jacques. *Of Grammatology*. Baltimore, MD: Johns Hopkins University Press, 1976.

———. *Writing and Difference*. Chicago: University of Chicago Press, 1978.

Desmond, Matthew, and Mustafa Emirbayer. *Racial Domination, Racial Progress: The Sociology of Race in America*. New York: McGraw-Hill, 2010.

Dobbs, Michael. "Universities Record Drop in Black Admissions," *Washington Post*, November 21, 2004. www.washingtonpost.com/wp-dyn/articles/ A2830-2004Nov21.html (accessed August 4, 2011).

Dowd, James J. "Prejudice and Proximity: An Analysis of Age Differences." *Research on Aging* 2, no. 1 (March 1980): 23-48.

Drane, John. *The McDonalization of the Church: Consumer Culture and the Church's Future*. Macon, GA: Smyth and Helwys, 2008.

D'Sousa, Dinesh. *The End Of Racism*. New York: Free Press, 1995.

Durkheim, Emile. *The Rules of Sociological Method*. New York: Free Press, 1982.

Dyson, Michael Eric. *Come Hell or High Water: Hurricane Katrina and the Color of Disaster*. New York: Basic Civitas, 2006.

Edsall, Thomas B. "White-Working Chaos," *New York Times*, June 25, 2012. campaignstops.blogs.nytimes.com/2012/06/25/white-working-chaos (accessed June 27, 2012).

Eliasoph, Nina. "'Everyday Racism' in a Culture of Political Avoidance: Civil Society, Speech, and Taboo," *Social Forces* 46, no. 4 (November 1999): 479-502.

Ensink, Titus. "The Frame Analysis of Research Interviews: Social Categorization and Footing in Interview Discourse." In *Analyzing Race Talk: Multidisciplinary Approaches to the Interview*, edited by Harry Van Den Berg, Margaret Wetherell, and Hanneke Houtkoop-Steenstra, 156-177. Cambridge, U.K.: Cambridge University Press, 2003.

Feagin, Joe R. *Racist America: Roots, Current Realities, and Future Reparations*. New York: Routledge, 2000.

———. *Systemic Racism: A Theory of Oppression*. New York: Routledge, 2006.

———. *The White Racial Frame: Centuries of Framing and Counter-Framing*. New York: Routledge, 2010.

Feagin, Joe R., and Clairece B. Feagin, *Racial and Ethnic Relations in the United States*, 9th ed. Upper Saddle River, NJ: Prentice Hall, 2010.

Feagin, Joe R., and Eileen O'Brien. *White Men on Race: Power, Privilege, and the Shaping of Cultural Consciousness*. Boston: Beacon Press, 2002.

Feagin, Joe R., and Melvin P. Sikes. *Living With Racism: The Black Middle-Class Experience*. Boston: Beacon, 1994.

Feagin, Joe R., Hernán Vera, and Pinar Batur. *White Racism: The Basics*, 2nd ed. New York: Routledge, 2001.

Forbes, Hugh D. *Ethnic Conflict*. New Haven, CT: Yale University Press, 1997.

Forman, Tyrone. "Color-Blind Racism and Racial Indifference: The Role of Racial Apathy in Facilitating Enduring Inequalities," in *Changing Terrain of Race & Ethnicity*, edited by Maria Krysan and Amanda E. Lewis, 43-66. New York: Russell-Sage, 2004.

Forman, Tyrone, and Amanda E. Lewis. "Racial Apathy and Hurricane Katrina: The Social Anatomy of Prejudice in the Post-Civil Rights Era," *Du Bois Review* 3, no. 1 (March 2006): 175-202.

Foster, John D. "Defending Whiteness Indirectly: A Synthetic Approach to Race Discourse Analysis." *Discourse & Society* 20, no. 6 (November 2009): 685-703.

Frankenberg, Ruth. *White Women, Race Matters: The Social Construction of Whiteness*. Minneapolis, MN: University of Minnesota Press, 1993.

Fraser, James, and Edward Kick. "The Interpretive Repertoires of Whites on Race-Targeted Policies: Claims Making of Reverse Discrimination." *Sociological Perspectives*, 43, no. 1 (Spring 2000): 13-28.

Gallagher, Charles A. "Miscounting Race: Explaining Whites' Misperceptions of Racial Group Size," *Sociological Perspectives* 46, no. 3 (Fall 1997): 381-396.

Gallup, George H. *The Gallup Poll, Public Opinion, 1935-1971*. New York: Random House, 1972.

Goffman, Erving. *Frame Analysis*. Boston: Northeastern University Press, 1974.

Gubrium, Jaber F., and James A. Holstein, *The New Language of Qualitative Method*. New York: Oxford University Press, 1997.

Guglielmo, Tom A. "Rethinking Whiteness Historiography: The Case of Italians in Chicago, 1890-1945," in *White Out: The Continuing Significance of*

Race, edited by Ashley W. Doane and Eduardo Bonilla-Silva, 159-172. New York: Routledge, 2003.

Gumperz, John J. "Sociocultural Knowledge in Conversational Inference." In *The Discourse Reader*, edited by A. Jaworski and N. Coupland, 98-106. New York, NY: Routledge, 2001.

Habermas, Jürgen. *Legitimation Crisis* (translated by Thomas McCarthy). Boston: Beacon Press, 1975.

Hak, Tony. "Interviewer Laughter as an Unspecified Request for Clarification." In *Analyzing Race Talk: Multidisciplinary Approaches to the Interview*, edited by Harry Van Den Berg, Margaret Wetherell, and Hanneke Houtkoop-Steenstra, 200-214. Cambridge, U.K.: Cambridge University Press, 2003.

Hartigan, Jr., John. *Racial Situations: Class Predicaments of Whiteness in Detroit.* Princeton, NJ: Princeton University Press, 1999.

———. "Who Are These White People?: 'Rednecks,' 'Hillbillies,' and 'White Trash' as Marked Racial Subjects," in *White Out: The Continuing Significance of Race*, edited by Ashley W. Doane and Eduardo Bonilla-Silva, 95-122. New York: Routledge, 2003.

Hass, R. Glen, Irwin Katz, Nino Rizzo, Joan Bailey, and Lynn Moore. "When Racial Ambivalence Evokes Negative Affect, Using a Disguised Measure of Mood." *Personality and Social Psychology Bulletin* 18, no. 6 (December 1992), 786-797.

Hayes, Dennis, and Robin Wynyard (editors). *The McDonaldization of Higher Education*. Westport, CT: Bergin and Garvey, 2002.

Hill, Jane H. *The Everyday Language of White Racism*. West Sussex, U.K.: Wiley-Blackwell, 2008.

Holstein, James A., and Jaber F. Gubrium, *The Active Interview*. Thousand Oaks, CA: Sage, 1995.

Hughey, Matthew W. *White Bound: Nationalists, Antiracists, and the Shared Meanings of Race*. Stanford, CA: Stanford University Press, 2012.

Isbister, John. *Promises Not Kept: Poverty and the Betrayal of Third World Development*, 6th ed. Bloomfield, CT: Kumarian Press, 2003.

Jackman, Mary R., and Marie Crane. "Some of My Best Friends Are Black: Interracial Friendship and Whites' Racial Attitudes." *Public Opinion Quarterly* 50, no. 4 (Winter 1986): 459-486.

Jhally, Sut, and Justin M. Lewis. *Enlightened Racism: The Cosby Show, Audiences, and the Myth of the American Dream*. Boulder, CO: Westview, 1992.

Kahlenberg, Richard D. *The Remedy: Class, Race, and Affirmative Action*. New York: Basic Books, 1996.

Kane, Thomas J. "Racial and Ethnic Preferences in College Admission." In *The Black-White Test Score Gap*, edited by Christopher Jencks and Meredith Phillips. Washington, D.C.: Brookings Institution, 1998.

Kaplowitz, Stan A., Bradley J. Fisher, and Clifford J. Broman. "How Accurate
    are Perceptions of Social Statistics about Blacks and Whites?" *Public
    Opinion Quarterly* 67, no. 2 (Summer 2003): 237-244.
Keen, Sam. *Faces of the Enemy: Reflections of the Hostile Imagination*. New
    York: Harper and Row, 1986.
King, Joyce E. "Dysconscious Racism: Ideology, Identity, and the Miseducation
    of Teachers." *Journal of Negro Education* 60, no. 2 (Spring 1991): 133-146.
Koole, Tom. "Affiliation and Detachment in Interview Answer Receipts." In
    Analyzing Race Talk: Multidisciplinary Approaches to the Interview, edited
    by Harry Van Den Berg, Margaret Wetherell, and Hanneke Houtkoop-
    Steenstra, 178-199. Cambridge, U.K.: Cambridge University Press, 2003.
Koppleman, Alex. "The Boy Who Cried Birther," *The New Yorker*, May 24,
    2012. newyorker.com/online/blogs/newsdesk/2012/05/bennett.birther.html
    (accessed July 13, 2012).
Lewis, Amanda. "Some Are More Equal Than Others: Lessons on Whiteness
    from School." In *White Out: The Continuing Significance of Race*, edited by
    Ashley W. Doane and Eduardo Bonilla-Silva, 159-172. New York:
    Routledge, 2003.
Mahoney, Martha R. "Segregation, Whiteness, and Transformation," *University
    of Pennsylvania Law Review* 143, no. 5 (May 1995): 1659-1684.
McIntosh, Peggy. "White Privilege: Unpacking the Invisible Knapsack." In
    Race, Class, and Gender: An Anthology, 5th ed., edited by Margaret
    Andersen and Patricia Hill Collins, 103-108. Belmont, CA:
    Thompson/Wadsworth, 2004.
McIntyre, Alice. *Making Meaning of Whiteness: Exploring Racial Identity with
    White Teachers*. Albany, NY: State University of New York Press, 1997.
McKinney, Karyn D. *Being White: Stories of Race and Racism*. New York:
    Routledge, 2005.
McKinney, Karyn D., and Joe R. Feagin, "Diverse Perspectives on Doing
    Antiracism: The Younger Generation," in *White Out: The Continuing
    Significance of Race*, edited by Ashley W. Doane and Eduardo Bonilla-
    Silva, 233-251. New York: Routledge, 2003.
Merton, Robert K. "Discrimination and the American Creed." In *Discrimination
    and National Welfare*, edited by Robert M. MacIver, 99-126. New York:
    Harper and Row, 1949.
Merton, Robert K., Marjorie Lowenthal, and Patricia L. Kendall. *The Focused
    Interview: A Manual of Problems and Procedures*, 2nd edition. London:
    Collier Macmillan, 1990.
Mills, C. Wright. "Culture and Politics: The Fourth Epoch." In *Power, Politics,
    and People: The Collected Essays of C. Wright Mills*, edited by Irving L.
    Horowitz. New York: Oxford University Press, 1963.
Myers, Kristen. *Racetalk: Racism Hiding in Plain Sight*. Lanham, MD: Roman
    and Littlefield, 2005.
Myrdal, Gunnar. *An American Dilemma: The Negro Problem and Modern
    Democracy*, vol. 1. New Brunswick, NJ: Transaction, 1996.

Eileen O'Brien, "The Political Is Personal: The Influence of White Supremacy on White Antiracists' Personal Relationships," in *White Out: The Continuing Significance of Race*, edited by Ashley W. Doane and Eduardo Bonilla-Silva, 253-267. New York: Routledge, 2003.

Omi, Michael, and Howard Winant. *Racial Formation in the United States: From the 1960s to the 1980s*, 2nd ed. New York: Routledge, 1994.

Orbe, Mark P. and Tina M. Harris, *Interracial Communication: Theory into Practice*.
Belmont, CA: Wadsworth, 2001.

Orfield, Gary. *Schools More Separate: Consequences of a Decade of Resegregation*. Cambridge, MA: Civil Rights Project, Harvard University, 2002.

———. *Historic Reversals, Accelerating Resegregation, and the Need for New Integration Strategies*. Los Angeles: Civil Rights Project, UCLA, 2007.

Padgett, Tim. "Still Black or White: Why the U.S. Census Misreads Hispanic and Arab Americans." *Time*, March 29, 2010. www.time.com/time/nation/article/0,8599,1975883,00.html (accessed August 4, 2011).

Patton, Michael Q. *Qualitative Evaluation and Research Methods*, 3rd ed. Newbury Park, CA: Sage, 1990.

Perry, Pamela. "White Means Never Having to Say You're Ethnic: White Youth and the Construction of 'Cultureless' Identities." *Journal of Contemporary Ethnography* 30, no. 1 (February 2001): 56-91.

Pettigrew, Thomas F., and Linda R. Tropp, "Does Intergroup Contact Reduce Prejudice? Recent Meta-Analytic Findings." In *Reducing Prejudice and Discrimination*, edited by Stuart Oskamp, 93-114. Mahwah, NJ: Lawrence Erlbaum.

Picca, Leslie Houts, and Joe R. Feagin. *Two-Faced Racism: Whites in the Backstage and the Frontstage*. New York: Routledge, 2007.

Pomerantz, Anita, and Alan Zemel. "Perspectives and Frameworks in Interviewers' Queries." In *Analyzing Race Talk: Multidisciplinary Approaches to the Interview*, edited by Harry Van Den Berg, Margaret Wetherell, and Hanneke Houtkoop-Steenstra, 215-231. Cambridge, U.K.: Cambridge University Press, 2003.

Potter, Jonathan, and Margaret Wetherell. *Discourse and Social Psychology: Beyond Attitudes and Behavior*. London: Sage, 1987.

Reed, Wornie L., and Bertin M. Louis. "'No More Excuses': Problematic Responses to Barack Obama's Election." *Journal of African American Studies* 13, no. 2 (June 2009): 97-109.

Reisigl, Martin, and Ruth Wodak. *Discourse and Discrimination: Rhetorics of Racism and Antisemitism*. London: Routledge, 2001.

Ritzer, George. *The Globalization of Nothing*. Thousand Oaks, CA: Pine Forge Press,

2004.

———. *The McDonaldization of Society 6*. Thousand Oaks, CA: Pine Forge, 2011.

Roberts, Sam. "Segregation Curtailed in U.S. Cities, Study Finds." *New York Times*, January 31, 2010. www.nytimes.com/2010/01/31/us/Segregation-Curtailed-in-US-Cities-Study-Finds.html?pagewanted=all (accessed June 10, 2012).

Robinson, Matthew B. "McDonaldization of America's Police, Courts, and Corrections." In *McDonaldization: The Reader*, 2nd ed., edited by George Ritzer, 88-101. Thousand Oaks, CA: Pine Forge Press, 2006.

Roediger, David. *The Wages of Whiteness: Race and the Making of the American Middle Class*. New York: Verso, 1991.

Schaefer, Richard T. *Racial and Ethnic Groups*, 12th ed. Upper Saddle River, NJ: Prentice Hall, 2010.

Sigleman, Lee, and Susan Welch. "The Contact Hypothesis Revisited: Black-White Interaction and Positive Racial Attitudes." *Social Forces* 71, no. 3 (March 1993), 781-795.

Smith, Christopher B. "Back and to the Future: The Intergroup Contact Hypothesis Revisted," *Sociological Inquiry* 64, no. 4 (November 1994): 438-455.

Steinhorn, Leonard, and Barbara Diggs-Brown. *By the Color of Our Skin: The Illusion of Integration and the Reality of Race*. New York: Plume, 1999.

Tannen, Deborah. "What's in a Frame?" In *Framing in Discourse*, edited by Deborah Tannen, 14-55. New York: Oxford University Press, 1993.

Tatum, Beverly D. *Why Are All the Black Kids Sitting in the Back of the Cafeteria?: And Other Conversations about Race*, revised ed. New York: Basic Books, 1993.

Thomas, William I. "The Relation of Research to the Social Process." In *W.I. Thomas on Social Organization and Social Personality*, edited by Morris Janowitz, 289-305. Chicago: University of Chicago Press, 1966.

Tuchman, Gaye. "Women's Depiction by the Mass Media." *Signs* 4, no. 3 (Spring 1979): 528-542.

Van Den Berg, Harry. "Contradictions in Interview Discourse." In *Analyzing Race Talk: Multidisciplinary Approaches to the Interview*, edited by Harry Van Den Berg, Margaret Wetherell, and Hanneke Houtkoop-Steenstra, 119-137. Cambridge, U.K.: Cambridge University Press, 2003.

Van Dijk, Teun. *Communicating Racism: Ethnic Prejudice in Thought and Talk* London: Sage, 1987.

———. "Discourse and the Denial of Racism," *Discourse and Society*, 3, no. 1 (January 1992), 87-118.

———. *Elite Discourse and Racism*. London: Sage, 1993.

———. *Ideology*. London: Sage, 1999.

Weber, Max. *Economy and Society: An Outline of Interpretive Sociology*. Berkeley, CA: University of California Press, 1978.

———. *The Protestant Ethic and the Spirit of Capitalism*. Los Angeles:

Roxbury, 1996.

Wetherell, Margaret. "Racism and the Analysis of Cultural Resources in Interviews." In *Analyzing Race Talk: Multidisciplinary Approaches to the Interview*, edited by Harry Van Den Berg, Margaret Wetherell, and Hanneke Houtkoop-Steenstra, 11-30. Cambridge, U.K.: Cambridge University Press, 2003.

Wetherell, Margaret, and Jonathan Potter. *Mapping the Language of Racism*. New York: Columbia University Press, 1992.

Wingfield, Adia Harvey, and Joe R. Feagin. *Yes We Can?: White Racial Framing and the 2008 Presidential Campaign*. New York: Routledge, 2009.

Wodak, Ruth. "Turning the Tables: Antisemitic Discourse in Post-War Austria." *Discourse and Society* 2, no. 1 (January 1991): 65-83.

———. "The Genesis of Racist Discourse in Austria since 1989." In *Texts and Practices*, edited by Carmen R. Caldas-Coulthard and Malcolm Coulthard, 107-128. London: Routledge, 1996.

———. "Daus Ausland and Anti-Semitic Discourse: The Discursive Construction of the Other." In *The Language and Politics of Exclusion: Others in Discourse*, edited by Stephen H. Riggins, 65-87. Thousand Oaks, CA: Sage, 1997.

———. "Discourses of Silence: Anti-Semitic Discourse on Post-War Austria." In *Discourse and Silencing: Representation and the Language of Displacement*, edited by Lynn Thiesmeyer, 124-156. Amsterdam: Benjamins, 2004.

———. "Critical Linguistics and Critical Discourse Analysis." In *Handbook of Pragmatics*, edited by Jan-Ola Ostman and Jef Verschueren (in collaboration with Eline Verluys). Amsterdam: Benjamins, 2006.

Wodak, Ruth, and Martin Reisigl. "Discourse and Discrimination: European Perspectives." *Annual Review of Anthropology* 28, no. 1 (October 1999): 175-199.

Index

ABZ Company Hybrid, 109–10, 111, 119n24, 156, 159
absurdity, 73–74, 99, 109, 121, 148
active interviewing, 14–15
affirmative action, 89, 90, 93, 96, 97, 101, 105, 106; hostility towards, 102; as racial quotas, 104
African Americans. *See* black Americans
Ailes, Roger, 54n9
Alexander, Michelle, 57
Allport, Gordon, 59, 75, 159, 162
Al-Queda, 122
ambiguous statements, 60–61, 63, 71, 96, 132, 140, 144, 166, 168
ambivalence, 4, 8–9, 18, 53, 60, 61, 108, 128, 129, 152, 177; projections of, 178; towards racial injustices, 33; toward racism, 19, 124; towards racial Others, 58; towards racist jokes, 19, 122, 141–42; towards whiteness, 36; towards white supremacy, 132
Americans of color. *See* minorities
American Apartheid, 57
American History X (film), 131
Americans, white, non-Hispanic. *See* white Americans
Anglo-Saxon heritage, 29, 49–50
anti-discrimination measures, 95
antiracism, 72, 85, 156, 171
apparent disagreement, 124
appeal to the recipient, 42, 68, 107, 117, 177
As Good As It Gets (film), 146
Autobiographical accounts, 156

BRD (black race discourse), 184
backchannelling, 14
backstage, 148, 156
Bakke decision, 104
Banton, Michael, 59
Beloved (film), 166
beneficial contact, 58, 75, 162, 178; low, 59–61; prerequisites of, 59, 162
beneficiality, 178
Bin Laden, Osama, 137
biologization of culture, 63–64
birthers, 121, 152n2
black Americans, 1, 66, 90, 96, 101, 117–18; 136, 138, 160, 174, 182, 185; as complaining too much, 48–49, 78, 81; as criminal in media, 52; deny agency of, 174; as deviant, 48; fear of, 82–83; feared in the workplace, 44; "good" versus "bad," 84–85, 100; as hostile, 78-79; as hypersensitive, 146-47, 151, 177; ignore freedoms of, 139–41; as irresponsible, 82, 141; misrepresentations of, 73; onus placed on, 77–80, 101; as self-serving, 49; as troublemakers, 47–48, 77; as unappreciative, 101; as unreasonable, 76, 98
black job applicant, 111, 119n24; not equal to white applicant, 111–12
Blacksville, 45
Bloomberg View, 57
Bok, Derek, 90
Bonilla-Silva, Eduardo, 2, 22n37, 22n39, 91, 109, 184
Bonnett, Alastair, 10
borderline whites, 77, 136, 141
Border Patrol (video game), 153n6

Bourdieu, Pierre, 22n39
Bowen, William G., 90
Brown, John, 156
Brown, Will, 48, 55n43
bureaucratic actions, 5, 53
bureaucratization of WRD, 19, 53, 58, 174, 175–76
Bush, George W., 20n9, 48, 90, 139
Bush, Jeb, 90
Byrd, Jr., James, 138

CNN, 132, 153n6
caste system, 2
Caucasians. *See* white Americans
Cheerful Robot, 22n36, 30
Civil Rights Movement, 1, 4, 7, 27, 35, 103, 118, 177; backlash towards the values of, 102, 105; counterattack against, 1
Clinton, Hillary, 20n7, 89, 118n6
Coach Carter (film), 165
Columbine high school, 167
color-blindness, 35, 43, 53, 63, 116, 124; mask of, 64, 94
color-blind pretense, 9, 22n42
Communists, 127
Confederate flag, 133
confessions, 156
constructivism as a mechanism of preserving whiteness, 39–40
contact, 59–60; hypothesis, 75
contradictions, 2, 3, 12, 13, 14, 29, 38, 58, 86, 98, 101, 102, 117, 122, 123, 140, 173; as face-saving devices, 5, 6
The Cosby Show (television series), 69
Crane, Mary, 59, 69

delusions of grandeur, 91–96
Democratic Party, 89
desegregation, 58
dialectic, 3
diminutive, 37, 60, 73, 140, 147, 174
disclaimer, 28, 31, 32
discourse, 29, 30, 33, 122, 138, 144, 152; color- and power-evasive, 34–35; interview, 31; supremacist, 121
discourse-historical approach, 11
discrimination, 99, 102, 104, 108, 117, 155, 156, 177, 180; covert forms of, 166; generational effects of, 167; hiring, 116, 158–59; institutional, 125
diversity, 42, 102, 112, 113, 118, 135; victims of, 19, 100; sacrificed in the name of, 102–05
double-consciousness, 34
D'Sousa, Dinesh, 19n2
dysconsciousness, 60

Edsall, Thomas, 118n1
empathy, 167
English-Americans, 50
epiphany, 158
equality, 135
E.R. (television series), 69
essentialist racism, 35, 95
essentialist theorizing, 9
Ethnic Notions (film), 165, 166
ethnicity, 156
evasiveness, 38

face maintenance, 98, 108, 115, 155, 160
face-saving mechanism, 5, 6, 126, 131, 182
Fair Housing Act of 1968, 57
falling intonation, 14
Feagin, Joe, 11, 22n38, 59, 178
focused interview, 14
follow-up questions, 14, 15
formal rationality, 30, 146
Forman, Tyrone, 8, 9, 10, 109
Fox News, 53n6
frames, 11, 30–31; of abstract liberalism, 8, 184; and blacks, 8; incompatible, 4, 6; minimization of racism, 30–31; naturalization, 96, 100, 116, 117; "us versus them," 65
frame switching, 6
France, 169
Frankenberg, Ruth, 14, 97, 159, 183
Frankfurt School, 11
freedom of speech, 136; in Germany, 169; limits on, 136, 169
friendships, 58, 59, 60, 163, 185; fictive, 66; interracial, 162
frontstage, 3, 8, 13, 16, 17, 156, 157
frustration-aggression hypothesis, 158
Fubu, 134, 135

gender, 5, 106, 110, 115, 116, 149, 151, 152
Gerbner, George, 153n5
Glaeser, Edward, 57
Glory (film), 165
"golden rule" for black men, 48
goyim, 135
Gubrium, Jaber, 14
Guess Who (film), 143–44

habitus, 6
hair weaving, 73–74
Hartigan, John, 10, 60
Hass, R. Glen and colleagues, 8
hegemonic power, 5, 6
hillbillies, 71
Hill, Jane, 22n37
Hispanics, 128, 131
Holmes, Jr., Oliver Wendell, 153n7
Holstein, James, 14
honorary whites, 142
Hurricane Katrina, 1, 69, 139, 140; collective memory of, 5

ignorance claim, 36, 180
illegals, 50, 51, 158
immigration, 50
impersonal nouns, 60, 80, 86
impression management, 6, 8
in-depth interviews, 13, 14
individualism, 5, 60, 96, 102, 118
integration, 106
interjection, 116–17
intermarriage, 109
International Baccalaureate (IB) program, 47
interracial contact, 166; disapprove of, 179
interracial dating, 63, 65, 68, 70, 160, 182
interracial families, 29
interracial interactions, 18, 53, 63; high-anxiety, 70-72
interviewer's role in producing discourse, 50, 144, 176; and gender, 184–85; and race, 184
intruder alert, 149
iron cage, 8

irrationalities of rationality, 54n15
Isbister, John, 152n3

Jackman, Mary R., 59, 69
Jackson, Jesse, 49
Japanese Americans, 108
Jewish Americans, 38; as honorary whites, 136, 141, 142; as a minority status, 38
Jewish respondents, 19, 81, 142, 167
Jim Crow, 166

KKK. *See* Ku Klux Klan
Kahlenberg, Richard, 89
King, Rodney, 170
Koole, Tom, 17
Ku Klux Klan, 122, 130, 131, 137, 139, 152, 167, 168

laissez-faire capitalism, 135
Latinos, 20n9
life chances, 8

Manhattan Institute, 57
March on Washington, 2, 20n10
Massey, Douglass, 57
McCain, John, 89, 118n6, 143
McDonaldization, 19, 28, 30; characteristics of, 30–33, 175
McIntosh, Peggy, 34
McVeigh, Timothy, 27
measurement error, 10, 11, 12
media influence, 129–30
Merton, Robert K., 54n25
Mexican Americans, 83
Mexicans, 132
Middle Eastern descent, 49, 55n44
Mills, C. Wright, 22n36, 30
minimization, 147, 165
miscommunication, 73–76, 86
Muslims, 27

NPR. *See* National Public Radio
National Public Radio, 27, 28
Nation of Islam, 139
neo-apartheid system, 7, 22n37
The New Jim Crow, 57

New Orleans, 1; ethnic cleansing of, 141
Neo-Nazis, 152
new racism, 22n37
"nice but racist," 71
nonracism, 3, 64, 174
nonwhites, 2, 3, 10, 11, 12, 28, 41, 43, 46, 58, 59, 60, 64, 83, 127, 128, 142, 143, 146, 152, 158, 162, 184

Obama, Barack, 1, 20n7, 90, 121, 152n2; as counterfeit, 121; white support for, 1-2, 20n9, 89
Olin Foundation, 1
Omaha Riot of 1919, 48
One Florida Plan, 90
optimistic robots, 7, 22n36, 173
O'Brien, Conan, 143
O'Reilly, Bill, 20n5, 27, 28
Orfield, Gary, 86n6

passive voice, 140
Picca, Leslie, 22n38
political correctness, 184
Politically Incorrect with Bill Maher (television series), 153n4
post-racial society, 21n24, 155
praxis, 9
prejudice, 68, 85, 125, 155, 156, 182; antiblack, 36, 67; anti-Other, 159; antiwhite, 128
progressive whites, 7
Proposition 209, 20n4, 90
Puerto Ricans, 66
purposive action, 32, 178
purposive sampling, 13, 16

quality contacts, 19, 21n22
quality relationships, 3

race, 1, 28, 29, 35, 158, 178, 179, 180; avoidance of, 112–15; beyond, 1; as binary oppositions, 45; concept of, 3; devoid of, 34; don't see, 33; equated with racism, 122, 124–25
race discourse, 3, 28, 30, 34; contradictory, 2; definition of, 21n14; a kind of "nothingness," 33; McDonaldization of, 30–33
race relations, 5, 7, 162, 171

races, 1, 30, 33, 35, 45, 50, 52, 69, 72, 125, 140, 145, 157, 158, 165
race-sensitive admissions policies, 90, 105, 107, 109, 173, 177, 178
racespeak. *See* racetalk.
racetalk, 2, 4, 7–8, 12, 19, 20n14, 28, 29, 30, 33, 34, 53, 54n10, 179, 180, 184
racial apathy, 8–9
racial attitudes, 58; antiblack, 67; of whites, 178
racial categories, 39; reification of, 39, 40
racial discrimination, 11, 22n38, 31, 95, 96, 102, 108
racial grammar, 2
racial identity, 10, 17, 18, 35, 36, 44, 100, 102, 103, 125, 163, 169, 173
racial ideology, 2, 91
racial inequality, 7, 8, 9, 18, 43, 138, 163; indifference toward, 9
racial integration, 58, 62; sincere fictions of, 69–70
racial order, 3, 31, 80, 176, 183; reproduction of, 4–7
racial Other, 64, 65, 66, 85, 141; as animal-like, 82; continuum of, 65; fear of, 82–83; as illegal, 50; as "weird," 44, 74; negative presentation of, 46; suspicious of, 72, 75
racial privilege, 102, 106
racial purity, 32
racial tension, 58, 70, 85, 132, 133; caused by "black pride," 78, 81; downplayed when caused by whites, 71; in the dorm, 73–74, 78
racialized social system, 7, 60, 66, 92, 97
racism, 1, 37, 52, 60, 69, 85, 122, 135, 184; atomistic view of, 71, 96–98, 103; avoid charge of, 61, 81; biological, 7; capable of, 77, 124; complacency towards, 39; is decreasing, 123; dismiss charges of, 43; end of, 1; equate with prejudice, 124; as human nature, 125–26; justify, 184; reduced to personal opinion, 125; white-on-black, 123
racist jokes, 124, 141, 146, 174; covert, 148–50; is everywhere, 123; fear expressing disapproval of, 150–51; as

harmless, 141; indifference towards, 141–42; on the Internet, 149–50
rationalization, 3, 4, 5, 6, 18; of racism, 47; of segregation, 72–85
rapport with the interviewer, 51, 156
Reagan Democrats, 89
rednecks, 71
reparations, 19, 51, 93, 97, 106, 107
repertoire, 3, 6, 28, 94, 96, 141, 148, 175, 184; color-blind, 178; discursive, 35; of law and order, 48; "privilege-cognizant," 35
reported speech, 76
resegregation, 58
retrogression, 90, 105–06, 118, 119n15
reverse racism, 19, 52; victims of, 90, 177
rising intonation, 38, 41, 98, 124, 177
Ritzer, George, 19, 28, 30, 175
rules of WRD, 19, 156, 173, 179–83; avoidance, 179-80; bailouts, 182–83; conversation terminators, 180–81, 182; semantic moves, 181–82;

Saturday Night Live, 143
Schenck vs. United States (1919), 153n7
segregation, 5, 66, 114; admitted, 67-68; excuse for, 75; naturalization of, 61–64, 85; residential, 57, 58; in the workplace, 68
self-segregation, 79–80
semantic move, 32, 41, 46, 73, 75, 80, 86, 92, 103, 106, 115, 124, 131, 157, 160
sexual orientation, 156, 168
shameface, 42
Sharpton, Al, 49
skinheads, 132
Sigleman, Lee, 59
sincere fiction, 81, 84; of race in U.S. society, 178; of the white self, 3
slippage, 17, 146, 148, 149, 182
slavery, 166
Smith, Christopher, 59
Smith, Shepherd, 20n5
social class, 5
social control, 7

social Darwinism, 95
social structure, 5
sociological imagination, 180
split personalities, 34
Steinem, Gloria, 156
stereotypes, 36; antiblack, 36, 44, 46, 47–49, 125, 143, 178
storylines opposing anti-discrimination policies, 91; "can't stop it anyway," 93–94; "I didn't own any slaves," 97-98; "it's their problem," 99–101; "past is the past," 91–93, 180; "wish it away," 94–96
Stowe, Harriet Beecher, 156
stratification, 109
structured incoherence, 5, 61, 65–66, 104, 129, 136
Supreme Court, 89
symbolic violence, 184
systemic racism, 4, 18, 19, 91, 101, 105, 106, 118, 175, 176

Tannen, Deborah, 11
Texas 10 Percent Plan, 90
"three strikes" sentencing guidelines, 57
"tie-breakers," 114
"no Timberlands at the door," 135
Training Day (film), 165
Trump, Donald, 121
typification, 47. See also stereotypes

unjust enrichment, 97, 104

Van Den Berg, Harry, 13
Van Dijk, Teun, 9, 23n44, 184, 85
virtual integration, 58, 69, 85

War on Drugs, The, 57
Weber, Max, 29, 30, 33
WRD. See white race discourse
Welch, Susan, 59
West, Kanye, 48, 139–41
Wetherell, Margaret, 14
white Americans, 28, 33, 34, 43, 48, 60, 77, 96, 121, 128, 155; antiblack attitudes of, 59; as antiracist, 156; as Cheerful Robots, 29; as close-minded,

51; in Detroit, 60; as raceless beings, 45, 124; overexaggerate number of black friends, 69–70, 85; preferential treatment of, 51–52
welfare, 101
white bubble, 51, 60, 131, 167
white fear, 64-66
white flight, 58
white habitus, 7, 60
white man's burden, 104
whites. *See* white Americans.
whiteness, 4, 9, 10, 11, 15, 18, 19, 29, 30, 53, 60, 69, 123; bureaucratization of, 29; defined as legal, 50; defined as normative, 35, 155; defined through the Other, 43–49; house of, 34; iron cage of, 33; is more resources, 51; as a liability, 104; is natural, 40; preserve the face of, 51; selective consciousness of, 35–37; sincere fictions of, 7, 163; as social stigma, 41; is under attack, 40–43
whiteness studies, 9–12; "constructivist" camp of, 9–10; "systemic racism" camp of, 9–12
white privilege, 34–35, 50, 60, 118, 156, 177, 178, 179
white race discourse, 2, 3, 4, 19, 96, 105, 117, 156, 157, 163, 175–76, 182, 183; alternative to, 183; back-and-forth character of, 34; sources of, 184
white racial frame, 11–12, 13, 58, 59, 60, 64, 65, 75, 80, 90, 101, 114, 184; validation of, 80–85, 177
white racism, 69, 77, 92, 105; blamed on a few bad apples, 118; defeatism towards, 101; legacy of, 90; waste of, 178
white supremacists, 122, 127, 131, 155, 179; activities of, 127, 129, 130, 132, 134, 139, 152; altercation with, 167; are decreasing, 131; on the Internet, 185; serious yet irrelevant, 123–24; are terrorists, 136, 137
white supremacy, 2, 48, 122, 123, 178; defense of, 179, 184; implicit acceptance of, 134-36; poor conceptualization of, 132–34; as trivial, 138
Williams, Juan, 27–28, 30
Wise, Tim, 156

Wodak, Ruth, 10

About the Author

JOHN D. FOSTER is assistant professor of sociology at the University of Arkansas at Pine Bluff. He received his Ph.D. from the University of Florida in 2006. John focuses his studies on the different methods used to rationalize and perpetuate social inequalities. He is the author of several articles published in academic journals, including *Discourse & Society* and *Ethnic & Racial Studies*. He is the winner of the 2012 Dovie Burl Mentor Award for the Ronald McNair Scholars program. He lives with his wife Srey and son Wijett in Pine Bluff, Arkansas.